Fortress Europe?

Annette Jünemann · Nicolas Fromm
Nikolas Scherer
(Eds.)

Fortress Europe?

Challenges and Failures of Migration and Asylum Policies

Springer VS

Editors
Annette Jünemann
Helmut Schmidt University
Hamburg, Germany

Nikolas Scherer
Hertie School of Governance
Berlin, Germany

Nicolas Fromm
Helmut Schmidt University
Hamburg, Germany

ISBN 978-3-658-17010-3 ISBN 978-3-658-17011-0 (eBook)
DOI 10.1007/978-3-658-17011-0

Library of Congress Control Number: 2017935813

Springer VS

Editor: Jan Treibel

Printed on acid-free paper

This Springer VS imprint is published by Springer Nature
The registered company is Springer Fachmedien Wiesbaden GmbH
The registered company address is: Abraham-Lincoln-Str. 46, 65189 Wiesbaden, Germany

Content

EU migration policies: An ambiguous picture of "Fortress Europe"

Germany's integration debate: Migration as a societal challenge

Acknowledgements

The editors wish to thank the Dahrendorf Forum for its generous support and two years of stimulating inspiration. As a joint initiative of the Hertie School of Governance, the London School of Economics and Political Science (LSE), and Stiftung Mercator, the Dahrendorf Forum fosters research and open debate on issues of political relevance. The topic of the last project cycle 2015–2016 was 'Europe and the World', comprising numerous high-level events on Europe's relations with five major regions. We had the honour to participate in the "Europe and the MENA Region" working group, chaired by Prof. Cilja Harders (FU Berlin) and Prof. Claus Offe (Hertie School of Governance). Together we organized the workshop on 'Fortress Europe? Rethinking European and German Migration and Asylum Policies' at Helmut Schmidt University in November 2015. This book is a follow-up of the workshop, which would not have taken place without the overall support of the Dahrendorf Forum and its MENA working group.

We are also highly grateful to Kati Bojang and Mathias Krämer, both from Helmut Schmidt University, for their tremendous work in editing the manuscripts. Finally, we thank the Bundessprachenamt and Daniel Ross for their careful proofreading of all the submitted articles. Together they made a great contribution to the final result presented here.

Hamburg and Berlin, December 2016
Annette Jünemann, Nicolas Fromm, Nikolas Scherer

The kaleidoscope of migration

Theoretical perspectives and conceptual considerations

Annette Jünemann, Nicolas Fromm and Nikolas Scherer

A globally unprecedented number of people is currently on the move. Millions have made their way to Europe. The reasons for this movement are as manifold as the migrants themselves: war, and thus personal and economic insecurity, is just one possible motive. Since 2015, the so-called refugee crisis, which we prefer to understand as a "humanitarian crisis of refugees", has been at the top of the political agenda in Europe. Europe, the EU and its member states, are struggling over how to respond to the increased inflow of people and the biggest "refugee crisis" since the end of World War II. Large sections of European societies are responding with anxiety and mistrust, fearing substantial changes in their living conditions. Their feelings can easily be exploited and are grist on the mills of extreme right-wing movements and parties. As a consequence, Europe finds itself at a crossroads: Nationalist, anti-migrant parties from Slovakia over Germany to the UK are gaining increasing support among the electorate, challenging not only the political "establishment", but also ideas of an open and humanitarian society. The political mainstream is under pressure and in search of viable and durable solutions. While the search for solutions has not yet ended, a pattern seems to be emerging: Border fences are getting higher and higher. Fortress Europe is in the making.

Against the background of war, civil war, state failure and violent conflict in Europe's direct neighbourhood and beyond, focusing on legal and material restrictions to immigration appears to be a deficient and somehow helpless approach to tackle a problem as complex as migration. Repressive strategies can at best address the symptoms of the problem; to cope with its manifold root causes, however, they seem to be short-sighted and misleading. Not only that. The making of Fortress Europe through fences and legal barriers is also somehow anachronistic in a globalizing world with global markets, global communication and global capital flows. In fact, it overlooks that migration is deeply intertwined with globalization and the lowering of barriers to international trade and investment.

In the emerging global economy, not only businesses are relocating their production sites to countries with lower labour costs, but also an increasing number of people are following those jobs to improve or escape their economic situation. Their remittances are important not only for their families, but also for the national budget of their home countries. In addition, improved communication and lower transportation costs have done their bit to facilitate not only trade and investment, but also the free movement of people. In fact, the number of people living outside their country of birth has never been greater, according to the UN (see International Migration Report 2015). Broad transnational networks connect people. Migration is inevitably part of globalization. Moreover, we believe it is very unlikely that any border fence can stop people migrating either from the Global South to the Global North or within a region. Border fences are not tight and never will be. Nevertheless, deterrence is one of the most important aspects in the complex EU migration regime. Given the numbers of migrants dying on their dangerous journey across the Mediterranean and the numbers of those still reaching Europe, however, one has to conclude that the EU migration regime is based on flawed assumptions and, due to that, is neither humanitarian nor efficient. Against this backdrop, migration and asylum policies not only in Europe, but also in its southern neighbourhood need to be reconsidered thoroughly. This, however, first of all requires a better understanding of the phenomenon of migration with all its manifold dimensions.

This book builds upon an international workshop held at Helmut Schmidt University in Hamburg in November 2015[1]. In an effort to stimulate a more evidence-based discussion and promote an "outside-in" perspective, experts from the Southern Mediterranean[2] and Europe gathered in Hamburg to analyze the root causes of migration, concepts, mechanisms, and side effects of inter-regional migration regimes, as well as the manifold stumbling blocks hampering migrant integration in receiving countries. At the time, the "refugee crisis" had reached a peak. In a moment of acute crisis, the German chancellor, Merkel, had just decided to open the German borders almost unconditionally. A "Willkommenskul-

1 The "Fortress Europe? Rethinking European and German Migration and Asylum Policies" workshop was part of the Dahrendorf Forum's project cycle 2015–2016.

2 EU migration policies depend heavily on close cooperation with South Mediterranean countries, most of them both sending and transit countries for migrants. The transnational and inter-regional dimension of migration therefore needs to be taken into consideration. This does not mean that we are unaware of the many refugees coming from Central Asian, sub-Saharan or other countries. All these countries, however, are at the fore of EU border control to a much lesser degree.

tur" (welcome culture) still dominated Germany's civil society[3]: Broad segments of society provided immediate humanitarian assistance to those seeking shelter. Times have changed since. Merkel's decision has increasingly met with harsh criticism not only from within the EU, especially from Hungary and Poland, but also from within her own country and party. Heated and extremely simplified debates about the right way forward have structured the political discourse in Germany ever since.

Unfortunately, few of these public debates, indeed if any, explore the structural root causes and dynamics of migration, the motives and routes of migrants or societal challenges more thoroughly. The aim of this book is to overcome precisely these deficits: It wants to highlight the different structural and personal motives underpinning migration. It wants to add complexities, details and nuances where others simplify. It wants to overcome the unproductive pro/contra debate that can be followed in European societies.

To live up to this ambition, we collected various perspectives. The book contains contributions from academics and practitioners alike, including voices, in English and French, from both shores of the Mediterranean. Most of the book's contributors were also participants at the Hamburg conference. Yet, to deepen various aspects, we invited fellow colleagues to join. The formats of the contributions are multifaceted, ranging from theoretically informed research articles to clear-cut policy-oriented essays. We also hope to contribute to stimulating a debate between academics and politicians.

Analytically, we opted for an interdisciplinary approach. Migration is too complex a phenomenon to be left alone to the Political Science and International Relations community. Historians, for instance, can tell us that migration is just as old as mankind; economists can tell us that migrants are far from being a burden to "national" economies; lawyers can tell us that existing frameworks – or the lack of them – are very much a cause of irregular migration. We believe there is added value to be gained when different disciplines come together and speak to each other. Ontologically, we reject the idea that although it is certainly a powerful actor in the political landscape, the state is the only decisive (f)actor in shaping migration dynamics. The decisions and challenges associated with migration are shaped by a number of actors and structures. Migration dynamics comprise, for instance, also sociological, socio-economic and ideational factors. Moreover, these factors often *transcend* national borders. Trade regimes, security frameworks, diaspora family networks and the transnational human trafficking industry serve as cases in point here. All these factors have a high impact on people's lives and the choices they

3 Also in Hungary, Austria, Greece and Italy, to cite only some examples, civil society activists provided refugees with humanitarian support.

make. Accordingly, we did not want to confine the analytical perspective to government policies in order to capture migration and its dynamics, but to appreciate these complexities in order to gain a broader understanding.

In contrast to the mainstream public discourse, we conceive migrants as individuals with identities, beliefs and interests of their own and do not conceive them as masses that are passively channelled by human traffickers on the one hand and governmental migration regimes on the other.[4] Migrants are actors and, with their actions, also shape the space in which they move. We believe that their agency should be taken seriously, not first of all as a matter of ethics, but also as a matter of policy relevance. Neglecting their agency is one of the main reasons why so many government measures to control migration fail. People who are forced to leave their country do not refrain from doing so just because there are some new laws in Berlin, Brussels or Rabat. Whenever countries introduce new restrictions to resettlement, people who are pressured to leave their country for all sorts of political or economic reasons will adapt to the new situation and look for new ways to achieve their goal. Fully understanding the driving forces of migration requires therefore the understanding and appreciation of migrants' perspectives in the political context.

The starting point of this book is the assumption that political processes are shaped through the co-determination of agents and structures. Change and stagnation in political interactions are neither solely the result of an actor's interests and dispositions nor merely determined by structural conditions. It has been the merit of social constructivist approaches in the discipline of International Relations to explicate that agents and structures co-determine each other (see Wendt 1987). This is to say that collective or individual agents follow certain logics of action that are made up of interests, beliefs and internalized norms.[5] Likewise, structures, such as culture or political discourses, display certain logics that provide templates for (individual) political action. From this perspective, the Euro-Mediterranean migration regime is shaped both by a multitude of actors (political institutions, non-governmental organizations, individual migrants etc.) and

4 One aim of the Hamburg conference was to empower migrants by giving them a voice and a stage. Ruham Hawash, a Syrian refugee and political activist living in Hamburg, represented the migrant's perspectives in a round table discussion at the conference; a theater play conceptualized and performed by and with refugees was an additional approach taken to give back agency to refugees.

5 Logics of Action is an analytical approach to analyse political processes and phenomena specifically in the Euro-Mediterranean political space. See Jakob Horst et al.: Logics of Action in the Euro-Mediterranean Political Space: An Introduction to the Theoretical Framework. In: Horst et al. (eds.): Euro-Mediterranean Relations after the Arab Spring. Persistence in Times of Change, Routledge 2014.

by specific structures. Material structures shaping the Euro-Mediterranean migration regime include e.g. economic or political push and pull factors, but also legal settings of EU treaties and repatriation agreements between the EU and MENA countries. Ideational structures of relevance are discourses that frame migration e.g. either as a security threat or as a solution to the aging of societies in Europe. These interregional dynamics are further shaped by broader global events and dynamics. The terror attacks of ISIS and the increasing securitisation of migration serve as cases in point. The *interplay* of actors and structures means that structures shape, but are at the same time themselves shaped by the logics of action in this specific policy field. Such deep analyses enables us to really understand the shortfalls of migration regimes and is a precondition for the identification of badly needed improvements.

This book is structured in three parts, moving from the general to the particular. The first part covers some of the root causes of migration in the Euro-Mediterranean space, taking account of legal, economic and diplomatic aspects. The second part shifts attention to the EU's migration policies, in theory and practice. The final part focuses on some of the main challenges linked to the arrival of migrants in receiving societies like Germany.

The first part seeks to capture in particular the *transnational* dynamics and linkages in the Euro-Mediterranean space that drive people out of their country. It suggests that binary analytical distinctions between 'political' and 'economic' refugees or 'legal' and 'illegal' migrants all too often have little to do with the reality of the migrants, and yet they have an enormous impact on their lives. When categorised as an 'illegal' person, for instance, a person is deprived of fundamental rights. In this sense, Parastou Hassouri challenges what she sees as the primary concern of so-called destination countries in Europe and North America, namely that of separating "genuine" or "bona fide" refugees from other migrants, economic migrants in particular. In her contribution, she examines some of the criteria that are used to determine who is a refugee, pointing to the limitations and protection gaps in the current legal framework.

Another popular analytical distinction that requires re-consideration is the distinction between sending and receiving countries. As the analyses reveal, all too often the 'receiving' country is part of the problem of the 'sending' country, due to the inherent political and economic interdependencies. The case of Morocco, which is a sending, transit and receiving country all in one, reveals the artificiality of such simplistic images and might help us to overcome such categories. In his contribution, Mehdi Lahlou underlines that demographic pressure, dramatic prosperity gaps and political insecurity act as key drivers for migration both on the African continent and in the Mediterranean basin. He also questions the political solutions currently in place to manage the movement of people in the region and discusses some alternative measures, focusing on sustainable economic development. The primary importance of socio-economic factors such as a lack of employment opportunities, which are pushing especially young people to migrate north, is further specified in Ummuhan Bardak's contribution. She emphasizes the structural role of labour emigration in Mediterranean economies and Europe, but also includes external shocks on the political macro level in her framework of analysis. As her overview shows, specific labour market constellations have repeatedly proven more significant than political crises for explaining peaks in migration in recent decades.

Within this inter-regional political context, which is structurally marked by socio-economic factors, the agency of Southern governments following their own goals with regard to migration policies may not be ignored: As Gerasimos Tsourapas shows, taking Egyptian regional emigration between 1970 and 1989 as an example, inner-regional migration policies have been put in place to support the ruling regime and used as a tool to foster cooperation between autocratic regimes.

The second part of this book explores the European approach towards migration. It indicates, first of all, that EU-coordinated migration policies are much more comprehensive than is commonly known and presented: Michael Köhler illustrates that the EU is using the full range of political, legal and cooperation tools and acknowledges the social and economic benefits of regular migration for itself and third states. Accordingly, additional development funds have been allocated and dialogue between the EU and third states has been enhanced to foster economic integration and education.

Jan Völkel's view of the EU is, by contrast, much more critical. In his contribution, he notes the 'securitisation of migration' through EU member states and points out dreadful side effects. He illustrates the record numbers of people who arrived in the European Union via the Mediterranean Sea – and people who lost their lives during that passage. Völkel concludes that the EU's approach of conceiving migrants as a potential security threat leads to the paradoxical result that the EU is failing to achieve either: security for the EU and security for migrants.

Also very critical, Catherine Teule shows that the EU is increasingly externalizing migration control through tools such as readmission agreements. She suggests that EU member states nowadays seem to attribute only minor importance to human and legal standards when it comes to developing migration policy strategies. Pursuing a 'remote control approach' southern partner countries are included in this game. She claims that the EU is concluding readmission agreements with Mediterranean partner countries that can hardly be labelled as 'safe', given their low human rights standards.

For those migrants who make it to Europe, a second journey starts – the arduous process of integrating into society. As the third part of this book shows, this implies a twofold challenge both for migrants and 'receiving' societies such as Germany. In her contribution, Naika Foroutan highlights Germany's ambivalence towards immigrants. She identifies Muslims as a primary target group of the anti-immigration debate and draws an overall worrying picture of the anti-Muslim sentiment prevalent in large sections of German society.

Hannes Schammann focuses on German immigration policies and its discontents. Drawing on the example of the political movement PEGIDA and the right-wing political party AfD, he analyses to what extent an 'opinion-policy gap' can explain social discontent with national immigration and integration policies. Jana Sinram, in turn, inquires the recent rise in so-called hate comments in social media, racist remarks often dehumanising and thereby threatening refugees, politicians, volunteers and journalists. How should media and society deal with this new quality of verbal aggression and how does it affect the relationship between the political establishment, the media and the people?

As this kaleidoscope of approaches to different aspects of migration to Europe demonstrates, the continent indeed faces a historical challenge that should be neither downplayed nor trivialized. Europe, however, is not as helpless and overstrained as one might believe according to the popularised discourses. It 'just' needs to appreciate the complexities involved in migration patterns and migration policies. It is probably this complexity that also frightens many people in Europe, resulting in a highly emotionalised public debate on migration. Annette Jünemann argues in her contribution that emotions themselves are a decisive factor in understanding the logics of action in the policy field of migration. Against the backdrop of Germany's welcome culture on the one hand and rising xenophobia on the other, she explores the impact of emotions on reactions to the "refugee crisis". Given that people with deviant opinions – including xenophobia – join the same peer-groups like families, circles of friends and colleagues, it is suggested that people actively involved in the support of refugees or at least sympathetic to their admission should collectively create the necessary environment for empathy to develop and to ideally function as an antidote against xenophobia. Because the thickest wall of "Fortress Europe" is in the heads of the Europeans.

Migration: Legal, economic and political determinants

Challenging established categories and exploring intersections

A critical assessment of common notions in migration discourse

Parastou Hassouri

Abstract

Although freedom of movement and the right to seek asylum are rights conferred to all persons under the Universal Declaration of Human Rights and other international covenants, it is commonly accepted that today's nation states may, in the exercise of sovereign powers, regulate and control entry and exit across their borders. However, states are also obligated to respect the principle of non-refoulement, the cornerstone of the international legal framework, enshrined in the 1951 Convention Relating to the Status of Refugees, which forbids states from returning refugees and asylum seekers to territories where their lives and/or freedom would be threatened. As such, a primary concern of many states, particularly so-called 'destination' countries (such as those in Europe, or North America) is to separate 'genuine' or 'bona fide' refugees from other migrants, economic migrants in particular. In the context of today's mass displacement from countries such as Syria, Iraq and Afghanistan (to name but a few), where the bulk of those displaced first seek protection in neighbouring countries that may or may not be signatories to the 1951 Convention, and where the UNHCR acts as a 'gatekeeper', my contribution will aim to examine some of the common notions in migration discourse, as well as the policies and criteria that are used to determine who is a refugee and who gets 'resettled' (i.e. access to a third country in Europe, North America or Australia). I argue that some of the limitations and protection gaps in this current framework, particularly when it comes to the seeking of 'durable solutions', may indeed contribute to the phenomenon of 'irregular migration'.

1 Introduction

The so-called refugee crisis in the Euro-Mediterranean region has dominated news headlines for well over a year now. Although the forced displacement of persons heading towards Europe should not have come as a surprise as the underlying conflicts and political problems leading to this displacement go back several years (and in some cases decades), the world began to focus on the issue only once the displaced started to make their way to Europe in large numbers using increasingly 'irregular' means. In this contribution I seek to shed light on the legal notions to capture this movement and explore the shortcomings – not to say the failure – of the current international legal framework to adequately address the unfolding humanitarian crisis. I will highlight not only that the current international legal categories and framework fails to adequately address the needs and vulnerabilities of displaced persons but also that it is precisely the existing migration and asylum policies that create this 'irregular' movement of displaced persons.

2 Legal classifications and their limitations

To understand why this movement is happening in an *irregular* manner, we must first acknowledge the fact that arriving in Europe *legally* is all but impossible for most of those coming.

All human beings theoretically enjoy the right to freedom of movement. Article 13 of the Universal Declaration of Human Rights (UDHR) (1948)[1] and Article 12 of the International Covenant on Civil and Political Rights (ICCPR) (1976)[2] both stipulate that individuals should enjoy the right to free movement within the borders of their own countries, and the right to leave any country, including their own, and to return to it. However, though both instruments grant all persons the right to leave their country, they are both silent with regards to a right to *enter* other countries. Article 12(3) of the ICCPR states that the right to free movement within and out of one's country 'shall not be subject to any restrictions except

1 The Universal Declaration of Human Rights, adopted by the United Nations General Assembly on 10 December 1948, arose directly from the experience of the Second World War and represents the first global expression of what are believed to be the rights to which all human beings are inherently entitled. Though not a treaty, it is a constitutive document of the United Nations and a powerful tool in applying diplomatic and moral pressure to governments that violate any of its articles. For a text of the UDHR, see United Nations (UN): http://www.un.org/en/universal-declaration-human-rights/.

2 A multilateral treaty ratified by 168 state parties, which constitutes part of the International Bill of Rights.

those which are provided by law, are necessary to protect national security, public order, public health or morals or the rights and freedoms of others, and are consistent with the other rights recognized in the Covenant'. In today's world, however, it is assumed that all sovereign states have the right to regulate the entry and exit of non-citizens (and even their own citizens) into and out of their countries. In short, the freedom of movement exists only in theory. In practice, the ability of any individual to leave his or her country and enter another is circumscribed by the passport they hold (and of course other practical matters, such as having the economic means to travel). And the passports held by most of the persons arriving on Europe's shores are not ones favoured.

Furthermore, although Article 14(1) of the UDHR states that 'everyone has the right to seek and enjoy in other countries asylum from persecution', practically speaking, this right does not exist in an absolute sense. Most nation states have laws and regulations delineating who can enter their country, for how long, and the terms of their stay. As foreigners, the right to enter a country is predicated on the assumption that the stay in that country will be temporary, and for a specific purpose (tourism, study, work). Generally speaking, 'to seek asylum' is not a purpose for which one can seek permission to enter a country. However, many states are bound by the principle of non-refoulement, which forbids states from sending or pushing back refugees to *territories* where their life or freedom would be threatened. The principle of non-refoulement, crystallised in Article 33 of the 1951 Convention Relating to the Status of Refugees, is the cornerstone of the international legal framework that governs refugee protection today. The 1951 Convention emerged and was drafted in the aftermath of two world wars which devastated Europe and led to large-scale displacement, and has since been ratified by 148 state parties. The non-refoulement principle has been elevated to hold the status of customary international law, meaning that all states are bound by this principle regardless of whether or not they have become signatories to the 1951 Convention.

What the non-refoulement principle circumscribes is that no state may deport, expel or push back a refugee, not only to the country he or she fled for fear of persecution (usually the country of origin), but also to countries where they would be at risk of refoulement. There have been many debates about the parameters of the non-refoulement principle: at what point is a state 'bound' by this principle? When is someone actually on their territory? Who is bound by the principle? Who does it protect? A detailed discussion of the non-refoulement principle is beyond the scope of this paper and has been examined extensively elsewhere (UN High Commissioner for Refugees 2001). For the purpose of this paper, it should suffice to state the following key points: (1) a state's obligation to abide by the non-refoulement principle begins as soon as the person seeking asylum is subject to that state's jurisdiction; (2) the prohibition on refoulement applies in any circumstance where the state and its organs, or any agent authorised to act on behalf of the state, is involved; and (3) the non-refoulement principle applies to asylum seekers and refugees.

From a legal standpoint, the term 'refugee' is reserved for those who have undergone some sort of formal determination procedure, and have been found to fulfil the legal definition of a refugee (set out in Article 1(a) of the 1951 Refugee Convention and adapted into the domestic legislation of many countries that use their own domestic legal framework for adjudicating refugee status). Until this formal declaration is made, the term used for persons seeking refugee status is 'asylum seeker'. However, since the non-refoulement principle protects refugees and asylum seekers, states may not deport or push back asylum seekers until their status has been clarified. And, as mentioned above, the non-refoulement principle is triggered not only when the asylum seeker is physically on the territory of the state, but as soon as he or she is subject to the state's jurisdiction (at the border, transit zones, territorial waters). It is for this reason that classifications such as migrant versus asylum seeker are significant.

In the current so-called refugee crisis gripping the Euro-Mediterranean region, the majority of those seeking protection in Europe are from Syria. The conflict in Syria has raged for more than five years and received a significant amount of media coverage. Because of this, the term refugee has been used to categorically refer to those fleeing Syria. But would the term also be used for those fleeing lesser known conflicts? Some of those seeking refuge are not fleeing countries in the grip of war, but countries ruled by authoritarian, repressive regimes. Although the asylum system is, theoretically, supposed to be apolitical, an asylum seeker stands a better chance of obtaining refugee status when fleeing a regime that is maligned and disliked by the countries of asylum, as opposed to one that has served as an ally. Those least in luck are persons fleeing countries that may be politically repressive, or undergoing some conflict, but which are also known to be impoverished. Those are persons labelled 'economic migrants' and therefore not deserving of international protection.

It is important to realise, however, that not *all* persons who flee war zones are automatically refugees. To be a refugee under the 1951 Convention, a person has to show that they are at risk of persecution based on one of five grounds: race, religion, nationality, political opinion or membership of a particular social group. In the context of a conflict, those who are disparately impacted in conflict due to their ethnic group or religion are more readily accepted as 1951 refugees (for example the Yazidis). However, the 1951 Convention is not meant to protect those fleeing generalised violence (there are other forms of complementary protection in such cases). Furthermore, even a person fleeing a war-afflicted country who may otherwise fit the 1951 refugee definition may be excluded from protection under the 1951 Convention if it is found that within their country of origin they could have fled to a safe area (what is usually termed an 'internal protection or flight alternative').

Economic migrants are excluded from the refugee definition. However, it is important to recognise that, in practice, things are not always so black and white. In many cases, economic impoverishment and political repression and corruption go hand in hand. Wars also lead to disruption of livelihoods and it is scarcity and economic pressures that compel some to flee during war. Is the need to feed your family morally any less compelling? If we decide that a political activist is more 'deserving' of international protection than, say, a Senegalese fisherman who has become destitute because big fishing industries have destroyed his livelihood, it is only because we have chosen to privilege civil and political rights over economic and social ones, and we need to be conscious of this.

3 The current 'refugee crisis' and its challenges

These distinctions become important when we consider the current forced displacement across the Euro-Mediterranean region and the manner in which those seeking asylum are classified and treated.

Turning specifically to the current 'crisis', we need to examine more broadly the area encompassing not only the Middle East and North Africa (MENA), but also the Horn of Africa and Central Asian regions.

Undoubtedly, much of the forced displacement witnessed today is a consequence of the uprisings and subsequent conflicts that have engulfed the MENA region since 2011. The starkest example of this, of course, is Syria, where approximately 4.8 million Syrians have been registered with the United Nations High Commissioner for Refugees (UNHCR) outside the country (UNHCR 2016), and more than 6.6 million are thought to be displaced internally (Internal Displacement Monitoring Center (IDMC) 2016a). These figures represent nearly half the population of the country.

Aside from Syria, there have been conflicts in Libya and Yemen (where an estimated 2.5 million have been internally displaced) (IDMC 2016b). With the emergence and sweep of the so-called 'Islamic State' in large parts of Iraq, there has been a consequent rise in internal and external displacement in that country. Palestinians residing in countries like Syria and Iraq have been forced into exile for a second or in some cases third time. Conflicts and unrest that predate 2011 have in some cases been reignited (Sudan, Afghanistan) and politically repressive regimes in the region continue to steadily fuel waves of migration (Eritrea, Iran). In fact, Eritrea is a leading origin of asylum seekers (Laub 2015).

Violence has also disrupted traditional labour migration within the region. For instance, many Egyptian workers in Libya have been forced by the chaos to return to their home country (Aman 2015), where high unemployment and a poor economy is prompting many to seek better opportunities in Europe.

In addition, it is important to bear in mind that despite the uproar and panic in Europe over the so-called migration crisis, the number of migrants who have come to Europe represents only a fraction of those who fled their homes and are residing in host countries within the region.

According to the UNHCR, the three largest refugee host countries are currently Turkey, Pakistan and Lebanon (UNHCR 2015). As mentioned previously, most refugees originate from Syria. Of the estimated 4.8 million Syrians registered with the UNHCR, more than 2.6 million are registered in Turkey, and more than 1 million are in Lebanon (UNHCR 2016).

The UNHCR recently stated that displacement has hit an all-time record high (Edwards 2016). What is particularly significant about this is the fact that increasingly larger numbers of refugees are experiencing 'protracted crises', defined as a situation in which '25,000 or more refugees originating from the same country have sought asylum in another country (or countries) for at least five consecutive years … and find themselves in a long-lasting and intractable state of limbo. Their lives may not be at risk, but their basic rights and essential economic, social and psychological needs remain unfulfilled after years in exile' (UNHCR 2004).

As the Syrian crisis extends into its sixth year, the situation of Syrians who have been residing in host countries in the MENA region may now be described as a 'protracted crisis'. Asylum seekers coming to Europe include not only Syrians but also other nationalities (in particular Afghans and Somalis), some of whom are fleeing conflicts, unrest and political repression that have gripped their countries for much longer.

4 The failure of durable solutions and conditions of host countries

The UNHCR's mandate includes finding 'durable solutions' for refugees (UNHCR 2007). The three durable policy solutions are: local integration, repatriation and resettlement. Although there is, technically speaking, no hierarchy among the solutions, legal historians have observed that, over time, the international community has favoured certain solutions over others (Chimni 1999). In the aftermath of the Second World War, the international community looked at resettlement as the preferred solution for those fleeing the 'Eastern Block' to the West. With the end of the Cold War, the preference shifted to 'containment', either through the encouragement of repatriation or local integration in host countries (which has been attempted through the building of refugee camps, which are not truly conducive to integration) (Chimni 1998). Regardless of how one views the evolution of practices, it is clear that these 'durable solutions' have failed, or revealed themselves as inadequate to address the current levels of displacement.

In order to understand what compels asylum seekers to undertake the costly and high-risk journey to Europe[3], it is important to better comprehend this inadequacy and also consider the host countries' context.

Local integration

Local integration as a durable solution involves three dimensions: legal, economic and social/cultural (UNHCR 2008). As a legal process, it entails a refugee acquiring a broader range of rights in the host state (especially as their period of stay there increases). As an economic process, it means that the refugee must have the right and reasonable opportunity to establish a livelihood and attain a standard of living comparable to citizens of the host country. Finally, it is a social and cultural process of adaptation and acceptance that enables the refugee to make contributions to the host country without fear of discrimination. True local integration is a process that takes time. However, the principle is established in international refugee law and Article 34 of the 1951 Convention exhorts contracting states to 'facilitate the assimilation and naturalization of refugees', suggesting that the ideal and natural culmination of local integration is a refugee obtaining citizenship status in the host country.

Unfortunately, at least within the MENA region, refugees are living in circumstances which are not at all conducive to true local integration. Most of the countries in the MENA region are not signatories to the 1951 Convention (for example, Jordan and Lebanon), and even in countries like Egypt which are a signatory to the 1951 Convention, the reservations made to the convention make the process of integration very difficult. In addition, most of the countries of the region lack a domestic legal framework for asylum/refugee status. Consequently, for instance, refugee status does not automatically confer upon those holding it the right to work in the host country. Like other foreigners, refugees are obligated to comply with a burdensome sponsorship scheme, which leads many of them to work illegally and risk arrest/detention.[4] Residence in the host countries as refugees does not, in

3 For instance, in 2015, the International Organization for Migration estimated that 3,771 persons lost their lives trying to cross the Mediterranean; see International Organization for Migration (2016).

4 For example, arrest for working illegally is the main reason why Syrian refugees are detained in Jordan. See: Al-Masri and Gillespie (2013).

most cases, lead to lawful permanent residence or citizenship, and access to education, healthcare and other services may be quite restricted.

Voluntary repatriation

Another durable solution is the *voluntary* repatriation of refugees to their country of origin. The key element of this solution is that, ideally, the return should be voluntary, based on an informed decision when conditions prevail that allow return in safety and dignity. The idea of safety here comprises safety that is physical (no dangers are posed to the returnees from the government or any other armed groups), legal (there is no longer a fear of persecution) and economic (there are conditions that would allow for the material security of refugees).

In the context of mass displacements caused by civil wars or armed conflict, host governments are advised not to put pressure on refugees to return upon the ceasing of hostilities or even after the execution of a peace agreement. The changed conditions in the country of origin must be 'fundamental' and 'durable' (UNHCR 2003). What this means is that the circumstances that led to a refugee's flight must have changed in a way so complete that the refugee no longer has any fear of returning to his or her country, and those changes must be enduring. If there is any chance that hostilities could re-erupt, for instance, then refugees should not be made to repatriate.

As mentioned above, a defining feature of many of today's refugee crises is their protracted nature. Many of the conflicts in the countries of concern – Afghanistan, Iraq, Somalia, Sudan and Syria – have been ongoing and flare up even after some periods of relative calm. In fact, despite the difficult conditions that they face in the host countries, returns to country of origin remain quite low. For instance, according to the UNHCR, over the course of 2014, 126,800 refugees returned back home – the lowest number since 1983 (UNHCR 2015). In general, the longer the period of exile continues, the more difficult and unlikely it becomes for refugees to return.

Resettlement

Resettlement, the third 'durable solution', refers to the transfer of refugees from the country in which they have sought asylum to another state that has agreed to admit them as refugees and grant them permanent settlement and an opportunity for eventual citizenship (UNHCR 2011). It is important to understand that resettlement is not a 'right'. Resettlement is seen as serving two primary functions: first, it serves as an important protection tool for particular refugees whose particular protection needs may not be addressed in the country of asylum; second, it is meant to be a tangible expression of international solidarity (occasionally referred to as 'burden sharing'), allowing states to share the responsibility as opposed to placing it all on host countries. As previously mentioned, host countries in the developing world generally bear the greatest responsibility in this regard and are made to absorb the largest numbers of refugees. Generally, the UNHCR makes submissions to countries of resettlement, which in turn interview the refugees and make a decision on whether to accept them. There is no obligation to accept refugees for resettlement and countries of resettlement may have particular admission criteria. It is also important to recognise that on a global level only a minority of refugees are resettled. For instance, in 2014, the UNHCR submitted 103,890 refugees for resettlement, of which 73,331 actually departed (UNHCR 2014). The 2014 figures were an increase from 93,226 in 2013 and 75,080 in 2012 (UNHCR 2015).

In a way, resettlement represents the 'legal' means by which refugees facing problems in host countries can get to countries of resettlement. However, aside from the fact that the number of refugees who are resettled is a minority of the total number of registered refugees, there are some other problems with the process that reduce its effectiveness as a tool to address situations of forced displacement.

First, the process may also be bureaucratically burdensome and quite lengthy. The first stage involves being selected by the UNHCR (based on criteria that will be discussed below), and then being referred to one of the resettlement countries, which, in turn, conducts interviews and background checks before admitting a refugee into their country. With an annual quota of 70,000, the United States is the world's leading resettlement country (Migration Policy Institute 2015). However, the United States also conducts quite extensive background checks and has stringent admission criteria, which notoriously take a long time to administer. It is quite common to hear of people waiting well over a year after being referred to the United States to find out whether they will in fact be resettled.

Second, when particular refugee crises are thrust into the spotlight and get media coverage and result in increased resettlement numbers, it impacts negatively on other refugees. It can happen both in terms of numbers (unless the total resettlement quota of a country is increased to accommodate the regular refugee load *and* the refugees now suddenly in the spotlight), or in terms of simply pushing the other refugees to the back of the queue in terms of priority and increasing their wait for resettlement. Of course it also creates a great deal of resentment within refugee communities against one another – when one group is perceived to be receiving 'favourable' treatment. The refugees from neglected countries lose faith in the system and are more likely to explore irregular migration routes and are more susceptible to traffickers.

Third, resettlement referrals are generally made based on vulnerability criteria determined by the UNHCR (among them: legal and/or physical protection needs, women and girls at risk, medical needs, etc.) (UNHCR 2003). While it is on the face of it understandable that the UNHCR should establish particular criteria for making these determinations, in practice it is extremely difficult for UNHCR staff to make these determinations when confronted with a population who all face vulnerabilities. The reality is that the desire to 'fit into' the vulnerability criteria does lead to abuse and in turn creates a situation of distrust for refugees.

Lastly, the resettlement system tends to disfavour 'secondary movers', a term used to refer to refugees who have moved onwards to a third country after having initially sought and found protection elsewhere. Sometimes, refugees will move onwards for protection reasons that relate to their original flight (for instance, if a refugee has fled to a neighbouring country and fears that intelligence agents from his country of origin are active and cooperate with agents in the host country). At other times, the onward movement may have been caused by other protection or survival issues. However, the refugee regime tends to favour those 'coming directly' from countries where their life and/or freedom was threatened. Consequently, it is not unusual to find that secondary movers, though they will be registered, will not be referred for resettlement (except in extreme cases of vulnerability). Again, this means that this group will also be more likely to seek irregular channels of migration.

In sum, the traditional durable solutions do not adequately address the current needs of the displaced. As discussed, local integration is not occurring in a meaningful sense in most of the host countries. Repatriation remains a remote possibility given the intractable nature of some of the conflicts and the fact that instability and violence continue to be defining characteristics of many of the refugee source countries for the foreseeable future. Lastly, resettlement, the 'legal' means for migration, addresses the needs of a fraction of those forcibly displaced.

The failure of the international refugee regime to address this unprecedented displacement and the mentality that labels this phenomenon a 'refugee crisis' for Europe neglects to consider the reality that forced displacement, for both political and economic reasons (which are related, despite all attempts by policymakers to separate the two), will continue for the foreseeable future.

5 Conclusion

Given these shortcomings, how might a future solution look like? The answer is not a straightforward one. Clearly, any attempts to resolve the 'refugee crisis' must be comprehensive: it must address the underlying causes of migration as well as those people who are, in fact, already displaced.

Against this background it is, first of all, important to cease viewing the movement of refugees and other migrants solely as a matter of a single country defined by its domestic affairs; the movement is a consequence of political and economic policies and circumstances in which the international community, and in particular its most powerful states, as well as international economic and financial institutions play a crucial role and are deeply involved. More robust cooperation and concerted actions are needed to protect civilians in conflicts, including those internally displaced. Some have argued that the 1951 Convention must be replaced with a broader convention to address the various causes of those who seek refuge (including internally), be it war, political oppression or climate change. The states absorbing the largest numbers of refugees must be given more assistance to integrate them. And more expeditious processes must be put in place to resettle refugees who have crossed borders and continue to have protection needs. Undoubtedly, there are no easy or immediate solutions, but it is clear that the current system is inadequate and untenable.

References

Al-Masri, Abdulrahman and Gillespie, Kristen. 2013. Jordan demands Syrians obtain work permits, but work permits illegal for Syrians. Syria Direct. http://syriadirect.org/main/30-reports/873-syrian-labors-in-jordan. Accessed: 20 September 2016.

Aman, Ayah. 2015. Egyptian workers endangered in Libya. Al-Monitor. http://www.al-monitor.com/pulse/originals/2015/03/egypt-workers-copts-victims-libya-militias-war.html. Accessed: 20 September 2016.

Chimni, B.S. 1998. The geopolitics of refugee studies: a view from the south. *Journal of Refugee Studies,* Vol. 11 (4): 350–374.

Chimni, B.S. 1999. *From resettlement to involuntary repatriation: towards a critical history of durable solutions to refugee problems.* New Issues in Refugee Research, Working Paper No. 2. May.

Edwards, Adrian. 2016. Global forced displacement hits record high. UNHCR. http://www.unhcr.org/news/latest/2016/6/5763b65a4/global-forced-displacement-hits-record-high.html. Accessed: 20 September 2016.

Internal Displacement Monitoring Center (IDMC). 2016a. Syria IDP Figures Analysis. http://www.internal-displacement.org/middle-east-and-north-africa/syria/figures-analysis. Accessed: 20 September 2016.

Internal Displacement Monitoring Center (IDMC). 2016b. Yemen IDP Figures Analysis. http://www.internal-displacement.org/middle-east-and-north-africa/yemen/figures-analysis. Accessed: 20 September 2016.

International Organization for Migration (IOM). 2016. IOM Counts 3,771 Migrant Fatalities in Mediterranean in 2015. http://www.iom.int/news/iom-counts-3771-migrant-fatalities-mediterranean-2015. Accessed: 20 September 2016.

Laub, Zachary. 2015. Authoritarianism in Eritrea and the Migrant Crisis. Council on Foreign Relations. http://www.cfr.org/eritrea/authoritarianism-eritrea-migrant-crisis/p37239. Accessed: 20 September 2016.

Migration Policy Institute (MPI). 2015. U.S. Annual Refugee Resettlement Ceilings and Number of Refugees Admitted, 1980–Present. http://www.migrationpolicy.org/programs/data-hub/charts/us-annual-refugee-resettlement-ceilings-and-number-refugees-admitted-united. Accessed: 20 September 2016.

United Nations (UN). UDHR. http://www.un.org/en/universal-declaration-human-rights/. Accessed: 20 September 2016.

UN High Commissioner for Refugees (UNHCR). 2001. The Scope and Content of the Principle of Non-Refoulement (Opinion). http://www.refworld.org/docid/3b3702b15.html. Accessed: 20 September 2016.

UN High Commissioner for Refugees (UNHCR). 2003. Guidelines on International Protection No. 3: Cessation of Refugee Status under Article 1C (5) and (6) of the 1951 Convention relating to the Status of Refugees, HCR/GIP/03/03. http://www.refworld.org/docid/3e50de6b4.html. Accessed: 30 June 2016.

UN High Commissioner for Refugees (UNHCR). 2004. Protracted Refugee Situations. EC/54/SC/CRP.14. http://www.refworld.org/docid/4a54bc00d.html. Accessed: 20 September 2016.

UN High Commissioner for Refugees (UNHCR). 2007. Refugee Protection and Durable Solutions in the Context of International Migration. UNHCR/DPC/2007/Doc. 02. http://www.refworld.org/docid/4745a64f2.html. Accessed: 30 June 2016.

UN High Commissioner for Refugees (UNHCR). 2008. Local integration: an under-reported solution to protracted refugee situations. http://www.refworld.org/docid/4c2325670.html. Accessed: 20 September 2016.

UN High Commissioner for Refugees (UNHCR). 2011. UNHCR Resettlement Handbook 2011. http://www.refworld.org/docid/4ecb973c2.html. Accessed: 30 June 2016.

UN High Commissioner for Refugees (UNHCR). 2014. Global Resettlement Statistical Report 2014. http://www.unhcr.org/52693bd09.pdf. Accessed: 20 September 2016.

UN High Commissioner for Refugees (UNHCR). 2015. UNHCR Global Trends 2014: World at War. http://www.refworld.org/docid/558292924.html. Accessed: 20 September 2016.

UN High Commissioner for Refugees (UNHCR). 2016. Syrian Refugee Inter-Agency Regional Update. http://www.refworld.org/docid/56cecf554.html. Accessed: 20 September 2016.

Pourquoi part-on de façon irrégulière d'Afrique ?

La pauvre Afrique vs l'opulente Europe

Mehdi Lahlou

Résumé

Dans un contexte politique et social marqué par des débats qui présentent le phénomène migratoire comme une menace pour l'Europe, il faudrait d'abord appréhender les raisons principales qui poussent toujours plus de migrants venus du continent africain à traverser la Méditerranée. L'Afrique est aujourd'hui confrontée à trois défis importants qui ont pour noms démographie galopante, grande pauvreté et insécurité. La combinaison des trois facteurs représente désormais un puissant démultiplicateur des migrations sous toutes leurs formes, et notamment de la migration irrégulière. En Afrique subsaharienne, la pauvreté extrême continue de sévir comme nulle part ailleurs dans le monde, et les Maghrébins ont pour raisons essentielles de départ vers l'Europe, outre des considérations politiques et de sécurité, le chômage. L'effet est amplifié par les décalages croissants de PIB – et donc de salaire et de niveau de vie vis-à-vis de l'Europe. Mais, cette Europe qu'on cherche désespérément à fermer sur elle-même ne ferait-elle pas mieux d'ouvrir ses frontières ? Si ces jeunes personnes partent ailleurs, ils n'en sont pas pour autant moins utiles aux leurs et aux populations européennes auprès desquelles ils se sont installés. Ce chapitre va ainsi proposer quelques mesures concrètes pour mieux bénéficier de cette opportunité de développement économique.

1 Introduction

En 1985, l'Europe a entamé la mise en place de cette aire de « Liberté de circulation » que deviendra « l'Espace Schengen ». En 1989, elle va voir disparaître l'un des principaux symboles de la guerre froide en Europe occidentale, le Mur de Berlin. Mais, depuis la fin des années 1990, l'Espagne s'est barricadée derrière ses enclaves au nord Maroc, Ceuta et Melilla ; de 2012 à 2014, la Grèce et la Bulgarie en ont fait de même face à la Turquie, et au cours de l'été 2015, la Hongrie – pays qui avait ouvert tellement d'espoirs de liberté et de fraternité en Europe, à Budapest en 1956, face au Stalinisme – a fini d'édifier une barrière de 175 km à sa frontière avec la Serbie (Zerrouky 2015). D'autres barrières seront aussi érigées aux frontières de la Croatie ou encore de la Macédoine. Et celles qui séparent Ceuta et Melilla du Maroc seront relevées et renforcées davantage qu'elles ne l'étaient auparavant, y compris par les Marocains (Association marocaine des droits humain AMDH 2016). Le Maroc devenant ainsi, de fait, une vraie frontière sud de l'Europe.

Pourtant, en 2005 déjà – après les évènements douloureux vécus par des centaines de migrants de pays d'Afrique subsaharienne qui avaient alors tenté de passer le double mur de barbelés « protégeant » la ville de Ceuta provoquant la mort d'une vingtaine de personnes parmi elles – le Commissaire européen de l'époque, Franco Frattini, soutenant alors que la « Forteresse Europe est tombée »[1]. Cela, alors même que le nombre de réfugiés/immigrants impliqués était infiniment plus réduit que ce que l'Europe allait connaître au cours des années 2013/2014 et suivantes. Et aujourd'hui, dans le sillage des guerres civiles qui ravagent nombre de pays du Moyen Orient et de la Méditerranée, et en parallèle à l'accentuation des déséquilibres socio-économiques entre l'espace de l'UE et l'Afrique, cette forteresse n'est pas près de tenir. Même si politiquement et sur le plan « identitaire », nombre de responsables de pays de l'est-européen, de la Hongrie à la Pologne, et de politiciens d'extrême droite, de France, de Grande Bretagne ou de Danemark, notamment, tentent de la faire revivre matériellement et, surtout, dans les esprits.

Mais, cette Europe qu'on cherche désespérément à fermer sur elle-même – pour ne plus admettre que des citoyens de pays riches, et parfois même, que des chrétiens ou des non-arabes, des non-musulmans – ne ferait-elle pas mieux d'ouvrir ses frontières ? En raison de ses responsabilités historiques d'abord, notamment en Afrique (comme au Moyen Orient, par ailleurs), ensuite pour le respect de ses principes et valeurs fondateurs et, aussi, pour ses intérêts démographiques et économiques propres, combien évidents.

1 Franco Frattini, commissaire européen : Le Monde (Journal). 2005. La forteresse Europe s'est écroulée. Le Monde (journal) du 8 octobre 2005. Cité dans : OCDE. 2009. Les enjeux régionaux des migrations ouest-africaines. Cahiers de l'Afrique de l'Ouest. Editions de l'OCDE.

2 La pauvreté en Afrique, entre legs colonial européen et mauvaise gouvernance économique et sociale

Il est évident que l'Europe occidentale a des responsabilités directes et indirectes multiples sur tout ce qui se passe à présent au Moyen-Orient et en Afrique. Ce sont la Grande Bretagne et la France (bien avant les Etats-Unis d'Amérique et leurs multiples guerres d'Irak) qui ont façonné à leur guise la région moyen-orientale durant la première partie du 20ième siècle et qui y ont laissé germer tout ce qui y a explosé au cours des dernières décennies. Dans ce sens, il est possible de citer les accords Sykes-Picot, signés entre la France et le Royaume Uni, qui ont découpé à partir de 1916[2] la région en plusieurs zones : sur la carte jointe au Traité est dessinée une zone bleue française d'administration directe (Liban et Cilicie) ; une zone arabe A d'influence française (Syrie du Nord et province de Mossoul) ; une zone rouge anglaise d'administration directe (Koweït et Mésopotamie) ; une zone arabe B d'influence anglaise (Syrie du Sud, Jordanie et Palestine) ; une zone brune d'administration internationale comprenant Saint-Jean-d'Acre, Haifa et Jérusalem. Comme il est possible de citer les conditions d'émergence de l'Etat d'Israël. Soit l'essentiel de ce qui va, des Palestiniens aux Libanais et à présent aux Syriens et aux Irakiens, déraciner plusieurs centaines de milliers de familles et les mettre sur les chemins de l'errance. Avant même la guerre dévastatrice enclenchée contre l'Irak au printemps 2003.

C'est aussi l'Europe (Grande Bretagne, Belgique et France en tête) qui a dominé l'Afrique et ses richesses jusqu'aux années 1960 et qui y a laissé des systèmes politiques et économiques taillés sur mesure pour y préserver ses intérêts. Lesquels demeurent, dans certains pays, encore plus importants que ceux des populations domestiques, d'où les multiples déficits économiques, sociaux et de sécurité qui continuent de jeter des millions de jeunes Africains sur différents couloirs migratoires débouchant sur la Méditerranée, la Mer Rouge ou, encore, les Îles Canaries (comme ce fut le cas jusqu'en 2006).

C'est sûrement là un sujet de débats historiques importants, qui n'enlèvent rien aux responsabilités évidentes des élites africaines qui dirigent leurs pays depuis le départ des colons. Les uns ayant joint leurs actions aux autres, sciemment ou dans l'inconscience, et ont rendu l'Afrique si peu attrayante pour un grand nombre de

2 Les accords Sykes-Picot sont des accords secrets signés le 16 mai 1916, après négociations entre novembre 1915 et mars 1916, entre la France et le Royaume-Uni (avec l'aval de l'Empire russe et du royaume d'Italie), prévoyant le partage du Proche-Orient à la fin de la guerre (espace compris entre la mer Noire, la mer Méditerranée, la mer Rouge, l'océan Indien et la mer Caspienne) en plusieurs zones d'influence au profit de ces deux puissances.

ses habitants, lesquels auraient bien aimé rester et créer de la richesse sur les terres qui les ont vu naître.

S'il n'y avait pas la main mise européenne sur l'uranium du Niger (Servant 2008), sur le pétrole du Tchad ou du Nigeria (Le Monde 2013), sur les forêts du Gabon et de la République démocratique du Congo, sur les ressources halieutiques du Golfe de Guinée (Lahlou 2009), sur le fer de Mauritanie, sur les diamants du Libéria, sur le Cacao de Côte d'Ivoire, etc… ; s'il n'y avait pas en Europe et aux USA ces subventions pour le coton, qui ont détruit des dizaines de milliers d'emplois dans la filière cotonnière africaine ou s'il n'y avait pas bien d'autres aides pour les exportations agricoles européennes ou américaines, et si la Chine ne s'y est pas mise à son tour pour s'offrir à faible prix les matières premières dont son immense industrie a besoin, combien de millions de jeunes africains n'auraient jamais perdu leur emploi et leur espoir d'une vie digne chez eux. C'est cette histoire coloniale et post-coloniale, même si elle n'est pas la seule qui doit être incriminée, qui est pour une grande part responsable de la pauvreté qui prévaut dans ce continent.

L'évolution de la situation en Afrique – au sud du Sahara, en particulier – depuis le milieu des années 1960, et plus nettement au cours des deux dernières décennies, est globalement marquée par un ensemble de problèmes majeurs, qui résument l'ampleur et la profondeur de ce que beaucoup d'observateurs qualifient de « drame africain » en ce début de siècle et qui sont, pour une large part, à l'origine des flux de « migration économique » que l'Europe enregistre depuis de nombreuses années.

L'Afrique est aujourd'hui confrontée à trois défis importants qui ont pour noms démographie galopante, grande pauvreté et insécurité. Ainsi, l'Afrique qui comptait 221 millions d'habitants en 1950 et 8,7% de la population mondiale de l'époque, en compte aujourd'hui près de 1,3 milliard (soit près de 13,5% de la population mondiale), et devrait regrouper 2 milliards d'habitants en 2050 et 4 milliards en 2100. A cette date là, un habitant sur quatre vivant de par le monde sera africain. Cependant, si le facteur démographique joue un rôle plus ou moins significatif dans les mouvements de départ de populations d'une région à une autre ou d'un pays à un autre, cela ne se vérifie que si d'autres éléments sont réunis, qui deviennent dès lors les moteurs de la migration. Parmi ceux-ci il y a, en premier, le facteur économique et social.

Dans ce sens, il parait bien que la pauvreté continue de sévir en Afrique comme nulle part ailleurs dans les autres régions du monde (PNUD 2015). Ainsi, comme cela est indiqué dans le tableau 1 ci-après, parmi les vingt-cinq pays les plus pauvres au monde en 2015, 22 sont africains. En outre, non seulement les économies de ces pays sont bien pauvres – en totalisant en 2015 un produit intérieur brut (PIB) de 298 milliards de dollars pour une population totale de près de

Tableau 1 Classement des pays les plus pauvres du monde, BIP/habitant (2015)

Rang/pays	PIB par habitant (en $)	Population totale (en million)
1/Burundi	315,2	9,4
2/République Centrafricaine	338,7	4,8
3/Malawi	352,7	18,1
4/Gambie	384,2	2
5/Madagascar	392,6	24,2
6/Niger	403,4	17,6
7/Liberia	469,1	4,3
8/République démocratique du Congo	478,2	81,7
9/Guinée-Conakry	545,6	12,3
10/Togo	578,1	7,2
11/Guinée-Bissau	582,2	1,8
12/Afghanistan	*614,9*	32
13/Ouganda	625,3	39,9
14/Mozambique	626,2	27,1
15/Erythrée	630,3	6,8
16/Burkina Faso	631,4	17,9
17/Mali	672,2	16,3
18/Sierra Leone	675,2	6,3
19/Ethiopie	702,1	89,8
20/Bénin	709	10,9
21/Comores	736,8	0,8
22/Rwanda	742,9	11,4
23/Népal	*751,1*	28,4
24/Haïti	*829,6*	10,6
25/Sénégal	934,6	15

Source : Deleneuville, Matthieu. 2015. Classement PIB : les pays les plus pauvres du monde. Journaldunet. com. http://www.journaldunet.com/economie/magazine/1164746-pays-pauvres/

500 millions d'habitants – mais, en plus, elles s'appauvrissent davantage puisque ce même PIB s'élevait à 310 milliards de dollars une année plus tôt, soit en 2014. Individuellement, un Africain sur deux – globalement, hors Afrique du Nord et République Sud-Africaine – dispose pour tous ses besoins de près de 600 dollars par an, soit 63 fois moins qu'un Français ou 78 fois moins qu'un Allemand.

Conséquence de ceci et de cela, et de bien d'autres motifs intérieurs (coups d'Etat à répétition, absence de démocratie, diminution de ressources en raison du changement climatique, etc...) et extérieurs (pression pour la libéralisation des économies, multiplication des interventions extérieures, non contrôle des armements, etc...) l'Afrique connait depuis de longues années près de 30 guerres régionales et civiles et voit le terrorisme s'étendre dans l'ensemble de sa partie sahélienne.

Or, dans un monde où les distances semblent avoir disparu et où les frontières sont devenues bien difficiles à contrôler (déplacements internationaux plus nombreux et plus fréquents, baisse des prix de ces transports, libéralisation de l'obtention des passeports dans la plupart des pays à travers le monde, de la Chine à l'ensemble des pays de l'est de l'Europe ou d'Afrique, intrusion de mafias pour les passages irréguliers des frontières, etc...), la combinaison des trois facteurs ci-dessus représente désormais un puissant démultiplicateur des migrations sous toutes leurs formes, et notamment de la migration irrégulière. Et entre l'Afrique et l'Europe, soit entre des zones d'opulence et des régions de pauvreté absolue, il n'y a que 14 km constitués par le Détroit de Gibraltar.

Et, de fait, et abstraction faite de facteurs politiques d'ordre général (en rapport avec l'existence de l'Etat de droit, ou plus fondamentalement avec les conditions de sécurité prévalant dans un pays ou une région), il est bien évident qu'il existe une relation forte de cause à effet entre situation économique et sociale et mouvements migratoires. En terme d'appel, lorsque la croissance s'installe durablement dans un espace économique donné, et en terme de départ, lorsque la dépression dure longtemps dans une région déterminée, sans perspective crédible de « sortie de crise », tel que c'est le cas de nos jours dans une grande partie de l'Afrique.

Chez les pays africains du sud du Sahara, le motif déterminant de départ (dans les conditions où cela s'effectue) serait ainsi d'abord la pauvreté extrême. On serait alors dans une forme de « migration de survie ». Et c'est cela qui expliquerait l'installation de migrants dans un pays voisin plus riche (Burkinabais en Côte d'Ivoire – avant la crise que ce dernier pays a connue au cours des dernières années ; Nigériens et Maliens au sud de l'Algérie ; Nigériens, Maliens ou Tchadiens en Libye, avant que n'éclate la guerre civile dans ce pays à partir de 2011) ou les migrations transfrontalières de courte durée, notamment entre les pays sus-cités. C'est dans ce sens que les estimations disponibles sur ce type de migrations indiquent que sur 100 000 Africains du sud du Sahara passant en Afrique du Nord chaque année, près de 15 000 seulement tentent d'aller jusqu'en Europe (Lahlou 2003).

Plus proches de l'Europe, les Maghrébins auraient pour raisons essentielles de départ vers l'Europe, outre des considérations politiques et de sécurité (tel que cela a été confirmé par les conditions où se sont déclenchés les mouvements de départ massifs que l'Algérie a connus au cours des années 1990) le chômage. L'effet est amplifié par les décalages croissants de PIB – et donc de salaire et de niveau de vie – vis-à-vis de l'Europe, et du voisin immédiat, l'Espagne, en l'occurrence pour le Maroc ou l'Italie pour la Tunisie, et la France pour l'ensemble. Le cas de la Libye représente ici une exception : Les Libyens n'émigraient pas étant donné l'abondance de leur richesse pétrolière et qui, justement pour cette raison et pas pour des motifs de transit, accueillaient depuis les années 1980 des migrations de travail de nombreux pays d'Afrique subsaharienne, mais aussi – selon les circonstances politiques du moment – des autres pays du Maghreb, d'Egypte ou de Palestine.

Partout au Maghreb central, le taux de chômage se situait au début du siècle actuel à plus de 15 % en moyenne. En milieu urbain, il était de 25,1 % en Algérie, de 19,5 % au Maroc et de 15,6 % en Tunisie à la même année (Charmes et al. 2003). Par ailleurs, il apparaît bien que ce chômage, outre qu'il est d'abord urbain, affecte essentiellement les personnes dotées de formations supérieures, les illettrés trouvant généralement plus facilement un emploi. Ainsi, les données disponibles pour le Maroc, en indiquant pour 2014 un taux de chômage urbain de 14,8 %, montraient que le taux de chômage en milieu rural n'était que de 4,2 % à la même année. En cette période, 38,1 % des jeunes de 15 à 24 ans vivant en milieu urbain étaient à la recherche d'un emploi. Par ailleurs, les mêmes données montrent que le chômage affecte davantage la population active disposant d'un diplôme. Ainsi, en 2014, alors que le taux de chômage parmi la population active ne disposant d'aucun diplôme n'était que de 4,7 %, 24,1 % parmi les diplômés des universités et autres grandes écoles n'avaient pas d'emploi (Haut Commissariat au Plan du Maroc 2014).

Une partie de plus en plus grande de cette population urbaine et diplômée, mais sans emploi, et même une composante de celle qui dispose d'un emploi mais qui considère qu'il n'est pas conforme à ses aspirations dans l'ensemble des pays maghrébins, va chercher à émigrer en Europe, en Amérique du Nord ou en Arabie Saoudite et dans les Etats du Golfe. Et une telle prédisposition n'est pas non plus, bien évidemment, sans rapport avec les écarts importants de PIB/habitant qui existent aujourd'hui, notamment entre les principaux pays de l'UE récepteurs de migrants et les pays du Maghreb central, comme cela est montré dans le tableau 2 ci-après.

Tableau 2 Ecart de PIB par habitant entre certains des principaux pays de l'UE récepteurs de migrants maghrébins et le Maghreb central

Pays	Allemagne	Belgique	Espagne	France	Italie	Pays Bas
Maroc	14,97	14,83	9,31	13,4	10,04	16,34
Algérie	8,71	8,62	5,42	7,8	6,42	9,51
Tunisie	10,8	10,7	6,72	9,66	7,97	11,8

Source : Tableau fait par nous sur la base des données 2014, publiées par la Banque Mondiale. http://donnees.banquemondiale.org/indicateur/NY.GDP.PCAP.CD

3 De l'intérêt pour l'Europe à s'ouvrir

Maintenant, si ces jeunes personnes – du Maghreb, comme du reste de l'Afrique et d'autres parties du monde – partent ailleurs, ils n'en sont pas pour autant moins utiles aux leurs et aux populations européennes (comme nord-américaines) auprès desquelles ils se sont installés ou cherchent à vivre.

Ainsi, la migration a représenté, et représente encore, une aubaine démographique pour l'Europe, avec tout ce que cela comporte comme conséquences sur l'évolution de la population active, et donc sur les capacités humaines de production de richesses et aussi sur le financement des caisses sociales européennes. De la sorte, le flux de migrants, aussi important qu'il soit, ne peut pas être considéré comme « seulement » un problème, un fardeau, ou un risque pour les pays européens. Il continue de représenter, aujourd'hui, une réelle opportunité de développement économique national et à l'échelle des régions dans les pays d'accueil (développement de la recherche, opportunités nouvelles d'activité, sauvetage d'activités traditionnelles ou de secteurs menacés, tels la petite agriculture, etc.). Comme il est en mesure de représenter un facteur de stabilité régionale et de consolidation, entre autres, d'un espace euro-méditerranéen qui serait capable, sur les plans politique et économique, de tenir face au bloc asiatique mené actuellement par la Chine et, bien sûr, à la puissance américaine telle qu'elle se déploie aujourd'hui de par le monde.

La migration contribue aujourd'hui aussi, à travers les transferts de revenus qu'elle permet, au soutien économique des pays de départ. Ces transferts atteignent, par exemple, près de 7 % du PIB marocain, et participent notamment à certains investissements productifs, mais surtout à la réduction de la pauvreté dans de très nombreuses régions du Maroc. Cependant, si cette migration participe aussi, pour partie, à la réduction des pressions sur le marché de l'emploi dans différents pays africains, elle prive aussi leurs entreprises et leurs centres de recherche d'une part importante des personnels qualifiés que leurs écoles ont formés, malgré le peu de moyens dont leurs systèmes éducatifs disposent. Comme elle a tendance à vider des zones complètes de leurs ressources humaines vives, certaines régions n'étant plus habitées – en raison de l'émigration de la partie la plus dynamique de la population – que par des enfants et des personnes âgées.

4 De l'intérêt à avoir une approche plus humanitaire, plus équilibrée au sujet des migrations

A partir de ces divers éléments, qui indiquent combien les effets des migrations sont ambivalents, il est important de signifier que : a/ la plus grande partie des migrants partant du sud, d'Afrique notamment, sont forcés en cela par des raisons économiques, sociales ou sécuritaires ; b/ que les migrations sont, dans la plupart des cas, porteuses de conséquences positives autant pour les migrants que pour les pays qui les reçoivent ou d'où ils partent.

Faire en sorte que ces effets positifs soient dominants, en dernière analyse, implique fondamentalement de :

- Réduire les tensions actuelles autour du phénomène des migrations irrégulières, qui apparaît désormais comme étant le seul concerné par les débats sur la Migration, et qui dans tous les cas de figure doit être jugulé pour des motifs d'abord humanitaires et éthiques
- De rendre plus visibles les effets positifs des migrations sur le développement dans les pays de départ et d'accueil
- D'instaurer une relation plus équilibrée (moins déséquilibrée) entre les pays de l'UE, les pays du Maghreb, dont le Maroc, et l'ensemble de l'Afrique, de telle sorte qu'on tende vers une diminution de la propension à émigrer, notamment illégalement, de populations qui ont peu de chances d'être intégrées dans un pays autre que le leur.
- Prendre conscience du fait qu'il est largement plus profitable pour les Européens, et pour les Etats maghrébins, qui pourraient avoir tendance à privilégier une approche sécuritaire et de négation des droits humains pour résoudre les problèmes migratoires de l'heure, de faire des migrations dans un cadre légal, de toutes origines qu'elles soient, un moyen de développement partagé et, in fine, de faire de certaines régions importantes de départ, comme c'est le cas aujourd'hui du Maghreb, des relais de développement vers des régions moins avancées à l'image de ce qu'est aujourd'hui l'Afrique au sud du Sahara. On passerait ainsi d'espaces quasi-enclavés et très peu développés sur les plans économique et de respect des droits humains, à des espaces ouverts, réellement

en voie de développement et d'instauration de l'Etat de droit. Autrement dit, on passerait d'un système de « vigilance » renforcée, auquel l'Europe serait fermée et d'un vaste espace considéré a priori comme hostile, à une situation de confiance partagée et à des zones d'instauration progressive des droits politiques, sociaux et économiques fondamentaux de l'homme.

Références

Amnesty International. 2015. Fear and fences : Europe's approach to keeping refugees at bay. 17. 11. 2015.

Association marocaine des droits humain (AMDH). 2016. La situation à la frontière : Nador : terrain de mise en oeuvre des politiques migratoires d'externalisation. Avril.

Barroux, Rẽmi. 2013. Miguel, Marina, Carlotta… ces Espagnols qui fuient la crise au Maroc. Le Monde. http://www.lemonde.fr/planete/article/2013/06/20/miguel-marina-carlotta-ces-espagnols-qui-fuient-la-crise-au-maroc_3433199_3244.html.

Charmes, J., M. Lahlou and S. Musette. 2003. Employabilité au Maghreb.

Deleneuville, Matthieu. 2015. Classement PIB : les pays les plus pauvres du monde. Journaldunet.com. http://www.journaldunet.com/economie/magazine/1164746-pays-pauvres/

European Union. 2002. Presidency Conclusions. Seville European Council, 21 and 22 June 2002. Brussels, 24 October.

Everett S. Lee. 1966. A theory of migration. Demography. March, Volume 3, Issue 1.

GADEM (Groupe antiraciste d'accompagnement et de défense des étrangers et migrants – Maroc). 2015. Ceuta et Melilla, centres de tri à ciel ouvert aux portes de l'Afrique. Rapport conjoint. Décembre.

Haut Commissariat au Plan du Maroc, Direction de la statistique. 2014. Enquête nationale « Activité, emploi et chômage » pour 2014. Rabat, Maroc. http://www.hcp.ma/downloads/

Lahlou, M. 2003. Plan d'action pour gérer les migrations irrégulières à partir de l'Afrique. Programme des migrations Internationales. BIT Genève. Avril.

Lahlou, M. 2009. Migration & Development in ECOWAS Countries : what role for the Maghreb ? In Regional Challenges of West African Migration. African and European Perspectives, ed. Marie Trémolières, OECD West African Studies, 99–126. Paris.

Lahlou, M. 2015. Morocco's Experience of Migration as a Sending, Transit and Receiving Country. IAI, Rome, Italy.

Le Monde (journal). 2005. La forteresse Europe s'est écroulée. du 8 octobre 2005.

Le Monde. 2013. Pollution Pétrolière au Nigeria : la justice néerlandaise condamne la filiale de Shell. http://www.lemonde.fr/planete/article/2013/01/30/pollution-la-justice-neerlandaise-rejette-la-plainte-de-4-nigerians-contre-shell_1824317_3244.html

Médecins sans Frontières. 2013. Violences, Vulnérabilité et Migration : Bloqués Aux Portes de l'Europe.

OCDE. 2009. Les enjeux régionaux des migrations ouest-africaines. Cahiers de l'Afrique de l'Ouest. Paris : Editions de l'OCDE.

PNUD. 2015. Rapport sur le développement humain 2015. New York.

Servant, Jean-Christophe. 2008. Uranium au Niger, vers une nouvelle malédiction ? Le Monde Diplomatique. http://blog.mondediplo.net/2008-09-18-Uranium-au-Niger-vers-une-nouvelle-malediction.

Trémolières, Marie, ed. 2009. Regional Challenges of West African Migration. African and European Perspectives. Paris : OECD.

Zerrouky, Madjid. 2015. Migrants : quand l'Europe s'emmure. Le Monde. http://www.lemonde.fr/immigration-et-diversite/article/2015/09/03/migrants-quand-l-europe-s-emmure_4744960_1654200.html.

Root causes and changing patterns of migration in the Mediterranean

Ummuhan Bardak

Abstract

Given the structural significance of labour migration from the Mediterranean economies and with Europe as one of the main destinations, this paper identifies past and current migration dynamics based on a conceptual review of the forces driving migration. It is clear that the root causes of migration alone, understood as simple push–pull factors, do not explain the complexity of migration determinants. Nevertheless, a historical review of outflows up to the present largely confirms the primary importance of enduring negative socioeconomic factors in the region. Emigration flows from the region show four distinct peaks, each corresponding to specific socioeconomic factors, also affected by sudden shocks to the complex macro-political context. The current fragile structure of the region in terms of socioeconomic factors and the macro-political context still keeps migration pressures high. Despite the civil war in Syria and manifold violent conflicts in the region, the labour market trends and migration policies of destination countries seem to shape future changes most of all.

1 Forces driving migration: A conceptual overview

The current so-called refugee crisis has triggered a debate on the 'root causes of migration' and 'how to tackle these underlying causes'. What is meant by 'root causes' can be very broad, covering all the unmet security and development challenges in source countries that push people out of their territory, e.g. poverty, armed conflict, violence, social strife, political turmoil, prosecution, economic hardships, absence of jobs/prospects, unemployment/low wages, inequality, discrimination, corruption, human rights abuses, problems of governance and rule of law, lack of freedoms and increasing disparities between developing and developed nations.[1]

Most of the migration determinants discussed in the literature are typically linked to push and pull factors and gravity models. A review of migration theories from the neoclassical to new economics of migration provides us with a list of macro, micro and mezzo-level determinants of migration (Table 1), e.g. all socioeconomic factors spanning from wage and income differentials to inequality and relative deprivation, rural exit and segmented labour markets or networks. In reality, most people choose to migrate due to a combination of multiple and complex factors, which is certainly not a random process. Instead, it is socially structured and spatially patterned, driven by a range of contextual, economic and non-economic factors. As people make 'migration choices' under structural constraints, both individual willingness and capability (i.e. economic, social and human resources) are needed for migration to happen.

It must be noted that our understanding of the forces driving people to migrate is still limited and fragmented. The literature still needs to combine macro-level migration determinants (e.g. population growth, income level and poverty, environmental degradation) with individual migration motives and capabilities (behavioural link to the micro level), bringing together both economic and non-economic factors and voluntary and forced migration (De Haas 2011). According to De Haas, migration is a complex and messy social process, an intrinsic part of human development. For this reason, it cannot be reduced to a simple function of push–pull factors, which tends to ignore non-economic, sending-country and policy factors. Conventional ways of classifying migration into distinct types (labour/economic, refugee, family or voluntary vs. non-voluntary) is also problematic as these migration types reflect legal rather than sociological categories (De Haas 2011).

Tackling the root causes of migration can certainly help improve people's lives in the countries of origin, thus reducing the socioeconomic pressures for migration. However, it is not certain whether migratory movements would stop as a result. The relationship between migration and broader processes of development and social transformation is not always linear. According to Martin and Taylor (1996), a temporary increase in migration – 'migration hump' – has been a usual part of the process of economic development. In the early stages of development, an increase in wealth leads to a rise in migration since a certain threshold of wealth is necessary to assume the costs and risks of migrating. People's personal life aspirations and awareness of opportunities elsewhere increase the higher the

1 In 1900, the ratio of the average income of the five richest countries in the world to the five to ten poorest countries was about 9:1. Today that ratio is 100:1.

Table 1 An overview of migration determinants

Theory	Analysis level	Determinants of migration
1. Neoclassical migration theory – functionalist	Macro Micro	Push–pull or gravity models based on wage and income differentials, probability of employment. Migration is a function of spatial disequilibria; migrants are rational and income-maximising actors, who move on the basis of a cost–benefit calculation (assuming free choice and full access to information by individuals).
2. New economics of migration – conflictual	Micro Mezzo	Income inequality and relative deprivation in sending societies are major drivers of migration. Migration is a collective household strategy to overcome market failures and spread income risks – it can be a livelihood strategy used by families through remittances.
3. World system theory (historical/structural) – conflictual	Macro: global	Structural changes induced by the flow of capital. Migration is the direct outflow of the spread of global capitalism and the related marginalisation and uprooting of rural populations around the world. The move to cities (within and across borders) is unavoidable.
4. Dual labour market theory – conflictual	Macro: nation state Mezzo	Segmentation of labour markets that creates a permanent demand for cheap immigrant labour at the bottom, not taken by natives (lower end of the labour market). High consumption levels among the highly skilled also creates new demand for low-skilled services (e.g. cleaning, child care, restaurant work) filled by migrants.
5. Network theory	Mezzo Micro	Migrants' agency and strategies tend to create meso-level structures (migrant networks, diaspora) which facilitate migration even over formally closed borders.

Adapted based on the information from Kurekova (2011) and De Haas (2011).

level of education and access to information. This process, referred to as 'human development' is known to lead to increasing aggregate emigration propensities.

This paper focuses primarily on the 'socioeconomic factors' in the Mediterranean as one of the key migration determinants, taking into account also the broader political context. Linked to this focus, 'economic/labour migration' is chosen as the main framework to limit the study. In particular, the labour market dynamics of the region are reviewed to visualise push and pull factors. The macro context is included as another layer of analysis since general state policies play a crucial role in shaping and transforming migration patterns on both sides. For example, many 'non-migration' policies in countries of origin directly or indirectly affect its emigration patterns. The profile of a 'typical migrant' is largely shaped by the policies of the state they come from – its economic policies, human development policies (e.g. education and health services), labour market policies, income and taxation, social welfare, foreign policies, political exclusion, etc. Hence, socioeconomic factors driving people to migrate are far more complex than simplistic notions like the German term 'Wirtschaftsflüchtling'[2] suggests.

Policy decisions in the countries of destination also tend to shape immigration patterns; examples include colonialism, economic and labour market structures, required skill profiles, forms of migrant recruitments, visa requirements and demographic trends. Especially changes in migration policy typically facilitate the entry of particular groups of origin while simultaneously restricting the entry of other groups (patterns of migration selectivity by age, gender, education/skill levels, ethnic roots, country of origin, etc.). For instance, EU migration policy tries to facilitate higher mobility within EU member states (particularly new enlargement countries) while restricting the entry of third-country nationals. Even this explicit migration policy does not change the fact that the state influence is mostly felt through general (socioeconomic) policies that are not necessarily included in the migration discourse.

The paper is structured as follows. Section 2 starts with a historical review of migration outflows in the Mediterranean and their root causes. It identifies four phases of migration flows that are not only shaped by socioeconomic factors, but also affected by political developments. Section 3 shifts the focus from the past to today's migration determinants and analyses the current socioeconomic situation, taking the region's dynamic political context into consideration. Thus, the analysis of socioeconomic factors is supplemented with references to the macro context as well as micro-level strategies. Finally, section 4 brings together all prognostic as-

2 'Wirtschaftsflüchtling' is a polemic notion in German to delegitimise refugees. It can be translated as 'economic refugee' and suggests that they have no legitimate – that is political – reason to come to Europe.

pects discussed in order to come up with some ideas for the future. The paper aims to illustrate the key and continuous importance of the socioeconomic factors in sustaining migration pressures, though in a context of complex and dynamic interaction with the broader political environment in the region.

2 Historical review of migration outflows and their root causes in the Mediterranean

Labour emigration has been a structural feature of the Mediterranean economies since the 1960s. According to the World Bank (2016), 3.38 million Egyptians, 3.04 million Moroccans, 1.78 million Algerians, 810,000 Lebanese, 782,000 Jordanians and 670,000 Tunisians live outside their countries of origin. Following the protracted violence in Syria during the last few years, almost 6 million Syrians left the country as refugees,[3] in addition to the labour emigrant stocks of almost a million from the past. The proportion of emigrants in most countries' populations remains low due to continuous population growth.

This section presents the main migration flows in four chronological periods, each corresponding to different destinations and different socioeconomic and political factors. In line with the key migration determinants presented in Table 1, most of these migration outflows can be linked to the socioeconomic factors reviewed in the previous section (e.g. income differentials, inequality, relative deprivation, networks). In addition to the continuous pressures of the socioeconomic factors which sustain the migration flows, however, the macro-political context seems to create sudden shocks and/or some disruptions in these flows.

Migration towards continental and northern Europe in the 1960s and 1970s
This first flow took place mainly through bilateral labour agreements and consequent family reunification schemes between European countries (Germany, France, Belgium, the Netherlands, Sweden) and North African countries (Morocco, Tunisia and Algeria). Historical and geographical links, colonial pasts and labour needs of heavy industry in Europe attracted large numbers of unskilled and low-skilled migrants from the region in the 1960s. This went hand in hand with the demographic transition, transformation of traditional agriculture, rural exit and unemployment, and the generally low education and skill levels of the populations in the origin countries. Following the immigration restrictions introduced by European countries in the 1970s, most migrant workers settled down and fam-

3 There are more than 3 million Syrian refugees in Turkey, 1.4 million in Jordan and 1.2 million Lebanon. For more info see http://syrianrefugees.eu/.

ily reunification then became the new method of emigration. Later, economic considerations such as joblessness, low wages, poor career prospects and low standards of living became the main reasons for emigration, in particular wage and income differentials rather than unemployment levels. At the same time, the Arab–Israeli conflict and consequent wars in 1948 and 1967 were the source of the large amount of Palestinian refugees in the region. This created a sharp disruption in the movements of the Palestinian population and provided a continuous labour source in the neighbouring countries of Jordan, Syria, Lebanon and Egypt.

Migration towards oil-producing Gulf countries in the 1970s and 1980

This second flow was the result of the labour needs of the Gulf's booming economies after the 1973 oil crisis and the attraction of well-paid jobs available for Arab migrants, spanning the entire spectrum of skills and occupations from manual labourers to professionals. The intra-regional migration provided an important outlet for workers in the labour-exporting countries, such as Egypt, Yemen, Jordan, Palestine and Lebanon. Jordanians and Palestinians were generally skilled workers and professionals. Yemenis were mostly unskilled or semi-skilled, and Egyptian migrants spanned the entire spectrum of skills and occupations from manual labourers to advisors and managers. Labour migration towards the Gulf region seems to have peaked before the second Gulf war. Egypt, Yemen and Jordan (including Palestinians) were the most prominent groups, the first in terms of absolute numbers and the other two by virtue of large proportions of the labour force. This was the golden age of Arab expatriate workers in the Gulf, strengthened by the advantages of common language and culture and geographical vicinity.

Migration within the region during the 1990s and 2000s

This third flow came as a consequence of the crucial political events (e.g. Saddam's occupation of Kuwait and the Gulf wars) that led to a dramatic decrease of Arab migrants in the Gulf region. The Gulf crisis made clear the political risks of having many Arab immigrants in the authoritarian monarchies of the Gulf. The most immediate consequence of the crisis was the dislocation of many Arab workers from the Gulf labour market. During the 1990s about 2 million Arab migrants and their dependents had to leave their residence in Kuwait and other Gulf countries because of respective government policies (claiming the political sympathy shown towards Iraq by Arab migrants).[4] The political cleavages among the Arab nations

4 Particularly Palestinians, Egyptians, Jordanians and Yemenis were heavily affected by the crisis and expelled from Saudi Arabia, Kuwait and other Gulf emirates (Baldwin-Edwards 2011).

created a bias against the recruitment of certain Arab nationalities. The Gulf monarchies now recruit Asian migrants, who are not only cheap to bring in, but also socially and politically easy to manage. As they also experience high youth unemployment among their own populations, nationalisation policies are put in place in state sectors (Baldwin-Edwards 2011). Libya on the other hand continued to attract many Arab workers in this period. The Iraq war led to another sudden flow of refugees among the neighbours (especially in Jordan). At the same time, unskilled labour movements became common for seasonal work, particularly between Syria, Jordan, Lebanon, Palestine and Egypt due to the slight income differentials observed in this period. For example, the number of Syrians working in Lebanon was estimated at 1 million before the Arab Spring.

Migration towards southern Europe and overseas in the 2000s and 2010s
In the early 2000s the northern European destinations largely became saturated for low-skilled migrants. With the eastern enlargement of the European Union, the migrants from Eastern Europe started to fill in most medium-skilled jobs in the context of restrictions towards third-country nationals. This fourth flow has been shaped by the new opportunities that have arisen in southern Europe (Italy and Spain as well as Portugal and Greece to a lesser extent) for low-skilled migrant workers from Egypt, Tunisia and Morocco. After a long period of emigration, these southern European countries became new countries of immigration for low-skilled, low-paid jobs especially in agriculture, construction, tourism and domestic care sectors. This is largely explained by increased income differentials, as native workers no longer take low-paid jobs which are filled by cheap migrants. Another marginal increase was noticed in the high-skilled outflows overseas – to the USA, Canada, Australia and New Zealand – with limited intake as a result of selective migration policies (Bardak 2015). Indeed, this last period shows an increased volume of south–north migration despite immigration restrictions towards third-country nationals – several countries have raised barriers for particular categories of migrants (e.g. low-skilled workers and asylum seekers), although they also facilitated the immigration of other categories (e.g. family migrants and high-skilled migrants). This is also the period when the North African countries have become a transit area for the Sub-Saharan African migrants, with Libya being at the centre until the disruptive changes caused by the Arab Spring.

It is important to emphasise that each of these migration flows from different countries in different periods are far from homogeneous in terms of origin (rural or urban), education/skill levels and nature (temporary or permanent). To give an example, Moroccan migration towards Europe was part and parcel of the livelihoods of members of poorer communities from large, mostly rural areas for a long time, while Egyptian migration also involved the temporary movement of skilled individuals from urban centres to the Gulf, Iraq and Libya (ibid.). As a whole, Arab migration flows have historically been dominated by the low-skilled. Labour emigrants towards Europe typically included low-skilled or unskilled male workers who were followed by family members, while migration to the Gulf and overseas included relatively higher-skilled (male) workers (particularly from Lebanon and Jordan). Migration to Europe tended to be permanent, while migration to the Gulf has always been temporary (even long periods of temporariness).

3 The main migration determinants today in the Mediterranean

This section analyses the current socioeconomic situation in the region, without forgetting its specific and dynamic political context after the Arab Spring. One dramatic impact has been the protracted violence in Syria that led to millions of Syrian refugees fleeing to mainly neighbouring countries. Large numbers of Syrian refugees today dominate most of the intra-regional movements in Jordan, Lebanon, Turkey and Egypt and will provide a continuous labour source in the economies. Despite the main focus on the socioeconomic factors in the section, the structure of analysis includes two other layers. The first additional layer considers the macro context and the second captures individual motives (micro-level strategies). All three aspects – the macro context, socioeconomic factors and individual motives – continuously interact with each other; they are the main determinants that will continue to shape migration patterns in the region.

Macro context: political turbulence and economic challenges

The years 2011–2012 will be remembered for the 'Arab Spring', when a wave of revolts led by young people swept through the region. This led to regime changes in Tunisia, Egypt and Libya, pre-emptive reforms in Algeria, Morocco and Jordan, and violence in Libya and Syria, resulting in one of the biggest refugee crises in the modern world. The uprisings underlined the problems of poor governance at all levels (continuously deteriorated in the two decades preceding revolution) and the deep resentment of people regarding increasing inequalities, unemployment, corruption and lack of democracy (voice and accountability in particular). Five years after the Arab Spring, many things have changed, but the expectations of citizens have not yet been met in most countries. Moreover, the 'Syria example' is increasingly used as a valid excuse for further authoritarianism. The continuing political turbulence affects all policy fields (economy, labour market, education) but they largely remain at a standstill. The risk of political instability remains, as does the risk of sudden shocks and unexpected flows. The future will depend on the direction of transitions and the socioeconomic development model chosen in each country.

The Arab Spring (together with the global crisis) has deteriorated economic growth (to varying degrees) in the region. The effect of political turbulence and social unrest is still felt in shrunken tourism and manufacturing/export sectors and low foreign direct investment, in particular in Tunisia, Egypt and to a lesser extent Lebanon, while the whole system has almost collapsed in Libya and Syria. Economic prospects in Algeria depend on the fluctuations of international oil and gas prices, while Morocco has relatively stable growth rates (ETF 2015a). Beyond this, the biggest challenge in the region's economies is a lack of (decent) job creation and insufficient labour demand (in particular for the highly skilled). Key structural issues affecting job creation are high agricultural employment in some countries and a business-unfriendly environment dominated by micro, small and medium enterprises (ETF 2012, WB 2014). The sectors with highest job potential over the short term (agriculture, construction and tourism) are very sensitive to external factors (e.g. weather, global economy, political stability) and have low productivity, and are hence characterised by poor wages and working conditions, mostly in the informal sector.

Socioeconomic factors: demography and inequality

The Arab countries have very high levels of young people, a demographic trend that is likely to continue until the 2050s. Although slowly decreasing, the population growth rates remain over 1 % in Maghreb and over 2 % in Mashrek countries. The share of the population under the age of 30 years exceeds 60 %, and the working-age population (15–64 years old) is approaching 70 % (ILO). Thus demographic pressure is a key feature of job markets and education systems. On the other hand, on average only half (or even less than half) of the working-age population is economically active and part of the workforce in the region, which means the countries are largely missing out on the 'demographic opportunity window' of having a young population. Considering the high aspirations of youth for education, jobs, marriage, housing and many other consumption items, it puts a tremendous pressure on national political and economic systems and maintains strong push factors for the emigration of youth from the region.

Although the region is classified in the middle-income group by UNDP's Human Development Index (2015), there are large variations between the countries: the human development level in Lebanon, Tunisia and Jordan is rated higher than that of Morocco, Syria and Palestine. A comparison between human development and national income levels reflects the unequal development pattern: Morocco, Syria, Egypt and Algeria have education levels far below their income levels (ETF 2012). Moreover, large variations exist in terms of regional or territorial disparities that are closely correlated with the rural/urban and the manufacturing/agriculture divides. Gini coefficients have been increasing for most countries, indicating higher inequality, and a large proportion of the populations lives close to the poverty line and hence is vulnerable to poverty. This is linked to the high share of vulnerable employment/working poor (e.g. unpaid family workers, informal workers, high self-employment) and weak social protection. The indicators for economic and political participation also point to a large gender gap: none of the countries make it into the top hundred in the 2015 WEF Global Gender Gap report.

Highly segmented and difficult labour markets

Even before the Arab Spring, difficult labour market conditions and a lack of decent jobs for young people are well documented for the region (ETF 2012, Bardak 2014, OECD 2015). On average, the region has the lowest labour market activity rates in the world, varying between 40 % and 50 %, mainly due to very low female activity rates (an average of less than 25 % of working-age women). Labour markets have been segmented along public/private, formal/informal and modern/traditional lines, and are characterised by high informality and precariousness, very low female participation, high unemployment (especially for young females) and significant agricultural employment. Despite low activity levels, the region has the highest youth unemployment rate in the world (28 % in 2013 after the Arab Spring), and this is projected to increase further to 30 % by 2018 (ILO 2013). The majority of unemployed people (up to 80 % in some countries such as Egypt) are young, first-job-seekers with no previous work experience, while unemployment tends to increase with education.

The main factors affecting youth employment prospects are poor macroeconomic performance and growth (which further deteriorated after the Arab Spring), the development model that determines the intensity/type of job creation and skills requirements, and the imbalance between an increasing working age population and low labour demand. In addition, poor labour market functioning (rigidity of labour market regulations) and youth employability problems further exacerbate the situation. Studies point to shortcomings related to the functions of adequate education and training (Bardak 2014), e.g. a lack of generic and/or soft skills (literacy, numeracy, communication, teamwork, critical thinking, work discipline, IT, foreign languages) or the limited role of vocational education and training (VET) (unwillingness to enrol in VET programmes and learn manual work or craft professions). Overall, the business environment is not conducive for individual entrepreneurship, while opaque labour market information and weak job-matching services contribute to poor matching. High social expectations of youth from jobs ('clean' office work) further deteriorate the situation.

Exclusive educational systems and decreasing quality

Over the past 50 years the countries of the region have invested a lot of resources in education. The result of this investment has been a considerable improvement in access to education. Primary education has become almost universal, with increased enrolment in lower secondary education. The gross enrolment rate in upper secondary education ranges from 50 % to 75 %, but the share of VET students at upper secondary level is extremely small in the region – with the exception of Egypt with half of the students directed to VET streams (UNESCO Statistics). The educational expansion has come with decreasing quality in most cases, in addition to worryingly high youth illiteracy and dropout rates in some countries.[5] Skills polarisation between the relatively limited pool of highly educated and the large pool of low-educated workers (with few in between) is observed in many societies. Having left school early, a substantial number of youth are not in education, employment or training (so-called NEETs). For the 15–29 age group, the NEET rate extends to 41 % in Egypt for which data is available, 35 % in Palestine, 32 % in Tunisia and 29 % in Jordan (ETF, 2015b). This means that at least one out of three youth is not in education or training, and not employed.

On the other hand, the strong empowering effect of education is very visible in the mobility of people in the region (especially Morocco, Egypt, Palestine, Jordan, Lebanon and Tunisia), where overall education levels are far lower and graduate unemployment is higher. For example, higher-educated people from Egypt, Jordan, Morocco and Lebanon tend to be more mobile, but they also tend to return home after a period abroad (less so in Lebanon). The same is observed in the stable and relatively high number of international students from the region, reflecting a 'brain gain/circulation' and the high premium placed on education acquired abroad within the domestic labour market context. Higher education normally reduces the intention to migrate while increasing the opportunity to do so. Like education, employment also seems to increase opportunities for migration as employed people generally have better access to information and connections (ETF 2014).

Micro level: attractiveness of the migration idea

Migration has always been and continues to be an attractive idea for a way out of the region, especially for youth both for economic and non-economic rea-

5 Morocco is the most dramatic example of low education levels among the population aged 15 or over: 80 % of people have primary or basic education, 12 % have a medium level of education and only 7 % have higher education. According to UNESCO, more than 40 % of the population was illiterate in 2010. Moreover, the share of people with vocational training at secondary and post-secondary level is less than 5 % (ETF 2012).

sons (Bardak 2015). Youth surveys continuously document a high proportion of young people considering migration, mainly due to low wages, poor jobs and career prospects and low standards of living. According to the ETF surveys in Egypt, Tunisia and Morocco (WB&ETF 2010, ETF 2013), around half of the young population (more than half in Tunisia) would like to migrate, and the large majority of these people are young males. They also dream of migrating to the West via the Gulf and have the desire to live within Western cultures and lifestyles. This might be linked to the positive perceptions of Western lifestyles (e.g. individual liberties), possibly developed over the decades through exposure to the Western TV and cinema industry.[6] The digital revolution has further facilitated the global connection through the Internet and different social media tools that are popular among the young middle class, while the intellectual dominance of the West is still visible in school systems.

In the ETF surveys, there has been a consistent 10 % of young people who would like to migrate because they think that 'there is no future' in their country, and this is not only about material factors. A survey of Arab students and researchers in France (IOM& Arab League 2004) indicated that the main determinants of skilled migration were the general environment which does not sufficiently appreciate skills and competences, a lack of individual freedoms, lack of transparency in the administration of careers, difficult work conditions, and a scarcity of interesting and valuable job opportunities. These social and political reasons may illustrate the failure of policies by the state, universities and private sector to keep human capital at home. Although very small, another potential group is young educated women, who increasingly migrate to have lives independent from their male family members (Babar 2014). This is a special group of educated females coming from middle-class families and migration for them is a life project. They are rather an exception as the large majority of young women have limited mobility and freedoms due to social norms in these societies.

4 What changes can be expected in migration patterns?

By reviewing the past and current trends, the paper showed the primary importance of socioeconomic factors in sustaining migratory pressures in the region, though in the context of a complex political environment. The analysis indicated that most of the migration determinants continue to exist in the region. Con-

6 It should be remembered that virtually every house is connected to satellite television, which is still the primary entertainment tool for the absolute majority of the population in the region.

sidering the political and economic fragility of the societies, migratory pressures will continue if not increase due to demographic youth expansion, economic and labour market pressures and inequality – all long-term structural factors even without any political crisis. The frustration of young people who are increasingly well-educated but at the same time denied agency and acceptable futures that led to the Arab Spring still remains. The result will depend on the level of individual motives and capabilities and the opportunities available in different destinations.

Unfortunately, the global context is not favourable to migration, especially towards the low-skilled. Political, economic and labour market conditions of traditional destinations have evolved, leading to more restrictive immigration policies both in Europe and the Gulf. Low-skilled migrants are no longer needed in the northern European destinations, while the economies of southern Europe are still struggling with their own labour market problems. The Gulf countries also recruit far fewer Arabs for both political and economic reasons. The number and percentage of Arab migrants in the Gulf labour force has continuously decreased, and was at 2.4 million recently (mostly high-skilled) (Babar 2014). The probability of change in the restrictive immigration policies is quite low in both destinations, at least against the low-skilled. Given the current international context, negative public opinions against immigration are expected to continue in the near future.

Nonetheless, traditional migrant stocks in Europe and the Gulf will keep a low level of natural gravity for new migrant flows through diaspora knowledge and migrant networks in those destinations. Despite the restrictive immigration policies and some degree of saturation in labour markets, family reunification through networks largely keeps the path dependency of new flows (Bardak 2015). Thus, a small but sustained level of migrant flows is expected from these networks. Another factor of continuity is 'geography of migration', which interacts with 'migration culture'. While the intention to migrate is as strong in rural and urban areas, the ETF findings in Egypt, Tunisia and Morocco highlight significantly different regional patterns, learnt by seeing examples in the best-established out-migration areas (ETF 2013). In Morocco, for example, the regions with the highest proportions of potential migrants are the same traditional areas of emigration (i.e. Agadir and Souss), where people could observe the benefits of migration from neighbours over decades.

The typical profile of migrants from the region is still young men in their 20s, most likely 'single' with fewer family links (and no children) (WB& ETF 2010, ETF 2013). A primary education level is the most common among the potential migrants from Morocco, Egypt and Syria, secondary education for those from Algeria and Tunisia, and higher education for those from Lebanon and Jordan. This is very much linked to the general human development level of society since the education and skill levels of migrants largely reflect the overall education levels of the populations and the structure and performance of education systems (ETF 2014). An equally important factor is the established culture/patterns of migration in each country. For example, most of the young people learn to develop life strategies from their peers, so migration culture is typically diffused among the same or similar social groups. For instance, most university students in Lebanon and Jordan learn migration as a life strategy from their peers that keeps the established migration pattern.

The exception to the typical low-skilled profile is migration for education purposes (mostly for graduate and postgraduate studies). The region is the source of a stable and sizeable minority of international students in Europe and overseas (ETF 2014). Language is an important contextual factor in the direction of flows, though Europe is less attractive than the USA and Canada. For instance, English-speaking countries such as the UK and Ireland attract many students from countries where English is the primary foreign language, while France draws more students from Maghreb countries, where French is the primary foreign language. Although France is a destination for low-skilled labour migrants from the Maghreb, it seems at the same time a natural preference for higher education studies for French-speaking students from the region. Another emerging study destination is the Gulf countries, where intense investment in education made over the last decade has started to attract Arab students from neighbouring countries (Bardak 2015).

Although low and medium-skilled migrants will still be needed to fill certain segments of the economy when the crisis is over – in particular in rapidly ageing Europe – more opportunities are certainly available for the high-skilled given the increasing global race for talent. Besides the traditional immigration countries (USA, Canada, Australia and New Zealand), Europe tries to follow a similar strategy to attract high-skilled migrants (e.g. reform of the Blue Card Directive, researchers and students directive). However, the average low level and quality of education systems in the southern Mediterranean region is a barrier for the majority of people to compete with skills for the international market. Based on current education and skill levels, the region would provide a poor match to the medium and high skills needed in Europe. Competition from cheaper, more educated and motivated migrants from other countries also decrease their opportunities in international markets.

In conclusion, socioeconomic factors seem to be largely affected and/or indirectly shaped by state policies (mostly in non-migration areas). At the same time, they are deeply embedded in a broader political context, which has a history of sudden shocks or disruptions in the migratory flows. Therefore, the analysis of socioeconomic factors needs to be supported by other layers of analysis on the complex macro context as well as the micro-level strategies. Given the complex situation, it is quite difficult to disconnect socioeconomic factors from political factors in this region. The final migration outcome will depend on the interaction between socioeconomic factors, the macro-political context, individual motives and capabilities, and the opportunities available in migration destinations.

References

Babar, Zahra R. 2014. Mobility and Migration from the Southern Mediterranean States to the GCC. In *IEMed Mediterranean Yearbook 2014*. Barcelona.

Baldwin-Edwards, Martin. 2011. *Labour Immigration and Labour Markets in the GCC Countries: National Patterns and Trends*. London: LSE Global Governance.

Bardak, Ummuhan. 2014. Labour market and education: Youth and Unemployment in the Spotlight. In IEMed Mediterranean Yearbook 2014. http://www.iemed.org/publicacions/historic-de-publicacions/anuari-de-la-mediterrania/sumaris/iemed-mediterranean-yearbook-2014. Accessed: 13 September 2016.

Bardak, Ummuhan. 2015. Continuity and change in youth migration patterns from the Mediterranean. IAI Working Papers, Issue No:15|09. http://www.iai.it/en/pubblicazioni/continuity-and-change-youth-migration-patterns-mediterranean. Accessed: 13 September 2016.

De Haas, Hein. 2011. The determinants of international migration: conceptualising policy, origin and destination effects. Working Paper 32, DEMIG Project, University of Oxford, International Migration Institute (IMI). http://www.imi.ox.ac.uk/pdfs/wp/wp-32-11.pdf. Accessed: 13 September 2016.

European Training Foundation. 2012. UfM Regional Employability Review by Ivan Martin and Ummuhan Bardak. http://www.etf.europa.eu/web.nsf/pages/UfM_regional_employability_review. Accessed: 13 September 2016.

European Training Foundation. 2013. Migration and Skills in Armenia, Georgia and Morocco: Comparing the survey results by M. Collyer, U. Bardak, E. Jansova and O. Karkainen. http://www.etf. europa.eu/web.nsf/pages/Migration_and_skills_Armenia_Georgia_Morocco. Accessed: 13 September 2016.

European Training Foundation. 2014. Migration and Skills Development Agenda in ETF Partner Countries. ETF Position Paper by Ummuhan Bardak. Turin.

European Training Foundation. 2015a. The challenge of youth employability in Arab Mediterranean Countries: The role of active labour market programmes. http://www.etf.europa.eu/web.nsf/pages/Youth_employability_AMCs. Accessed: 13 September 2016.

European Training Foundation. 2015b. Young people not in employment, education or training (NEET): An Overview in ETF Partner Countries by U. Bardak, M. Rubal and F. Rosso. http://www.etf. europa.eu/web.nsf/pages/NEET_ETF_partner_countries. Accessed: 13 September 2016.

Fargues, Philippe and Christine Fandrich. 2012. Migration after the Arab Spring, MPC Research Report 2012/09. Florence: European University Institute. http://

www.migrationpolicycentre.eu/docs/MPC%202012%20EN%2009.pdf. Accessed: 13 September 2016.

ILO. 2013. *Global Employment Trends for Youth,* Geneva.

IOM and Arab League. 2004. *Arab Migration in a Globalised World*. Publication of the proceedings of a regional conference organised by League of Arab States and IOM. 2–4 September 2003, Cairo.

Kurekova, Lucia. 2011. Theories of migration: conceptual review and empirical testing in the context of the EU East-West flows. Paper prepared for Interdisciplinary Conference on Migration 6–9 April 2011, University College London. https://cream.conference-services.net/resources/952/2371/pdf/MECSC2011_0139_paper.pdf. Accessed: 13 September 2016.

Martin, P.L. and J.E. Taylor. 1996. The anatomy of a migration hump. In *Development Strategy, Employment and Migration: Insights from Models,* 43–62. Paris: OECD Development Centre.

OECD. 2015. Investing in Youth: Tunisia – Strengthening the Employability of Youth during the Transition to a Green Economy. http://www.oecd.org/countries/tunisia/Tunisia-a-reform-agenda-to-support-competitiveness-and-inclusive-growth.pdf. Accessed: 13 September 2016.

UNDP. 2015. Human Development Report 2015: Work for Human Development, United Nations Development Programme. http://hdr.undp.org/en/2015-report. Accessed: 13 September 2016.

WEF. 2015. The Global Gender Gap Report 2015, World Economic Forum. http://reports.weforum.org/global-gender-gap-report-2015/. Accessed: 13 September 2016.

World Bank-ETF. 2010. Migration and skills: the experience of migrant workers from Albania, Egypt, Moldova, and Tunisia by Alquézar Sabadie, J., Avato, J., Bardak, U., Panzica, F. and Popova, N. http://issuu.com/World.Bank.Publications/docs/9780821380796. Accessed: 13 September 2016.

World Bank. 2014. Jobs or Privileges: Unleashing the employment potential of the Middle East and North Africa. http://documents.worldbank.org/curated/en/2014/06/19794535/jobs-or-privileges-unleashing-employment-potential-middle-east-north-africa. Accessed: 13 September 2016.

World Bank. 2016. Migration and Remittances Factbook 2016. http://econ.worldbank.org/WBSITE/EXTERNAL/EXTDEC/EXTDECPROSPECTS/0,,contentMDK:21352016~pagePK:64165401~piPK:64165026~theSitePK:476883,00.html. Accessed: 13 September 2016.

The politics of Egyptian regional migration

Examining autocratic cooperation processes in the Arab world

Gerasimos Tsourapas

Abstract

What is the impact of labour migration on autocratic regimes? This article argues that labour migration affects processes of cooperation between autocratic regimes of the sending and host states. It focuses on Egypt between 1970, when the Egyptian regime under Anwar Sadat began the process of liberalising its migration policy, and 1989, when the economic embargo imposed upon Egypt by the League of Arab States in response to the Egypt-Israel Peace Treaty formally ended. It employs process-tracing in a broader qualitative methodological approach, where data are examined sequentially to draw descriptive inference and to disconfirm rival explanations. Primary materials are comprised both of semi-structured expert and elite interviews conducted in Cairo (n = 31), including current and former ministers, former Prime Minister Abdel Aziz Hegazy, and high-ranking government officials, and of emigration-related articles published in the three major, semi-governmental daily newspapers in Egypt *(al-Ahram, al-Akhbar, al-Jumhuriya),* and the non-Egyptian press. Through the case-study of Egyptian regional emigration, the paper demonstrates, firstly, that emigration is able to contribute to closer cooperation between authoritarian regimes and, secondly, that such cooperation is able to support the sending state's ruling regime.

1 Introduction

How does labour migration affect processes of cooperation between autocracies? Academic literature on authoritarian systems of governance has yet to explore the phenomenon of mobility as a separate field of inquiry. Thus far, it has only empirically highlighted regimes' strategies that aim to consolidate elites' power by restricting or encouraging citizen migration. It has not yet provided a solid theoretical claim to explain these processes. More often than not, research is framed solely around securing migrants' financial remittances or other macroeconomic determinants. The literature on the politics of migration has hitherto focused either on the latter's impact on liberal regimes or, to a lesser extent, on states' processes of democratisation. Yet, the global expansion of autocratic rule, coupled with the rise of migration flows into, out of and through non-democracies, implies that scholars still need to develop a comprehensive conceptual approach to explore the linkages between the two phenomena.

In the light of my tentative data, I argue that regimes promote emigration in pursuit of the aim to attain closer cooperation with other regimes. In other words, ruling regimes utilise domestic populations as resources to promote foreign policy aims such as the enhancement of bilateral cooperation.[1] This paper puts forward two hypotheses for further testing. Firstly, authoritarian regimes encourage labour migration to non-democratic countries for political reasons. As I will demonstrate in this paper, the Sadat regime encouraged Egyptian labour migration in order to distinguish itself from a contentious Nasserite legacy and to signal an ideological affinity with elites in the Arab Gulf. Secondly, the promotion of population mobility enhances the personalistic ties between authoritarian regimes of the sending and host states.

This paper focuses on Egypt between 1970, when the Egyptian regime under Anwar Sadat began the process of liberalising its migration policy, and 1989, when the economic embargo imposed upon Egypt by the League of Arab States in response to the Egypt-Israel Peace Treaty formally ended. Egypt has been selected for three reasons. First, it constitutes the largest supplier of migrant labour in the Middle East. Egypt boasts one of the largest emigrant populations in the world, estimated at 3.7 million in 2010, not including emigrants' descendants (Tsourapas 2015a, 2193). Second, state policy on emigration underwent a concrete shift at an identifiable point in history, and this allows greater analytical precision to be achieved: Egypt's restrictive emigration policy, which had been in place since 1952, was replaced by a fully liberalised, de-regulated policy in late 1971, and it has been in place ever since. Third, the Egyptian regime proved to be remarkably durable; holding power continuously between 1952 and the 2011 Arab uprisings, it recent-

1 In accordance with practices in the relevant literature, I principally employ the term "sending state" to refer to migrants' states of origin. I further differentiate between the term "state", which I consider politically neutral, and the terms "regime" or "government" (cf. Tsourapas 2015a).

ly resurfaced following a brief democratic experiment between 2011 and 2013[2]. As such, the Egyptian regime forms part of a broader universe of cases that includes Cuba, the People's Republic of China, North Korea and other regimes that engage in migration accords with other non-democratic regimes.

The paper is structured as follows: I first review relevant scholarship on authoritarianism and the politics of emigration, identifying a lacuna in theorizing how labour emigration is used by non-democracies. I then proceed to hypothesise that the promotion of population mobility is aimed at enhancing the collaboration between authoritarian regimes of the sending and host states. I test this hypothesis on the case of Egyptian labour migration across the Middle East in the 1970–1989 period. The paper's findings highlight how migration enhances cross-regime collaboration, firstly, by signalling an ideological affinity between elites in the sending and host states and, secondly, by the establishment of interpersonal relations with such elites. I conclude the paper with suggestions as to how this analysis might be extended.

2 Authoritarianism, regime cooperation & emigration

This section firstly establishes the claim that the broader scholarly research on authoritarianism and politics of emigration has yet sufficiently theorised the linkages between the two phenomena. It will then propose a novel approach based upon the emerging literature on authoritarian regime cooperation. I use Juan Linz's definition of authoritarian regimes as

> 'political systems with limited, not responsible, political pluralism, without elaborate and guiding ideology, but with distinctive mentalities, without extensive nor intensive political mobilization, except at some points in their development, and in which a leader or occasionally a small group exercises power within formally ill-defined limits but actually quite predictable ones' (Linz 1964, 255).

Scholars researching authoritarian regimes do not usually treat migration management processes as an independent variable. Instead, authoritarianism is mainly approached with the focus on domestic political factors (Posusney and Angrist 2004, Schlumberger 2007). O'Donnell (1973), for instance, point to the importance of technocrats in sustaining 'bureaucratic authoritarian' regimes. Drawing

2 For the purposes of this analysis, I treat the Egyptian authoritarian regime as homogenous within the 1952–2011 period, given that succession was straightforward (Nasser designated Sadat as his successor, and he, in turn, designated Mubarak).

on Skocpol, Eva Bellin (2004, 2012), by contrast, highlights the regimes' coercive apparatus and their use of force and emphasise the existence of a strong middle class. Geddes' work (2005) focuses on the role of political parties. He argues that single-party regimes are more stable than military or personalistic dictatorships. Other scholars investigate the role of elections in what have been termed "hybrid regimes" (Levitsky and Way 2010); the role of propaganda and leaders' "personality cult" (Wedeen 1999, Tripp 2007); the importance of keeping opposition forces under control (Albrecht 2013) or the "coup-proofing" of domestic institutions (Byman and Lind 2010). A small group of scholars attempt to move beyond domestic political determinants of authoritarianism and highlight the role of international relations, albeit without including migration in such analyses. Instead, they focus on how foreign intervention impedes democratisation either directly (Gasiorowski and Byrne 2004) or indirectly through military, financial or other aid (Brownlee 2012). Others point to the role of Western liberal regimes in supporting authoritarian structures in the Gulf Cooperation Council states (Vitalis 2007), North Africa (Tsourapas 2013), and Latin America (Blasier 1985).

Moreover, political scientists' examination of the effects of international migration traditionally focuses on the host state, and particularly on advanced, industrialised economies (Messina and Lahav 2006). Within the small, albeit growing group of scholars examining the politics of emigration within sending states (Østergaard-Nielsen 2003, Fitzgerald 2009, Collyer 2013), research usually seeks to account for the decision to foster state-diaspora linkages (Varadarajan 2010), particularly from the economics angle (as will be examined below). Processes of democratisation are traditionally approached either within liberal regimes (O'Mahony 2013), particularly Mexico (Pérez-Armendáriz and Crow 2010, Pfutze 2012), or within transitions from autocratic rule to democracy (Koinova 2009, Brand 2013). Authoritarian regimes are expected to be more likely to restrict emigration than either established liberal states (Messina and Lahav 2006) or many emerging democracies, which also actively encourage labour migration (Massey 1999). A notable exception is the emerging literature on authoritarian regimes' decision to introduce out-of-country voting: Brand focuses on the Algerian, Tunisian, and Moroccan regimes in an effort to demonstrate that 'in authoritarian contexts, expanding the franchise is aimed at increasing sovereignty over expatriates with resources to be tapped, or at reinforcing security through a different means of monitoring communities abroad' (Brand 2010, 97). Yet one wonders if migration may also serve authoritarian power in other ways, particularly given that out-of-country voting continues to constitute the exception, rather than the rule, in sending states globally.

I situate my analysis within the emerging strand of literature examining the international relations of authoritarian regimes and, in particular, the cross-regime patterns of cooperation that may emerge (Mattes and Rodríguez 2014). This paper uses Keohane's definition of the concept:

> 'Cooperation occurs when actors adjust their behaviour to the actual or anticipated preferences of others, through a process of policy coordination. To summarize more formally, intergovernmental cooperation takes place when the policies actually followed by one government are regarded by its partners as facilitating realization of their own objectives, as the result of a process of policy coordination' (Keohane 2006, 81).

Building on a strong tradition of researching the international dimension of democratisation, liberal value "diffusion," and "Europeanization," some authoritarianism scholars argue that non-democratic regimes 'deliberately use international cooperation to bolster their particular type of rule.' (Erdmann, Bank et al. 2013, 5–6). In fact, this research agenda is emerging, particularly on cooperation and different types of authoritarian regimes (Mattes & Rodriguez, 2014; cf. Svolik 2012). Yet, this literature continues to be highly fragmented, and its empirical and conceptual bases are shaky (Erdmann et al. 2013). In an effort to enrich this literature with a novel empirical case and re-conceptualise it through the prism of population mobility, the next parts of this paper focus on the linkages between authoritarianism, regime cooperation, and Egyptian migration across the Middle East.

I employ process-tracing in a broader qualitative methodological approach, where data are examined sequentially to draw descriptive inference and to disconfirm rival explanations (Beach and Pedersen 2013). I have relied on diverse primary and secondary material in Arabic, French, and English for the purpose of hypothesis formation through induction. Primary material is comprised of semi-structured expert and elite interviews conducted in Cairo (n = 31), including current and former ministers, former Prime Minister Abdel Aziz Hegazy, and high-ranking government officials. For the purposes of triangulation, I also draw on articles on emigration published in the three major, semi-governmental daily newspapers in Egypt *(al-Ahram, al-Akhbar, al-Jumhuriya)*, and the non-Egyptian press (Tsourapas, 2014).[3] Finally, I rely on archival material in Cairo drawn from the Ministry of Education and the Ministry of Manpower and Migration.

3 The three main Egyptian newspapers are referred to as semi-governmental because they were, at various points, formally nationalized media instruments of the regime, or loosely affiliated with various officials, operating under strict censorship. Thus, they are treated as broadly reflecting government views. For a similar approach, see Waterbury (1983).

3 Egyptian migration & Arab regime rapprochement

The Arab world is now in what may be termed the Saudi epoch in modern Arab history.

Muhammad Hasanayn Haykal[4]

Egypt in the 1952–1970 period was marked by Gamal Abdel Nasser's rule, who developed an Egypt-centred, pan-Arab rhetoric that combined 'anti-colonialism, Arab socialism and the ideal of Arab political union' and reverberated across the Middle East (Dekmejian 1971). However, the Arab masses' enthusiasm for the radical ideas of "Nasserism" was not shared by conservative Arab elites, who were especially distressed by the regime's ominous statements that 'we should differentiate between Egypt as a state' and 'Egypt as a revolution' (*al-Ahram*, 29 December 1961). In particular, Saudi Arabia's King Faisal saw 'Nasser's pan-Arabism as a direct threat to the survival of the Sa'udi ruling group' (Al-Rasheed 2010, 113). This uneasy tension between the Arab republics and the Arab monarchies, the so-called "Arab Cold War" (Kerr 1971), was exacerbated by the political activism of Egyptians abroad who promoted a pro-Nasser agenda across North Africa and the Middle East, the sole exception to an otherwise restrictive emigration policy (Tsourapas 2015a). Under Nasser, economic emigration was restricted, but migration for political purposes was commonplace. On the one hand, 'Egypt was a country at war, and it viewed its manpower as a much needed source' (Roy 1991). In fact, the success of Nasser's statist-developmentalist agenda relied on a strong domestic labour force that would allow Egypt to embark on construction programmes as well as ensure Nasser's promises of free education for all (Mountjoy 1972, Ayubi 1995). As Ibrahim (1982) describes:

> 'This was the period in which central planning, the public sector, workers' participation in management, land reform, and rent controls were all in vogue. The share of industry in Egypt's GNP was steadily rising, and the transformation of Egypt's labour force to modern sectors looked irreversible. With such socioeconomic forces at work, the thought of massive labour transfer to other countries was unthinkable' (Ibrahim 1982, 65).

On the other hand, Egypt promoted regional, short-term migration for distinct foreign policy purposes, in order to "export" Egyptian revolutionary ideals abroad – primarily Nasserism and pan-Arabist ideals. Egyptians abroad filled the positions of bureaucrats, educators, administrators and medical staff. They were jobs that

4 Quoted in *Al-Anwar* (Beirut), 20–23 May 1977.

the recently decolonised Arab states were unable to produce. A chief example is migration to Libya: 'I've never been so rich in my life,' one Egyptian administrator boasted to a *Sunday Times*' reporter in Tripoli. 'The Egyptian Government [...] pay my salary at home in addition to my salary here; they fly me home free for my annual leave' (*Sunday Times*, 28 March 1958). The *quid pro quo* consisted of heightened political activism of such Egyptians around issues of anti-Westernism and pro-Egyptian revolutionary ideals (Tsourapas 2016). In schools, for instance, Egyptian teachers taught a distinct, pro-Egypt version of history:

> 'The presence of Egyptian teachers explains why so many classrooms show the influence of Egyptian propaganda. Pupils do crayon drawings of Egyptian troops winning victories over Israel or Britain. In Benghazi, Libya, a complete course in Egyptian history is given to secondary school students. A display in a high school art exhibit showed pictures of the leading rulers of Egypt; on one side were the "bad" rulers, on the other the "good" rulers. The bad rulers began with the Pharaoh Cheops, who enslaved his people to build the pyramids, and ended with Farouk. The good rulers began with the idealistic Pharaoh Ikhnaton and ended with, of course, Gamal Abdel Nasser' (Wynn 1959, 137).

Nasser's death in 1970 marked the end of that era, although ambitions of confrontation with the conservative Arab regimes had already come to an end with the 1967 Arab-Israeli War. The time was ripe for a re-appraisal of Egypt's regional policy as Sadat, Nasser's successor, moved towards a stronger relationship with Egypt's neighbours, particularly the Gulf regimes and, chief among them, Saudi Arabia (Ayubi 1991). This policy shift was necessary given the military defeat in the 1967 war, which accelerated Egypt's economic collapse and led to a legitimacy crisis. In fact, the relevant literature has identified multiple reasons behind Sadat's wish to enhance cooperation with his Arab counterparts. Having faced massive financial problems since the mid-1960s, Egypt's military defeat signalled the shift of political and economic power to the increasingly prosperous Arab states of the Gulf (Richards and Waterbury 2009). Economic, military, and political support to post-1967 Egypt now depended very much upon the goodwill of its Arab neighbours (Feiler 2003). The role of migration was crucial in ensuring the longevity of such cross-regime cooperation.

Closer cooperation with neighbouring Arab states would only have been possible if Egypt demonstrated that it had abandoned Nasser's earlier path of regional confrontation and political agitation. This was accomplished, at least partly, through Sadat's espousal of labour migration and his decision to liberalise Egypt's emigration policy in the country's 1971 "Permanent" Constitution. Whereas Nasser had previously restricted labour emigration, rejecting free travel abroad until Egypt possessed 'a surplus of foreign currencies which we can spend on luxury and on summer vacations in Europe and America,' Article 52 of the "Permanent" Constitution now declared that 'citizens shall now have the right to permanent or temporary migration' (Arab Republic of Egypt 1971). Egypt's policy shift, which occurred six months after Sadat's "Corrective Revolution" of 15 May 1971 that marked the purging of remaining Nasserite forces from the regime, was ideological in nature. As Sadat declared, Egyptians' freedom to travel abroad corresponded to his personal liberal leanings. Under Nasser, he wrote (Sadat 1978), Egyptians had been 'turned into puppets. They became dummies *(dumā)* in the hands of their rulers, who did with them as they pleased. People were not allowed to travel [...]'. The regime now professed to espouse ideals of personal freedom, highlighting how they contradicted Nasserite-era socialist doctrines. As Sadat would frequently declare:

> '[...] I want to make it clear that if we do not hold to the complete freedom of the individual in the shadow of competition, we cannot realize any progress. He who wants to travel, let him travel' (Sadat, n.d., quoted in Cooper 1982: 97–87).

While this novel discourse was a distinct nod to manpower-poor Arab countries (an issue that will be explored below), it also constituted a sign that the era of Egypt's politicised migration and antagonism with other Arab regimes was over. While, in the past, 'Arab states' suspicion of Nasser's political motives was reflected in a reluctance to encourage the emigration of Egyptians' (Choucri 1977, 6), Arabs were now urged to abandon such scepticism. Prominent journalist 'Ali Amin underlined that 'Egypt will [now] never think of interfering with the internal affairs of any Arab state. Neither will it impose an opinion, a certain person, policy, or form of government on them, be it Beirut, Amman, Damascus, Tripoli, Kuwait, or the Arabian Gulf' (*al-Ahram*, 7 April 1974). Anis Mansur, the later editor-in-chief of the regime mouthpiece *October*, explained:

> '[An] Egyptian was looked upon as the man with the 'ugly face' throughout the Arab world. For twenty years, every Egyptian had seemed to turn into a spy or saboteur. Every Egyptian teacher was thought to have come to overthrow the standing rule and to distribute subversive literature. Every Egyptian doctor was considered a spy acting for Egyptian Intelligence Service to set one class against another. [...] Now he is not interested in other peoples' affairs. 'Give and take' is his motto. [Under Nasser] every Egyptian was treated as a persona non grata and he had to isolate himself to affirm that he had nothing to do with what happened in Egypt. [Under Sadat] this abominable picture changed and will continue to change to the better, for Egypt came to be governed by a ruler not by a leader [...] Egyptians abroad form a 'working army' for the sake of Egypt and all Arabism' (al-Akhbar, 13 March 1974).

In a similar tone, *al-Akhbar's* Mostafa Amin argued in a column entitled '"Ugly Egyptian" Image Removed' that the Egyptian migrant was formerly considered

> 'a hooligan holding a knife in his mouth and a heavy club in his hand. Unfortunately, the Egyptians helped maintain that ugly picture by their behaviour, and this explains to a great extent the pleasure that the world showed upon our 5 June 1967 defeat. Today the situation is totally different' (al-Akhbar, 23 May 1976).

Indeed, Egyptian regional migrants confirmed the regime's promises by developing a reputation of being apolitical – or, at the very least, less political than Egyptians abroad under the Nasserite era – to the delight of their host states. 'Statistics show,' Haddad argues (1987, 248), 'that both Saudi Arabia and Kuwait reduced the recruitment of Palestinian labourers' after 1970, opting instead to employ 'large numbers' of Egyptians who would not 'function as a fifth column and eventually endanger the host countries.' Of course, this is very difficult to prove categorically, but the opinion that Egyptians in the post-Nasserite era were less interested in politics was widely held. Importantly, this was propagated by the ruling regime itself: Under Sadat, the Egyptian state effectively ceased to promote migrant political activism abroad:

> 'It must be stressed that, for the most part [...], Egyptians go abroad for purely economic reasons. They may not like the conditions or the social values of the countries hosting them, but they are totally disciplined [not] to jeopardise the opportunity to earn money by indulging in political activities' (Roy 1991, 574).

The New York Times put it bluntly:

> 'In theory, it would be possible to replace the Egyptian expatriate work force with Palestinians, who constitute the region's other major pool of skilled labour. However, Palestinians are often discriminated against as political risks [...] Saudi Arabia tends to view Palestinians as potential fifth columnists and prefers Egyptians who may be less motivated but are more "harmless and submissive," as one Saudi employer put it' (*New York Times*, 8 July 1979).

Another indication of how migration was employed by the Sadat regime to distinguish the new leadership was that exit visas, a key feature of the Nasserite era, were abolished on 15 May 1974, the third anniversary of Sadat's "Corrective Revolution". Egypt's three main newspapers reported that

> 'The decision to abolish exit visas was taken in accordance with President Anwar

> el-Sadat's directives. It was also inspired by the principles of the Corrective Movement of May 15, which underlined the citizen's freedom and the removal of all restrictions on the exercise of his liberties. Exit visas have been required for Egyptians and foreigners for the past 25 years' (MENA, 15 May 1974).

While most analyses of Egyptian migration in the post-1970 era focus on its economic determinants, the argument that Egyptian elites promoted regional migration for material purposes is not entirely convincing. Firstly, as has been explained, Egypt had a distinct history of politically driven migration processes in the decades preceding Sadat's rise to power. In the decades leading up to 1970, therefore, Egyptian regional migration was not viewed as an instrument of economic development, but as a distinct foreign policy tool. At the same time, the decision to liberalise Egypt's migration policy in late 1971 was not a decision purely based on attracting economic remittances or addressing demographic pressures – after all, the decision to liberalise Egypt's emigration policy preceded the post-1973 Arab-Israeli War, the OPEC oil embargo and the rise of oil prices, by a few years. Finally, even in the post-1973 oil boom era, Egypt's liberalised migration policies actually strained the country's resources. One result was that domestic labour shortages soon appeared. Construction workers, for one, departed 'in such proportions, that project implementation schedules were slipping [and] crash training programs in construction trades were necessary to offset the high out-migration flow' (Socknat 1979, 27). Consequently, labour shortages in the 1970s fuelled 'inflationary havoc in the building industry,' as daily wages of skilled workers such as bricklayers topped those of architects and civil engineers by 1977 (Shazly, 2003, 177–8). In turn, this led to shortages in Egyptian agriculture, as 'some half a million agricultural workers left the sector' in the 1973–79 period in order to enter the construction field (Richards 2007). Overall:

> 'The occupational immobility prevailing within the rigidly compartmentalized domestic labour market has meant that internal readjustments to compensate for the exports of particular types of manpower have not been as extensive and successful as in other labour supplying countries, e.g. Jordan. This is the cause of the unexpectedly sudden shortages that have appeared in the numbers of technicians, tradesmen and craftsmen both among the formally and informally qualified' (Birks and Sinclair 1979, 301).

The regime itself was well aware of these strains on the national economy. Despite public warnings from the Minister of Education, Dr. Mustafa Kamal Hilmi, that the country suffered from a shortage of 25,000 educators in 1974, some 20,000 teachers were dispatched across 'Arab and friendly countries' in that year alone (*al-Ahram,* 17 June 1974). By 1979, the Ministry of Education would report that it had a shortage of 14,928 teachers in languages alone (*al-Jumhuriya*, 30 August 1979). In a report issued in 1979, the National Bank of Egypt argued that 'the main functional categories and professionals which are badly needed in Egypt... are [those] inclined towards migration.' It estimated that shortages in technicians and skilled workers reached 40–50 % (National Bank of Egypt, 1979). Sadat would respond that, as far as 'Egyptian emigration to Arab and African states [is concerned] Egypt will continue to meet the manpower requirements of these countries' (*MENA*, 5 January 1977). Egypt boasts a surplus of unskilled workers, as well as many categories of university graduates, but faces a shortage of skilled workers, as well as of some professional skills. Unregulated emigration created bottlenecks and 'acute shortages' (Birks and Sinclair 1979, 297). Thus, mass emigration led to the strange phenomenon of labour shortages within a labour surplus economy. Roy (1991) describes this problem in more detail:

> 'The basic problem with the approach is that there is absolutely no quality control over who goes. The Arab states have long since learned to distinguish between the truly able and productive Egyptian professional and the poorly trained incompetent one. They actively recruit in Egypt and have well-developed means by which to identify the most promising candidates. In this sense, Egypt may be exporting its most needed professionals while retaining the least able and experienced' (Roy 1991, 565).

Overall, this section highlighted how the Egyptian regime's wish to liberalise its emigration policy was driven by distinctly ideological reasons rather than economic ones. By the end of the 1970s, as concerns over domestic labour shortages were invariably bypassed for Arab states' developmental needs and any political economy cost was set aside in favour of its bilateral relations, Egypt's role as a regional supplier of labour had 'become a tradition' (Birks and Sinclair 1978, 43).

4 Egyptian migration & personalistic relations with Arab elites

This section discusses how, beyond ensuring a degree of ideological *rapprochement*, migration allowed Middle Eastern regimes to discuss and coordinate issues on a top level rather than through any institutional or bureaucratic process. Egypt's strategy on migration was 'always focused on bilateral agreements, according to Hegazy. The Arab League spoke about the use of Arab manpower, but did not have any power, and no policy on this issue,' arguably given the weakness of the multilateral organisation in the face of bilateral relations (*Personal Interview*, 27 April 2014). This allowed the Egyptian regime to use migration matters in order to benefit from closer, stronger ties to other Arab regimes. One example of this is the amendment of Law No. 97/1969, which under Nasser prohibited former government officials and ministers from working in the Arab world for five years after the termination of their work in Egypt. The new version, No. 38/1973, vested the President himself with the power to make exceptions as he deemed fit. The reason cited for this amendment was the need of Arab countries for Egyptian expertise.

Again, this process was not adopted with the Egyptian regime having the state's or the migrants' best interests at heart. It set off a tradition by which migrant communities became victims of the regime's relations with host state authoritarian regimes. When bilateral relations flourished, migratory flows between countries increased: The 1972 dispatch of 6,000 Egyptian workers to Algeria, for instance, was agreed under the aegis of increased bilateral cooperation between the two countries (*Akhbar el-Yom*, 7 January 1972). When bilateral relations deteriorated, however, as in Libya, Egyptian migrants suffered imprisonment, expulsion, torture, even death (Tsourapas 2015). As Fergany (2001) wrote,

> 'Attempts to organize the pan-Arab labour market have fizzled out into ineffective declarations of intent that have been impeded in reality by perceived narrow national interests, particularly of countries of employment, acting the mind set of buyers in a buyers-market [...] Labour movement in the Arab region has been captive to the ups and downs of Arab politics, sometimes with devastating consequences to the welfare of embroiled migrants' (Fergany 2001, 37).

As the regime abolished exit visas, it replaced them with two types of bilateral agreements: first, those that would allow Egyptians entry to foreign countries such as Libya or Syria with any official document of identification and, second, those that set a limit to the numbers of immigrants that host states in the Arab world were willing to receive and regulated labour conditions abroad. At the time, the latter were an odd occurrence, as ever since the Middle East's 'labour movement has been spontaneous' (Birks and Sinclair 1980, 84). It is safe to assume that these frequently overlapping accords aimed less at regulating regional emigration than at consolidating intra-regime cooperation ties. These agreements 'only described very general principles of cooperation' (Collyer 2004, 11), avoiding more 'hot' topics such as medical care or end-of-contract bonuses (Farrag 1998); even then, they were rarely observed and the limits they set on the number of immigrants were not imposed. The 1971 protocol with Libya, for instance, was frequently violated. In fact, in a personal interview (2 April 2014), the former Minister of Manpower & Migration (2006–2011), Aisha Abd al-Hadi, admitted she was unaware of the content of many of these accords, which was typically not made public; in some cases she was not even aware of their existence. Overall, the utility of such agreements appears to be suspicious, given that most Egyptian officials admitted that regional migration processes were so complex that they could not be effectively regulated through intra-state accords (Lesch 1985).

The Sadat regime worked hard to ensure that Egypt continuously provided skilled and unskilled labour to accommodate Arab states' increasing labour market needs. Indeed, one of the goals of the Higher Council of Manpower and Training, newly formed through Presidential Decree No. 795, was the 'fulfilment of the needs of Arab and other friendly countries' (Messiha 1980, 12) At the same time, Egypt introduced training regulations ensuring that the state 'provides the specialized manpower required and regulates the supply of workers whose services are sought by the sister Arab states' (*al-Ahram*, 30 April 1974). By 1970, Egypt's population had grown from 21 million in 1952 to over 33 million. Labour migrants were relatively well-educated, as a result of Nasser's 1962 decision to make all levels of education free, while oil-exporting Arab countries had clearly stated their need for migrant labour well before the 1973 oil embargo dramatically increased their monetary resources and manpower needs. Already in 1970, the Saudi five-year plan reported that:

> 'The employment of non-Saudi personnel is considered a partial answer to the Kingdom's needs of manpower necessary for development processes because of the number of Saudis working in both the private and public sectors who possess academic qualifications and adequate training required for fast development will continue to be relatively low' (Barsalou 1985, 136).

'The supply of Egyptian manpower was essential for the Gulf countries, and the President realized the country's potential,' recalled Hegazy (*Personal Interview*, 27 April 2014). In 1974, the regime announced that:

> 'Evening classes will be arranged for government employees. Within the framework of planning to meet the requirements of Arab, African and foreign countries of skilled workers in building, electricity, factories and services, practical technical training centres will be set up in order to meet increased demand of Egyptian workers who receive high wages abroad. In view of the need of Egyptian teachers in the Arab and African countries, the ministry of higher education will set up special institutes to train those who wish to work as teachers abroad from among holders of university degrees and government employees' (*MENA*, 3 July 1974).

By 1979, Egypt put forward a plan for the creation of specialised offices in 'every faculty' of Egyptian universities that would supply students with accurate information on vacant employment posts across the Arab world (*al-Ahram,* 8 February 1974). Prime Minister Mamduh Salim had already officially declared that 'Egypt's policy is to encourage export of its manpower to the Arab world [...] so that Egyptians can participate in the development plans of sister Arab states' (*al-Akhbar,* 15 August 1975). Egyptian school curricula now taught that 'people emigrate, just like the birds' (*Al-Ahram al-Iqtisadi,* No. 745, 1983), while the 1977 preparatory school certificate examination asked students to write an essay on 'the joys of a person who could obtain work in an Arab country, thus managing to accumulate money and return home to start a new life' (*Al-Ahram,* 18 May 1977). The Undersecretary of the Ministry of Immigration supported such statements: 'we must supply the Arab countries with the manpower to develop [...] This is our duty. They need our manpower and we have good relations. They are our brothers' (*Cairo Today,* May 1984).

Overall, regional migration constituted a key policy for the Egyptian state, which employed it as part of a broader policy of *rapprochement* with the Arab states. 'Migration helped restore the relationship between Egypt and the Arab countries,' Hegazy recently recalled (*Personal Interview,* 27 April 2014). The dispatch of 6,000 Egyptian workers to Algeria in 1972, for instance, was agreed under the aegis of increased bilateral cooperation between the two countries (*Akhbar el-Yom,* 7 January 1972). In the 1980s, Algeria's decision to replace French teachers in the sciences, mathematics, chemistry, and physics with Egyptians was also dependent on the cordial relationship between the two regimes (*MECS* 11, 1987). A similar 1973 agreement to dispatch Egyptian agricultural experts to Iraq was signed under similar rhetoric (*MENA,* 20 February 1973). During a visit to Kuwait in October 1971, Sadat received representatives of the '36,000 strong' Egyptian community, underlining the 'fraternal ties binding Egypt and Kuwait' (11 October 1971). By doing so, Sadat began a process of labour migration coordination through the heads of state – for instance, Oman's Sultan Qaboos did not hesitate to directly replace all Bahrainis working in the country with Egyptians, following his 1971 coup d'état (Graz, 1992).

5 Conclusion

> 'There is not a single Arab citizen or a single Arab country that is not indebted to the Egyptian people [...] for their sacrifices at all times [...] It is nationally incumbent on every true Arab to hasten to repay part of that debt so that giant and generous Egypt should continue to stand on its feet in full grandeur. We in Iraq are prepared to contribute to that duty, and that honour. Our doors are flung open to Egyptian farmers, workers, and intellectuals. They will be assured here of the same treatment as their Iraqi

brothers, without the least discrimination' (Interview, Saddam Hussein in *al-Ahram*, 21 February 1975).

What impact does migration have upon authoritarian regimes' patterns of international cooperation? This paper has attempted to go beyond the existing literature by exploring how migrants have been used by authoritarian regimes. It has aimed at enriching the emerging literature on regime cooperation by introducing migration as a key policy issue affecting cross-regime relations. Through the case study of Egyptian regional emigration, the paper has demonstrated, firstly, that emigration is able to contribute to closer cooperation between authoritarian regimes and, secondly, that such cooperation is able to stabilise the ruling regime. Beyond a novel argument of why and how sending states employ emigration policies, the paper has also offered a novel account of how population mobility has featured in the intra-Arab relations. It has shown how migration has influenced the course of post-Nasserite regional politics.

How does this theorization travel beyond the Egyptian case? A brief look at the strategies of other authoritarian regimes throughout the world appears to confirm this paper's argumentation: The Cuban regime, for instance, has developed a long, institutionalised process of dispatching medical personnel to a number of countries, through a strategy of "medical internationalism" that has distinct cooperation objectives. North Korea is currently dispatching thousands of workers to friendly states such as Russia, China, and some of the Gulf countries. There were similar processes between the Soviet Union and various Eastern Bloc countries in the pre-1989 period. Japanese migration to Latin American countries can also be examined under the paper's framework of enhanced cooperation. Having established a causal link between emigration and authoritarianism in the Egyptian case, this paper aims to pave the way for future research across, and within, multiple cases.

References

Al-Rasheed, M. 2010. A History of Saudi Arabia. New York: Cambridge University Press.

Albrecht, H. 2013. Raging Against the Machine: Political Opposition Under Authoritarianism in Egypt. Syracuse: Syracuse University Press.

Arab Republic of Egypt. 1971. Dustur Jumhuriyat Misr al-'Arabiyya. Cairo: Ministry of Information.

Ayubi, N. 1991. The State and Public Policies in Egypt Since Sadat. Reading: Ithaca Press.

Ayubi, N. 1995. Over-Stating the Arab State: Politics and Society in the Middle East. London: I.B. Tauris.

Barsalou, J.M. 1985. Foreign Labor in Sa'udi Arabia: The Creation of a Plural Society. Columbia University. Ph.D.

Beach, D., and R.B. Pedersen. 2013. Process-tracing methods: Foundations and guidelines. Ann Arbor: University of Michigan Press.

Bellin, E. 2004. The robustness of authoritarianism in the Middle East: Exceptionalism in comparative perspective. Comparative Politics 36(2): 139–157.

Bellin, E. 2012. Reconsidering the robustness of authoritarianism in the Middle East: Lessons from the Arab Spring. Comparative Politics 44(2): 127–149.

Birks, J.S., and C.A. Sinclair. 1978. Human Capital on the Nile: Development and Emigration in the Arab Republic of Egypt and the Democratic Republic of the Sudan. Geneva: International Labour Organisation.

Birks, J.S., and C.A. Sinclair. 1979. Egypt: A Frustrated Labor Exporter? Middle East Journal 33(3): 288–303.

Birks, J.S., and C.A. Sinclair. 1980. International Migration and Development in the Arab Region. Geneva: International Labour Organization.

Blasier, C. 1985. The Hovering Giant (Revised Edition): U.S. Responses to Revolutionary Change in Latin America, 1910–1985. Pittsburgh: University of Pittsburgh Press.

Brand, L. 2010. Authoritarian states and voting from abroad: North African experiences. Comparative Politics 43(1): 81–99.

Brand, L. 2013. Arab Uprisings and the Changing Frontiers of Transnational Citizenship: Voting from Abroad in Political Transitions. Political Geography 41.

Brownlee, J. 2012. Democracy Prevention: The Politics of the U.S.-Egyptian Alliance. Cambridge: Cambridge University Press.

Byman, D., and J. Lind. 2010. Pyongyang's survival strategy: tools of authoritarian control in North Korea. International Security 35(1): 44–74.

Choucri, N. 1977. The New Migration in the Middle East: A Problem for Whom? International Migration Review 11(4): 421–443.

Collyer, M. 2004. The Development Impact of Temporary International Labour Migration on Southern Mediterranean Sending Countries: Contrasting Examples of Morocco and Egypt. Brighton: Sussex Centre for Migration Research.

Collyer, M., Ed. 2013. Emigration Nations: Policies and Ideologies of Emigrant Engagement. London: Palgrave Macmillan.

Cooper, M. 1982. The Transformation of Egypt. London: Croom Helm.

Dekmejian, R.H. 1971. Egypt Under Nasir: A Study in Political Dynamics. Albany: State University of New York Press.

Erdmann, G., et al. 2013. International cooperation of authoritarian regimes: Toward a conceptual framework. GIGA Working Papers(229).

Farrag, M. 1998. Emigration Dynamics in Egypt. Emigration Dynamics in Developing Countries. R.T. Appleyard. Aldershot: Ashgate: 44–88.

Feiler, G. 2003. Economic Relations Between Egypt and the Gulf Oil States, 1967–2000: Petro-Wealth and Patterns of Influence. Brighton: Sussex Academic Press.

Fergany, N. 2001. Aspects of Labor Migration and Unemployment in the Arab Region. Almishkat Center for Research.

Fitzgerald, D. 2009. A nation of emigrants: How Mexico manages its migration. Berkeley: University of California Press.

Gasiorowski, M.J., and M. Byrne. 2004. Mohammad Mosaddeq and the 1953 Coup in Iran. Syracuse: Syracuse University Press.

Geddes, B. 2005. Why parties and elections in authoritarian regimes? annual meeting of the American Political Science Association.

Graz, L. 1992. The Turbulent Gulf. London: IB Tauris.

Haddad, Y. 1987. Islamic "Awakening" in Egypt. Arab Studies Quarterly 9(3): 234–259.

Hollifield, J. 2004. The Emerging Migration State. International Migration Review 38(3): 885–912.

Ibrahim, S.E. 1982. The New Arab Social Order: A Study of the Social Impact of Oil Wealth. Boulder: Westview Press.

Keohane, R. 2006. Cooperation and International Regimes. In Little, R, and M. Smith. (eds.) Perspectives on World Politics. London: Routledge.

Kerr, M. 1971. The Arab Cold War: Gamal 'Abd al-Nasir and His Rivals, 1958–1970. London: Oxford University Press.

Koinova, M. 2009. Diasporas and democratization in the post-communist world. Communist and Post-Communist Studies 42(1): 41–64.

Lesch, A.M. 1985. Egyptian Labor Migration: Economic Trends and Government Policies. Fieldstaff Reports – Africa: Northeast Africa Series(38).

Levitsky, S., and L. Way. 2010. Competitive Authoritarianism: Hybrid Regimes After the Cold War. Cambridge: Cambridge University Press.

Linz, J.J. 1964. An Authoritarian Regime: The Case of Spain. In E. Allardt & Y. Littunen (Eds.), Cleavages, Ideologies, and Party Systems: Contributions to Comparative Political Sociology, 291–342. Helsinki: Transactions of the Westermarck Society.

Massey, D. 1999. International migration at the dawn of the twenty-first century: the role of the state. Population and Development Review 25(2): 303–322.

Mattes, M., and M. Rodríguez. 2014. Autocracies and International Cooperation. International Studies Quarterly 58(3): 527–538.

Messiha, S.A. 1980. Export of Egyptian School Teachers to Saudi Arabia and Kuwait: a Cost-Benefit Analysis. Cairo: American University in Cairo Press.

Messina, A.M., and G. Lahav. 2006. The Migration Reader: Exploring Politics and Policies. London: Lynne Rienner Publishers.

Messiha, S.A. 1980. Export of Egyptian School Teachers to Saudi Arabia and Kuwait: A Cost-Benefit Analysis. Cairo: American University in Cairo.

Mountjoy, A.B. 1972. Egypt: Population and Resources. Populations of the Middle East and North Africa: A Geographical Approach. J.I. Clarke and W.C. Fisher. London: University of London Press Ltd.

O'Donnell, G.A. 1973. Modernization and bureaucratic-authoritarianism; studies in South American politics. Berkeley: Institute of International Studies.

O'Mahony, A. 2013. Political Investment: Remittances and Elections. British Journal of Political Science 43(04): 799–820.

Østergaard-Nielsen, E. 2003. International Migration and Sending Countries: Perceptions, Policies and Transnational Relations. Basingstoke: Palgrave Macmillan.

Pérez-Armendáriz, C., and D. Crow. 2010. Do Migrants Remit Democracy? International Migration, Political Beliefs, and Behavior in Mexico. Comparative Political Studies 43(1): 119–148.
Pfutze, T. 2012. Does migration promote democratization? Evidence from the Mexican transition. Journal of Comparative Economics 40(2): 159–175.
Posusney, M.P., and M.P. Angrist. 2004. Authoritarianism in the Middle East: regimes and resistance. London: Lynne Rienner.
Richards, A. 2007. Ten Years of Infitah: Class, Rent, and Policy Stasis in Egypt. Journal of Development Studies 20(4): 323–338.
Richards, A., and J. Waterbury. 2009. A Political Economy of the Middle East. Boulder: Westview Press.
Roy, D. 1991. Egyptian Emigrant Labor: Domestic Consequences. Middle Eastern Studies 27(4): 551–582.
Sadat, A. 1978. al-Bahth 'an al-Dhat [in Arabic]. Cairo: Modern Egyptian Library.
Schlumberger, O., Ed. 2007. Debating Arab Authoritarianism. Dynamics and Durability in Non-Democratic Regimes. Stanford: Stanford University Press.
Shazly, S. 2003. The Crossing of the Suez. San Francisco: American Mideast Research.
Socknat, J.A. 1979. The Potential Relationship of International Migration for Employment and a Middle East Peace Settlement: An Assessment. Middle East Review 11(4): 58–64.
Svolik, M.W. 2012. The Politics of Authoritarian Rule. Cambridge: Cambridge University Press.
Tripp, C. 2007. A history of Iraq. Cambridge: Cambridge University Press.
Tsourapas, G. 2013. The Other Side of a Neoliberal Miracle: Economic Reform and Political De-Liberalization in Ben Ali's Tunisia. Mediterranean Politics 18(1): 23–41.
Tsourapas, G. 2014. Notes from the Field: Researching Emigration in post-2011 Egypt. American Political Science Association, Migration & Citizenship Newsletter 2(2): 58–62.
Tsourapas, G. 2015a. Why Do States Develop Multi-Tier Emigrant Policies? Evidence from Egypt.' Journal of Ethnic & Migration Studies. 41 (13): 2192–2214.
Tsourapas, G. 2015b. The Politics of Egyptian Migration to Libya. MERIP Reports.
Tsourapas, G. 2016. Nasser's Educators and Agitators Across al-Watan al-'Arabi: The Development and Politics of Regional Egyptian Migration, 1952–1967. British Journal of Middle Eastern Studies 43 (3): 324–341.
Varadarajan, L. 2010. The domestic abroad: diasporas in international relations. New York, NY: Oxford University Press.
Vitalis, R. 2007. America's Kingdom: Mythmaking on the Saudi Oil Frontier. Stanford: Stanford University Press.
Waterbury, J. 1983. The Egypt of Nasser and Sadat: The Political Economy of Two Regimes. Princeton: Princeton University Press.
Wedeen, L. 1999. Ambiguities of Domination: Politics, Rhetoric, and Symbols in Contemporary Syria. Chicago: University of Chicago Press.
Wynn, W. 1959. Nasser of Egypt: The Search for Dignity. Clinton, MA: Colonial Press.

Newspaper

Arabic

al-Ahram
Al-Ahram al-Iqtisadi
al-Akhbar
Akhbar el-Yom
Al-Anwar (Beirut)
al-Jumhuriya
National Bank of Egypt. *Economic Bulletin*, June 1974

English

Cairo Today
MENA (Middle East News Agency)
Middle East Contemporary Studies series

EU migration policies: An ambiguous picture of "Fortress Europe"

Comprehensive crisis management[1]

Michael Köhler

Abstract

The European Union (EU) must continue to uphold its moral and legal obligations to offer international protection and humanitarian assistance to those in need. However, short-term humanitarian actions do not solve the underlying problems of the migration and refugee crisis. Therefore, the EU is also using the full range of political, legal and cooperation tools to tackle root causes of migration while also acknowledging the social and economic benefits of regular migration for itself and third states. Europe supports the long-term accommodation and if possible integration of refugees and migrants in host countries, which could benefit both the host country as well as the migrants. The EU is contributing to this through additional development funds and enhanced cooperation with third states, focusing in particular on livelihoods/economic integration and education. In addition to concrete cooperation, the EU is also offering policy dialogue and works towards concluding agreements on readmission and legal migration. Moreover, strengthening border management is crucial.

1 Introduction

The world is currently witnessing forced displacement on the largest scale since the end of World War Two (UNHCR 2015a). Sixty million people have been forcibly displaced, 20 million of them outside their own country (ibid.). On top of this,

1 I am greatly indebted to Laura McDonald of the European Commission's Centre of Expertise on migration in the Directorate-General for Neighbourhood and Enlargement Negotiations for her assistance in drafting this article and putting it into the right shape.

irregular migration flows have also increased.[2] The numbers of migrants and asylum seekers seeking to enter the European Union are unprecedented (BBC 2016). Daily, people risk their lives to make the treacherous journey across the Mediterranean to Europe, in search of a better life.

Europe cannot ignore, and in fact has not ignored, the extent of the crisis in terms either of numbers or of duration. It is increasingly clear that current trends are set to continue, with the crisis in Syria unlikely to be resolved in the short to medium term; ongoing and new conflicts elsewhere; as well as the threat to livelihoods caused by climate change and continuing economic problems in many parts of the developing world. The shocking deaths in the Mediterranean in April 2015 shook Europe into action. But EU Member States are also facing political problems at home around the integration of refugees, particularly in a context of high unemployment and disappointing economic growth, where immigrants are blamed for problems that are not of their making. In this political climate, the positive contribution of migrants to European society is too often ignored.

It is critical that we continue to uphold our legal and moral obligation to provide international protection to those in need. As part of this we must work to save lives at sea. However, we are also working to address the root causes of irregular migration and refugee flows, in order to reduce or at least stem the numbers of displaced persons worldwide and to seek an end to individuals risking their lives in highly dangerous journeys, often assisted by unscrupulous smugglers. Our approach has evolved in response to the current crisis, building on existing measures in the remit of the EU's development and neighbourhood policies but also going beyond these to comprehensive crisis management. The most important feature of EU policy, and what will be the key to its success, is that it runs the full gamut, from humanitarian assistance to long-term development and security. At every stage, solidarity is the guiding principle: between European countries; with host countries in our neighbourhood and beyond; and most importantly with those individuals in need of international protection who have often made long and difficult journeys in order to obtain it. The EU has been using a range of tools to address the crisis, including financial assistance, technical assistance, and dialogue and cooperation. We must not forget in all this, though, that migration also offers an important opportunity. Europe must continue to attract labour that will be necessary to fill skills gaps and counter the effects of an ageing population. The range

2 We use IOM's (International Organization for Migration) definition, according to which an irregular migrant is '[a] person who, owing to unauthorized entry, breach of a condition of entry, or the expiry of his or her visa, lacks legal status in a transit or host country… The term "irregular" is preferable to "illegal" because the latter carries a criminal connotation and is seen as denying migrants' humanity' (IOM).

of tools and themes is essential to addressing the migration and refugee crisis as it affects not only Europe but also our neighbours and our partners in the developing world.

2 From humanitarian assistance to development

The arrival of over one million irregular migrants, asylum seekers and refugees in EU countries in 2015 represented a huge increase in numbers on previous years (BBC 2016). The onset of the crisis has shown that many existing EU tools can be used to address irregular migration and forced displacement, and to harness the development benefits of migration. In recent months, 40 % of arrivals to Greece and Italy have been Syrian, and 90 % come from the top ten countries of origin (UNHCR). Protection, rather than irregularity, is the key issue. First and foremost, we must uphold our moral and legal obligation to offer international protection and humanitarian assistance to those in need. We already do this through the Instrument contributing to Stability and Peace (IcSP) and through funding from the EU's humanitarian agency (ECHO). Since 2014, the Commission has allocated € 8.76 million for humanitarian aid in Libya. With this, the Commission supports the UN, international organisations and international non-governmental organisations (INGOs) in their emergency response targeting internally displaced persons (IDPs) and migrants in Libya.

However, an approach that focuses on the protection of refugees, rather than addressing their long-term developmental needs, is limited by its short-term nature. It makes it more difficult for refugees to be integrated into host communities as active participants. This means that host communities lose out on the important social and economic benefits refugees can bring, such as filling skills gaps. For refugees themselves, it can make secondary displacement towards Europe more attractive, if they are unable to access job markets or their children cannot attend school in their first country of destination. This is particularly important because 45 % of the internationally displaced population is subject to 'protracted displacement', where members of a certain community have been displaced for over five years (UNHCR 2015a, p. 11). Syrians will soon be included in these numbers. In this context, finding long-term solutions is essential. Our experience with the Regional Protection Programme (RPP), introduced in 2005, is a good example of how the EU is seeking to address the long-term development needs of refugee communities. RPPs were intended to enhance the protection capacity of regions hosting refugees and to better protect the refugee population. These programmes aimed to provide durable solutions through voluntary return, local integration or resettlement in a third country. The emphasis was on humanitarian response.

A review of RPPs pointed to the need to consider protracted displacement as a developmental, economic and political challenge, rather than simply a humanitarian one. As a result, the programmes have been renamed Regional Protection and Development Programmes, to include a more developmental and sustainable approach to displacement. These programmes aim to improve access to services, job skills and livelihood opportunities.

3 Addressing developmental frustrations

EU funding tools have been used to address some of the root causes of migration for many years. However, they need to be reoriented to allow a greater focus on migration specifically. The European Development Fund funds projects in partner countries across the developing world. Development cooperation has a twofold role in addressing the root causes of irregular migration. Firstly, it tackles socio-economic instability. Secondly, it can help partner countries to make migration management more effective. The EU is one of the biggest funders of development programmes in sub-Saharan Africa, the region with the biggest increase in forced displacement in recent years after Syria (UNHCR 2015b). Building resilience to food insecurity and improving access to basic services is an important way of addressing pressures that can contribute to migration. The SHARE programme (Supporting Horn of Africa Resilience) is a good example of this. The €50 million project in southern and eastern Ethiopia aims to improve access to basic services and encourages income diversification in order to improve resilience to shocks. A €20 million job creation project in Mali seeks to increase youth incomes by creating 6,000 jobs in road maintenance. The project has been designed to respond to the fragile economic context in Mali and will mitigate pressure on young people to migrate. Rule of Law projects also seek to address the causes of insecurity and human rights abuses, which also spur people to migrate.

Similarly, the European Neighbourhood Instrument (ENI) funds projects in countries in our neighbourhood, importantly including North Africa, the Middle East, and the Eastern Neighbourhood and Ukraine. There is €15.4 billion of funding available for the period 2014–2020 (European Neighbourhood Policy Instrument 2016), which is allocated according to the traditional distribution key of two thirds for the South and one third for the East. This includes projects aiming to integrate migrants, as a key part of mainstreaming migration policy in our cooperation, addressing migration in sectors that are not principally concerned with this issue area. A €10 million project in Morocco promotes the integration of migrants there. This provided additional funding to two EU budget support programmes: to the Ministry of Education and Professional Training and to the Ministry of Health.

This has enabled regularised migrants in Morocco to benefit from medical coverage and for their children to be integrated into the education system. The effective integration of migrants has important benefits for hosting countries in our neighbourhood, as migrants' skills can be used in the local economy. It also reduces the likelihood of onward, irregular movement to the EU, as migrants are able to access work and services. A report commissioned by IOM found that Morocco's broad regularisation of migrants in 2013 reduced the incentive for secondary movements to the EU (Altai Consulting 2015).

The EU Instrument for Pre-Accession provides assistance to the Enlargement Region, specifically Turkey and the Western Balkans. These are key partners in managing the migration crisis, as countries of destination and transit. Several programmes address border management in the region. However, projects addressing migrants themselves have largely been limited to protection, especially of refugees, rather than longer-term integration and resilience.[3] This has been a clear limitation of EU migration policy in the region, especially with regards to Turkey, our main partner in managing the flow of refugees to the EU and the country hosting the largest number of refugees worldwide. In recognition of Turkey's importance, the EU–Turkey Joint Action Plan was introduced in October 2015. It is exemplary of the comprehensive, coordinated approach we are seeking with all our partners. Humanitarian assistance will continue, alongside greater integration of refugees into the local economy and enhanced migration management through the registration of all migrants and enhanced border controls.

The reorienting of the Regional Protection Programmes to include a greater emphasis on development is part of the recognition that traditional instruments have proved inadequate in dealing with the magnitude of the problem with which we are currently faced. For this reason, we have established two new EU Regional Trust Funds, one for Africa and one – also known as the 'Madad Fund' – to address the crisis in Syria. These are innovative funding mechanisms, designed to pool resources from different donors such as the EU budget, EU Member States and third countries to maximise impact. Importantly, the Trust Funds are rapid, flexible and enable the coordination of donor activities. Project design to implementation takes on average five months, rather than the two-year period typical under the development, neighbourhood and pre-accession instruments. The Trust Funds will allow us to respond more effectively to the crisis as it evolves, which has clearly been a limitation of other funding instruments, where resources are often already tied into existing projects. Moreover, by pooling donor resources, we are

3 In this context, resilience is understood to include livelihoods and economic self-sufficiency. This is important given that both irregular migrants and refugees report moving in search of economic as well as physical security (Altai Consulting 2015).

able to implement bigger, more joined up projects that are more efficient in their use of resources. The political buy-in of Member States in EU-funded projects is also increased in this way, since donors to the Trust Fund are directly involved in the process as members of the Board, and because they are co-funders of actions under the Trust Funds.

By the end of October 2015, nine Member States had already formally confirmed their participation in the Emergency Trust Fund for Stability and Addressing the Root Causes of Migration and Displaced Persons in Africa, committing a total of € 28.3 million, and five more had declared their intention to participate. This demonstrates the clear appetite for activities taking place under the Trust Fund and the recognition by EU Member States that tackling the root causes of migration, which is its primary aim, is a priority. This is crucial. In a political environment in which much of the focus has been on the effects of irregular migration and refugee movements on European countries, the willingness of these states to put political and monetary weight behind addressing root causes and issues in countries of origin and transit, often far beyond Europe's borders, is significant. It demonstrates that Member States' governments grasp the complexity of the current crisis, which cannot be solved at Europe's borders alone. Development aid can be a hard sell to domestic populations even in times of greater internal stability and economic prosperity, so the political courage this has demonstrated should be applauded.

By June 2016, € 733 million had been committed to the EU Regional Trust Fund in Response to the Syrian Crisis (Madad Fund) by the EU and Member States. It is currently funded from a variety of EU budget sources, 22 EU Member States and Turkey. The Madad Fund primarily addresses the longer-term resilience needs of refugees and host communities in countries neighbouring Syria. For example, € 12.5 million was provided to UNICEF's No Lost Generation initiative in Turkey. There is a strong emphasis on education actions under the Trust Fund, as education is critical to ensuring the life and livelihood chances of Syrian refugee children. Funding both from the Trust Funds and from more typical funding instruments is essential in harnessing the benefits of migration for host countries, and in preventing irregular migration and forced displacement in the first place. By allowing migrants and refugees access to job markets and educational opportunities, they are able to contribute to the host economy. This is an important move, as we increasingly look to building the long-term resilience of migrants, refugees and host communities, rather than merely providing short-term humanitarian assistance, though this will continue where it is needed. Moreover, it will demonstrate to host communities the opportunity that refugee populations represent, which will in turn reinforce the integration and security of refugees themselves.

4 Global solutions to a global crisis

Dialogue is also a critical tool for addressing the crisis. Without this, we cannot hope to work effectively with partner countries. Frustrations with development outcomes in the global South and poor job opportunities for young people in sub-Saharan African countries in particular mean that migration to the EU for what can crudely be termed 'economic reasons' is here to stay. We must recognise that Europe needs to deliver on legal migration and mobility if it wants commitment from our partners on the return and readmission of irregular migrants to their countries of origin. The revised European Neighbourhood Policy, which was revamped in November 2015, takes this into account, emphasising the need for priorities to be jointly defined with partner countries to ensure that their interests are properly addressed. For many of our African partners, the access of their citizens to jobs and education in Europe is an essential element of any migration strategy. The implementation of existing mobility partnerships and agreements on return and readmission, and the negotiation of new ones, is important in addressing these areas of concern to EU Member States and our partners. Programmes such as Euromed Migration III and IV, with a focus on cooperation between parties, also continue to help in this area. Moreover, dialogues such as the Rabat and Khartoum Processes with African countries, and the Budapest and Prague processes, which involve countries along the Eastern route to Europe, have already been and will continue to be essential to maintaining cooperation with countries of origin and transit for migration.

This is a global crisis, so the solutions must also be global in scope. With the Valletta Summit, the EU, its Member States and participating African countries demonstrated the success that dialogue can have by producing an Action Plan for dealing with migration in future, bridging the gaps between European and African players, and signing the constitutive act of the Emergency Trust Fund for Africa. Dialogue at the international level and between EU Member States themselves is important in addressing legal migration. Countries of origin and transit demand EU action on this issue, as it is important to their citizens. Moreover, skills transfer and remittances from the diaspora are important contributors to development.

Legal migration remains a Member State competence. However, the European Commission advocates a common European system. The Commission will support Member States in promoting a permanent dialogue and peer evaluation at European level on issues such as labour market gaps, regularisation and integration. Improving the access of potential migrants from our partner countries to European labour markets will be beneficial for us all. With Europe facing problems of an ageing population and skills gaps, attracting migration will be essential to our continuing social and economic health. More ambitious policy on legal migration will also reduce demand for migrant smugglers, if individuals are more easily able to reach the EU legally.

Demand for migrant smugglers will also decrease if we are able to demonstrate a credible threat of return for individuals entering the EU irregularly. Effective return and readmission policies require the cooperation of our partner countries and must go hand in hand with development and reintegration assistance. They must also be backed up with the ability to forcibly return individuals with no right to remain in the EU. This must be in line with the principle of non-refoulement, and must uphold migrants' fundamental rights. In 2014 and 2015, according to the European Commission's Directorate General for Migration and Home Affairs, only 40 % of those ordered to leave EU Member States because they were staying or had entered irregularly were successfully returned to countries of origin or transit (European Commission, Directorate General for Migration and Home Affairs). This figure must be improved if we hope to dissuade migrants from undertaking life-threatening journeys to Europe.

5 Security and defence to prevent irregular migration

Finally, operational activities are being undertaken. For example, Common Security and Defence Policy (CSDP) missions are increasingly tailored towards migration. Similarly, we have strengthened the capacity of Frontex, the EU border management agency. This is essential in addressing the most pressing and immediate concern: saving lives on the migration route. Disrupting the business model of migrant smuggling networks is an essential part of this. More than 22,000 migrants have died trying to reach the EU since 2000 (Hagen-Zanker and Mallet 2015). When more than 700 people died off the Libyan coast in April 2015, we learnt the hard way that Search and Rescue operations are not in themselves a pull factor: the end of Operation Mare Nostrum did not see a significant reduction in the numbers of people attempting to reach Europe via the Central Mediterranean. As an immediate response, the EU tripled the capacities and assets for Frontex joint operations Triton and Poseidon. Moreover, these operational activities can tackle the criminal networks which are able to thrive in conditions of instability, and which may seek to maintain conflict for their own ends. Trafficking and smuggling are interlinked, though distinct, activities and there is often overlap in the actors involved, as well as with other forms of transnational crime and terrorism. Security responses, integrated border management and strengthening the rule of law and judicial systems in countries of origin and transit are therefore crucial if we are to shift trafficking in human beings and migrant smuggling from 'low risk, high gain' to 'high risk, low gain' activities (European Commission 2015). The profits to be made in migrant smuggling are huge, with individual migrants paying thousands of euros for their passage.

EUNAVFOR MED Operation Sophia was launched in May 2015 to tackle migrant smuggling and trafficking networks by undermining the business model. Operation Sophia includes search and rescue operations, which have saved thousands of lives (European Council 2016). But smugglers have responded by shifting routes. In the second half of 2015, the Western Balkans route, including the Eastern Mediterranean, was the busiest path to Europe, though the Central Mediterranean remained the deadliest. Importantly, we still lack sufficient understanding of how the networks operate, where the key nodes are and who is involved. It is essential that this situation is not allowed to continue if we are to prevent the loss of life on the migration route and to reduce the amount of irregular migration to Europe. The military operations already in place, as well as agreements with third countries, are already having a significant effect. But their work must continue to improve, especially through coordinated responses and information sharing.

6 Conclusion

When managed effectively, migration brings important benefits to host countries, countries of origin, and migrants themselves. The sharp rise in global forced displacement and in irregular migration to the EU and our neighbours has made effective management difficult. However, we have stepped up our response, both within the EU and, the focus of this article, with our partners. The most pressing concern is saving lives at sea. The deaths of more than 700 migrants and asylum seekers in the Mediterranean in April 2015 was a wake-up call and led to renewed and more effective action in this area. Moreover, the EU is committed to upholding our legal and moral obligations to offer international protection to those in need, and also continues to offer real support to humanitarian responses to the refugee crisis. However, migration management must address the root causes that push individuals to migrate. The Trust Funds for Africa and for the Syria crisis seek to improve the coordination and speed of our actions in this area. Improved cooperation and dialogue with our partners, in the neighbourhood and enlargement regions and beyond, will enable host countries in all regions to better harness the benefits of migration through improved integration and legal channels.

References

Altai Consulting (for IOM). 2015. Migration Trends across the Mediterranean Connecting the Dots.

BBC. 2016. Migrant crisis: Migration to Europe explained in seven charts http://www.bbc.com/news/world-europe-34131911. Accessed: 4 March 2016.

European Commission. 2015. A European Agenda on Migration.

European Commission, Directorate General for Migration and Home Affairs. 2016. Return and Readmission. http://ec.europa.eu/dgs/home-affairs/what-we-do/policies/irregularmigration-return-policy/return-readmission/index_en.htm. Accessed: 30 June 2016.

European Council. 2016. EUNAVFOR MED Operation Sophia: mandate extended by one year, two new tasks added. (20/06/2016) http://www.consilium.europa.eu/en/press/press-releases/2016/06/20-fac-eunavfor-med-sophia/. Accessed: 30 June 2016.

European Neighbourhood Policy Instrument. 2016. The European Neighbourhood Instrument. http://www.enpi-info.eu/ENI. Accessed: 26 July 2016.

Hagen-Zanker, Jessica and Richard Mallett. 2015. Migration Policy: Three Things to Know about Fortress Europe. ODI.

IOM. 2016. Key Migration Terms. http://belgium.iom.int/key-migration-terms%2%80%8B. Accessed: 26 July 2016.

UNHCR. 2016. Refugees/Migrants Emergency Response – Mediterranean. http://data.unhcr.org/mediterranean/regional.php. Accessed: 1 June 2016.

UNHCR. 2015a. World at War. http://www.unhcr.org/556725e69.html. Accessed 26 July 2016.

UNHCR. 2015b. Mid-Year Trends. http://www.unhcr.org/56701b969.pdf. Accessed: 26 July 2016.

When Interior Ministers play diplomats

Fatal ambiguities in Europe's securitised migration policy

Jan Claudius Völkel

Abstract

The year 2015 brought record numbers of people into the European Union via the Mediterranean Sea – and people who lost their lives during that passage. This dramatic swell in the numbers of refugees has revived debates within the EU about suitable counter-strategies. Solutions discussed in Brussels and member state capitals are meant to achieve two goals: to increase security at the EU's external borders and to decrease the number of people dying in the Mediterranean. The article argues that while the European Commission has tried to keep the humanitarian aspect of the migration crisis on the agenda, the governments of the EU member in particular stress on the security aspect. Yet, it is exactly this concentration on the potential security threat that is leading to the paradoxical result that the EU is failing in achieving either more security for itself or more safety for the immigrants. With the aid of six examples, the article shows that an abandonment of the securitised perception of irregular immigration is needed to achieve both more security and more safety. In this logic, the article recommends fundamental changes to the EU's approach towards immigration and calls for a comprehensive revision of the EU's immigration policy.

1 Introduction

In November 2015, the European Union (EU) hosted an extraordinary summit in Valetta with top representatives of various African countries to discuss ways to reduce the record figures for undocumented migration[1] from the global south to Europe (Völkel 2016c). For 2015, the UNHCR counted more than 1,015,078 people who crossed the Mediterranean Sea for Europe irregularly, with 3,771 losing their lives or becoming missed at sea. These were by far the highest figures for undocumented immigration to the EU since it came into being.

Until 2011, Europe was rather successful in keeping the number of people migrating from the southern and eastern Mediterranean low, thanks to the stability of the autocratic regimes existing across the Middle East and North Africa and the functioning cooperation between EU member states and them (Völkel 2014b, p. 265f.). Italy, for instance, concluded a 'friendship pact' with Libya in 2008 that included joint migration control (Lucht 2013, p. 174). Germany established a readmission agreement with Syria in July 2008 which went into effect on 3 January 2009 (BAMF 2010, p. 39).

The member states' restrictive actions were in remarkable contrast to the EU's legal framework, particularly its Asylum Directive and the European Charter for Fundamental Rights, which constitute the world's most advanced asylum regulation framework. This article will notably argue that there is a fundamental difference between migration-related practices (mainly pleaded by the EU member states in the Council of Ministers) and migration-related discourses (mainly pleaded by the European Commission and the European Parliament).

The Arab Spring and the subsequent state crises, particularly in Libya and Syria, triggered unprecedented numbers of arrivals. This made European decision-makers refer back to their elaborated range of restrictive measures, which according to many scholars strengthen the 'securitisation' of the migration issue (Léonard 2010, 2015). The much debated March 2016 'deal' with Turkey, initiated mainly at the instigation of the German government, is but one of these measures. They all derive from a view in which undocumented immigration is primarily perceived as a *security problem* and much less as a *humanitarian disaster.*

---

1 Among many terms and expressions, I prefer 'undocumented (im)migrants' as the collective term for all people crossing a border without being registered by border guards despite requirements to the contrary. This includes refugees, i.e. people who are forced to leave their country due to violence or devastating life circumstances (after natural disasters, for instance), as well as economic migrants, i.e. persons who voluntarily leave their country in search of better living conditions. While a distinction between the two groups is necessary for evaluating their chances in obtaining the right to stay in a destination country, border protection measures affect them both in the same manner.

After discussing the phenomenon of 'securitisation' in EU migration policy (next chapter), this article will show with the help of six examples (in section 3) that this approach has yielded paradox results: problems are being increasingly exacerbated and prolonged, but not solved. Based on Düvell's observation (2011, p. 275) that 'regulations that are meant to prevent unwanted migration often have unintended side-effects and instead encourage irregular migration', this article argues that strict concentration on securing Europe's borders is leading to the high number of deaths and injuries among undocumented immigrants. Yet it is not increasing the level of security within the EU.

2 EU migration policy: security versus protection

Weiner (1992, p. 105f.) identified five ways in which undocumented migrants might be perceived as a security threat for the receiving country in terms of (1) political opposition (including violent action) (2) economic hardships and/or (3) cultural challenges; likewise, they might become (4) a burden for the relations between the host and the sending country and (5) might be instrumentalised by the host government against the sending government. Referring to the EU, Huysmans (2000) broke these risks down by classifying unregulated immigration as a perceived threat to culture, the socio-economy and internal security.

While the 'Copenhagen School' around Barry Buzan et al. (1998) and Ole Wæver (1995) developed the initiating thoughts on securitisation, i.e. 'the intersubjective establishment of an existential threat with a salience sufficient to have substantial political effect' (Buzan et al. 1998, p. 25), it was the scholars of the 'Paris School' around Didier Bigo (1998, 2002, 2008, 2011, 2014) and Thierry Balzacq (2005, 2010, 2011, 2015) who broadened the focus from states to also non-state actors as relevant players in securitising politics (Rychnovská 2014, p. 11f.). In addition, they consider *practices* crucial for securitisation (Balzacq 2011; Wæver 2015, p. 122; Williams 2015; cf. Hansen 2011, p. 359ff.), hence broadening the Copenhagen School's focus on *speech acts*, understood in their performative form as 'not normally thought of as just saying something' (Austin 1962, p. 7); performative speech acts make a difference, as they 'transform social reality' (Balzacq et al. 2015, p. 2).

EU migration policy consists of discourses that can be considered speech acts (such as directives or declarations that produce an effect) and practices (implemented measures such as border control, quotas initiatives, etc.). Bigo (2002, 2014) identifies a 'field of insecurity', where external and internal securities overlap and 'insecurity professionals' (i.e., police officers, border guards, intelligence officers, database analysts) deal with issues like migration, asylum, terrorism and drug trafficking, all of which 'have been handled through the exclusive lens of security, at the expense of other possibilities, such as social inequality of global justice' (Balzacq et al. 2015, p. 12). In sum, officials and agencies from the EU and its member states, but also media, interest groups, civil society and analysts not only *talk* securitisation, but *make* it.

The EU bases itself in its documents on 'the values of respect for human dignity, freedom, democracy, equality, the rule of law and respect for human rights, including the rights of persons belonging to minorities' (Lisbon Treaty, Article 2). The promotion of the Charter of Fundamental Rights of the European Union as compulsory further stresses the importance of value-based decision making (Mink 2012, p. 142). Indeed, the EU has elaborated a globally advanced asylum mechanism with its European Asylum Directive and the European Asylum Support Office (Kaunert and Léonard 2012a).

Yet, these laudable achievements are in stark contrast to the EU's asylum and refugee practices, where the guiding principle is keeping the gateways into the EU as narrow as possible. As most decisions on EU migration policy are taken in the Justice and Home Affairs Council, which consists of the member states' interior and justice ministers, in cooperation with the Council's High Level Working Group on Migration and Asylum (HLWG) and the European Commission's Directorate-General for Home Affairs (DG Home), securitisation of immigration policy is on the rise. With 'Ministries of Interior-like actors playing at diplomats' (Carrera et al. 2013), the humanitarian dimension of asylum seekers, refugees and immigrants plays less of a role, while the fear of an increasing influx of criminal networks or terrorists along with the refugee trails is gaining ground. That was already the case in the 1990s, when the many refugees from the Balkans arrived in the EU, and it is again the case now, where the reduction of immigration figures is the prime target of the European governments (den Hertog 2016, p. 207).

Across the EU, the invigoration of populist and sometimes openly racist parties is causing speech acts and practices to increasingly overlap. Woefully, words are leading to anti-immigrant deeds, in a manner that is unprecedented in post-1945 Europe. Securitisation 'succeeds when a target audience accepts this framing and endorses employing extraordinary measures to address it, thus removing the issue from normal politics to a mode of emergency' (Lupovici 2014, p. 394). Speech acts of the 'target audience' in Europe, particularly anti-immigrant voices, have already taken on a decidedly hostile tone (Chryssogelos 2013). Every 'wave of immigration [a term that can easily be attributed to the speech act related mechanisms of securitisation; comment of the author] to Europe and the United States raised similar objections to successive waves of newcomers who were accused of being too numerous, too dissimilar from natives, too criminal in their behaviour, and too alien national traditions' (Chebel d'Appollonia 2012, p. 6). More than 1,000 criminal attacks against asylum seekers in Germany in 2015 alone sadly speak for themselves (Schumacher 2016). Even regular immigrants are now often perceived as a security threat – UK's Brexit campaign has been an alarming sign of what racist behaviour securitisation discourses can provoke (Thielemann and Schade 2016).

The dichotomy between speech acts and practices is an important distinction for judging European migration policy. Neal (2009) and Boswell (2006), for instance, answer the question of whether EU migration policy has undergone securitisation since 9/11 in completely different terms: the former, analysing practices, in a positive way (yes, it has securitised, for instance through the creation of Frontex); the latter, concentrating on EU speech acts, in a negative way (no, it hasn't, the EU is still globally leading in immigrant rights) (Balzacq and Guzzini 2015, p. 98).

In its Communication on the 'European Agenda on Security' of 28 April 2015, the European Commission (2015a: 18) links external aspects of security with internal aspects of it and connects undocumented migration with illegal smuggling. Built on this, the 'European Agenda on Migration' of 13 May 2015 proposes four pillars to improve control of migration (European Commission 2015b): (1) reduction of incentives for irregular migration, (2) improvement in border management with the aim of saving lives and securing external borders, (3) strengthening of the EU's common asylum policy and (4) establishment of new approaches to legal migration, such as reviving the Blue Card initiative.

These proposals are hardly new and try to reconcile the EU's normative claims with the perceived security needs. Therefore, while the EU's asylum policy remains quite advanced in its core (in the form of speech acts), its border protection practices assure that as few people as possible can enjoy these rights, mainly due to the member state governments' worries about economic and societal difficulties (Kaunert and Léonard *forthcoming*).

3 Disastrous effects of Europe's securitised migration policy

Looking at undocumented migration primarily through the security lens is Europe's 'cardinal sin' and one cause of the high number of deaths at sea every year, particularly since 2011. As Caillault (2012, p. 137f.) states:

> "Instead of reducing migration, intensified border controls have led to a rise in irregular migration, the use of new and more dangerous migration routes, thus increasing the risks and costs for the migrants involved, and leading to the professionalization of smuggling methods."

In the subsequent sections, six disastrous effects of Europe's securitised approach to migration are discussed. They illustrate the paradox consequences it has both for migrants and European citizens. It will become clear that the negative results by far outweigh the hoped-for positive implications.

3.1 The EU saves people whom it pushed into clandestine migration before

With the Frontex Triton mission since November 2014 and the EU Naval Force Operation Sophia since May 2015, the EU patrols the Mediterranean Sea with military vessels in order to prevent smugglers from bringing more irregular migrants to Europe and to rescue immigrants in distress (Tardy 2015). Indeed, thousands of people have been saved through these missions. Yet, this moral obligation gets shaken by the observation that search and rescue activities apparently 'act as a magnet to migrants and ease the task of smugglers, who would only need their vessels to reach the high seas' (UK House of Lords 2016, p. 3).

The main reason for people embarking unsafe boats, however, is Council Directive 2001/51/EC, which obliges air carriers to only allow passengers with valid visas aboard when flying into the EU. Refugees, asylum seekers and other irregular migrants are excluded, even if they have a valid ticket. Though 'this Directive is without prejudice to the obligations resulting from the Geneva Convention relating to the Status of Refugees of 28 July 1951, as amended by the New York Protocol of 31 January 1967', as its text stipulates, it de facto makes airport staff in Cairo, Tunis and Khartoum decide who might be eligible for asylum in Europe and who might not. A procedure that usually takes months, if not years, is hence meant to be applied by a single person in a minimum of time. In the end, as nobody without a valid visa is permitted to board a plane, the comparatively safe and cheap way of travelling to Europe is barred for refugees and migrants.

This directive erases the option of safe ways into the EU for refugees. French researcher Kamel Doraï estimates that 94 % of Syrian refugees would receive asylum status in France, but only 1.5 % of them would receive a visa from the French embassy in Beirut (quoted in Schlaefli 2016). The introduction of biometric Schengen visas in 2012 had a similar effect: by obliging travellers to leave their fingerprints at the embassy, applicants from 'safe countries' such as Egypt, Morocco or Algeria, who have little chance of obtaining asylum status, are incentivised to enter the EU clandestinely via the Mediterranean (Martin 2012, p. 281), as they do not want to be identified at later police checks, as this would facilitate their being returned to their home countries quickly. Similarly, people who intend to overstay their Schengen visas in order to live and work irregularly in the EU fear that they will be identified by means of their fingerprints. Stories of people who burn their fingerprints 'to prevent his prints being checked against migration databases, such as EURODAC' (Grant 2011, p. 148) are becoming more frequent (Trilling 2015).

3.2 By closing the easy transit routes, the EU fuels the fire at sea

The European states have been very successful in closing the traditional hotspots of Mediterranean migration in cooperation with their neighbouring countries. Figures for migration between Morocco and Spain (the Western Mediterranean Route), in the 1990s among the most used Mediterranean routes due to its geographic proximity (the route across the Strait of Gibraltar is only 14 km long), play no particular role anymore (see Table 1). This is particularly due to the functioning cooperation between Spanish and Moroccan border guards (Frontex 2016a, p. 21). Most boats using the Central Mediterranean Route come from Libya and Egypt, while the figures from Tunisia, the country closest to Italy as the distance between Tunis and Pantelleria is just 75 km, are very low, also thanks to the functioning coast control (Limam and Del Sarto 2015). The figures for the Eastern Mediterranean Route, meanwhile, mainly depend on the intensity of crises in Turkey's south-eastern neighbourhood (i.e., Afghanistan, Iraq, Syria).

Table 1 Arrivals via the three Mediterranean routes

	2008	2009	2010	2011	2012	2013	2014	2015
Western Mediterranean Route (Algeria/Morocco to Europe)	6,500	6,650	5,000	8,450	6,400	6,800	7,840	7,164
Central Mediterranean Route (Egypt/Libya/Tunisia to Europe)	39,800	11,000	4,500	64,300	15,900	40,000	170,760	153,946
Eastern Mediterranean Route (Turkey to Europe)	52,300	40,000	55,700	57,000	37,200	24,800	50,830	885,386

Source: Figures taken from the Frontex website, http://frontex.europa.eu/trends-and-routes/migratory-routes-map (26 June 2016).

The unprecedented surge on the Eastern Mediterranean Route in 2015 first triggered the re-erection of fences and border controls along the Western Balkans route and then the migration 'deal' with the Turkish government, de facto sealing the border to Europe for all but an annual maximum of 72,000 Syrian refugees (see Section 3.5).

However, these 'successes' are not reducing the overall figures, but are rather diverting refugee trails (Kasparek and Wagner 2012, p. 185). Indeed, Greece has reported a decline in the number of arrivals since the Turkey 'deal' (European Commission 2016), but this does not mean that the real figures are going down. Instead of crossing the sea via the shortest, and hence safest routes, passages are becoming longer, more dangerous and more expensive. Syrians may now board a boat directly at Syrian's coastline instead of wandering through Turkey first or embark boats that take the much longer route to Italy instead of Greece. In fact, the figures for the Central Mediterranean Route 'more than doubled' (Frontex 2016b) in May 2016, compared to the previous month, with the Turkey deal having its share in this (Frontex 2016c): Refugees are increasingly choosing Egypt as the country of departure now (Agence France-Press 2016), with the journey to Italy usually taking more than ten days.

3.3 Patrolling the Mediterranean does not help if people fly over

The Mediterranean Sea and the EU's eastern border are under massive surveillance, not only from the national coast guards and the Frontex operation 'Triton', but also through the 'Eurosur' programme (Rijpma and Vermeulen 2015) and, most recently, the EU naval operation 'Sophia'. The costs for these operations have increased exorbitantly over the last ten years: the annual budget of Frontex reached € 114.00 million in 2015, after initially being € 19.6 million in 2006, its first full operational year. Hayes and Vermeulen (2012, p. 51) estimate that the setup for Eurosur costs between € 318 million and € 913 million, while the annual operating costs come on top. Added to this is the national spending on border protection.

The generous spending on EU border protection, however, is surprising, given the fact that many irregular migrants within the EU, if not most, come by plane as tourists with a regular Schengen visa as with a temporary work/study permit and do not return after their visa expires (Triandafyllidou/Ambrosini 2011: 271f.; Caillault 2012: 137). Though there are no reliable statistics, the Italian interior ministry estimated that the share of sea immigrants among Italy's irregular population in 2006 was only around 13 % (Cuttitta 2007: 3), and the German government stated in August 2011 that the majority of irregular persons in the EU came into the EU via legal routes with a short-term visa and then overstayed (Bundesregierung

2011). Likewise, the Clandestino (2009: 7) project concluded that in many EU member states, "visa overstaying is the most relevant inflow into irregular residence", and also Frontex (2013: 18) admitted 'that overstaying is a very common modus operandi for irregular migration to the EU'. According to the European Commission (2016c: 2), some 50 million non-EU citizens visited the EU on a regular basis in 2015, compared to "only" 1.8 million irregular border crossings during the same year. Hence, patrolling the Mediterranean with satellite technology and military equipment at great expense does not help if many people, if not most, fly over and is in conflict with the EU's principle of proportionality.

3.4 EU readmission agreements cost a lot and help little

Since the Treaty of Amsterdam of 1999 and the inclusion of asylum matters into the 'Community Pillar', the European Commission has the principal responsibility for EU Asylum and Immigration Policy initiatives, which are then adopted by the European Parliament and the Council of Ministers. As a result, it has commenced negotiations with 18 countries about readmission agreements and successfully concluded them with many, for instance Russia, Ukraine and Turkey.

With regard to the southern Mediterranean, the EU has signed 'mobility partnerships' offering visa facilitation for partner country nationals in exchange for the conclusion of readmission agreements with Morocco, Tunisia (both in 2013) and Jordan (in 2014) (García Andrade et al. 2015, p. 31). While Tunisia was quick to sign the offered mobility partnership, hoping to stabilise its shaken economy and benefit from further EU privileges such as easier visa access, Morocco proved to be a difficult negotiation partner. The government insisted on making visa facilitation mandatory, though the Commission could not make substantial promises, as the granting of visas is still the responsibility of the EU member states. As the Commission therefore lacks credibility (Devisscher 2011, p. 93), the signing of agreements requires the EU to offer a lot of expensive incentives, a fact that, for instance, also applies to EU-Turkey migration cooperation (Karakaya 2016; see also the next section 3.5). It is precisely for this reason that Egypt has strictly refused to enter into any negotiations about a Mobility Partnership with the European Commission (Völkel 2014a, p. 158f.).

While negotiation costs are high, however, successful implementation is questionable, as even if an agreement is signed, there is no saying whether it will be sufficiently ratified and consistently observed (Coleman 2009, p. 27ff.; Triandafyllidou and Ambrosini 2011, p. 258f.).

3.5 The EU loses ground in other important negotiations

Particularly EU member state governments are looking for closer cooperation with neighbouring governments in order to externalise and to extra-territorialise border control through readmission agreements, joint operations, information exchange and the setup of detention centres in the neighbouring 'safe third countries' – of course, in exchange for 'substantial financial support' (Caillault 2012, p. 133). Indeed, the EU has set up an 'extensive system of security governance' (Pawlak 2012, p. 96) with the countries in its neighbourhood. Their 'pre-barrier territories' are becoming increasingly important for EU border control (Seiffart 2012).

Also, 'dubious devices as e.g. the concept of *safe third country* which [...] lack adequate guarantees, leave a far too large margin of appreciation to EU Member States and thus could necessarily lead to human rights violations' (Mink 2012, p. 121; own omission). The EU's serious pushes for closer cooperation with the governments of Sudan, Eritrea, Algeria, Egypt and others are odd against any human rights considerations (Völkel 2016a).

Due to its strong commitment to conclude readmission or similar agreements, the EU is weakening its arbitration position in other negotiations. For one thing, it is easy for 'partner governments' to demand greater EU concessions in exchange for a cooperative stance on readmitting immigrants. The Action Plan agreed upon by the European states and 35 African governments at the Valletta Summit in November 2015 contains almost € 2 billion in incentives for the African states – a remarkable 10 % plus on the already € 20 billion paid annually by the EU to Africa in development cooperation (ibid).

The fact that the EU is losing ground is further demonstrated by the deal with Turkey. Not only is its legality disputed (Fotiadis et al. 2016), but Turkey has also succeeded in pressing € 6 billion instead of the initially offered € 3 billion (Pop 2016), after the EU had pledged an additional € 1 billion in September 2015 as an incentive for the Turkish authorities to reduce the flow of outgoing migrants. It added another € 2 billion, offered accelerated membership negotiations and removed visa restrictions (Paul and Seyrek 2016). These, nota bene, were not to be granted for real improvements in Turkey, but as the 'price' for Turkey's willingness to cooperate. The existing readmission agreement ('Agreement between the European Union and the Republic of Turkey on the readmission of persons residing without authorisation'), signed in 2014 after lengthy and costly negotiations, includes third country nationals only from 01 October 2017 onwards, except for nationals from countries with which Turkey has bilateral readmission agreements (Sözen 2015, p. 59). Syrians and Iraqis, the two biggest refugee groups in Turkey, are not included in this agreement (Avci 2016). This shows how 'useless' the original readmission agreement is, despite all the negotiation efforts and cost.

The strong insistence on cooperation in migration is also leading to less EU pressure being applied in other critical areas, such as protecting the Mediterranean environment. Egypt's opening of a second Suez Canal lane on 6 August 2015 is a specific example: biologists fear a further deterioration of the Mediterranean Sea's biodiversity through the invasion of alien species. During the hasty preparations for the canal's enlargement, which took less than a year, the Egyptian representatives promised to conduct an environmental impact assessment, which would most probably have led to the instalment of locks and salinity barriers. However, they never delivered a clear assessment. Despite concerns, European diplomats remained silent, and '[o]bservers say that Brussels doesn't want to lean too hard on Egypt because President Abdel Fattah el-Sisi is cooperating in dealing with the refugee crisis' (Bishop 2016).

3.6 Repressive measures do not protect EU citizens, but harm them

It is a misbelief that increased border control and restricted reception offers, such as predefined maximum reception numbers as introduced by Austria in April 2016 (Huggler 2016), would increase internal security in Europe. If border checkpoints are closed for irregular migrants, they will avoid official registration even more and try to remain undetected. Clearly, the more refugees register with the authorities, the greater is the knowledge about them, and '[a] screening process would also provide better assurance that the refugees ultimately accepted for Europe are not would-be terrorists. ISIS might still try to infiltrate attackers into Europe, but a reduced flow of people arriving chaotically at sea would make that more difficult' (Roth 2016).

Shortly after the Charlie Hebdo attacks, the governments of Austria, Belgium, Denmark, Germany, Italy, Latvia, the Netherlands, Poland, Spain, Sweden and the United Kingdom published a Joint Statement on 11 January 2015 calling for increased cooperation in security matters, including an amendment of 'the rules laid down in the Schengen Borders Code to allow for broader consultation of the Schengen Information System (SIS II) during the crossing of external borders by individuals enjoying the right to free movement' (Bigo et al. 2015: 4). This 'Second-Generation SIS', in place since 09 April 2013 after several years of delay, and the other EU cooperation instruments such as the Visa Information System (VIS) or the European Dactylographic System (Eurodac) have often been criticised for their doubtful consideration of personal data protection and individual rights (Roe 2012; Occhipinti 2013). However, they offer much advancement regarding actual security within the EU (Pedersen 2015). In fact, it is not the lack of security cooperation *possibilities* that poses the real challenge – it is the lack of commitment of certain member states to seriously use them (Monar 2014). As the Brussels attacks of 22 March 2016 showed, all the attackers were on the lists of security forces before, yet the Belgian authorities did not integrate this information into their actions (Banks 2016). Hence, no matter what is written in EU agreements, more co-operation is needed in reality.

While the open borders within the Schengen area are not the problem, the re-introduction of comprehensive border controls would impair Europe's economy massively. The reintroduction of temporary controls at certain EU internal borders in 2015 was followed by a decline in local economic activity (Alderman and Kanter 2016). If controls were reintroduced at all the Schengen borders, Felbermayr et al. (2016) would expect 'an annual decline in trade volumes of € 221.34 billion'. The European Commission (2016b, S. 14) estimates 'that reintroducing internal border controls on a systematic and long term basis could cost between up to € 5 billion and up to € 18 billion in overall direct costs alone'. Given the existing economic difficulties in many EU member states, this would certainly put a massive strain on Europe's economy and social welfare systems and reduce both socioeconomic and other forms of security in Europe.

4 Conclusions

While mass demonstrations against immigrants and frequent arson attacks on refugee homes and non-nationals have poisoned public debate about immigrants, with politicians increasingly calling for more repressive measures and the UK even about leaving the EU, this article has shown that Europe's securitised migration policy has paradoxically yielded worse results for all those involved.

Differentiating between speech acts and practices, the EU is divided between making comparatively generous offers for asylum seekers once they have reached EU territory and trying to minimise the numbers of undocumented immigrants by adopting an increasingly securitised approach to border control. In fact, the European Commission has been much more supportive of a human rights oriented immigration policy than the EU member states governments, which care more about their (perceived) security and hope to keep rising racist oppositionists under control.

Yet, the ongoing humanitarian disaster in the Mediterranean, in which thousands of lives are being lost at sea every year, must prompt a serious reconsideration of current practices. The trend towards securitisation in recent years is misguided and wrong-headed. This approach simply compels individuals to opt for irregular entry into the EU and does not lead to a factual reduction of influx numbers. Mobility Partnerships with non-democratic governments are morally dubious and hardly keep what they promise. What the Commission is increasingly lobbying for and even found the applause of Frontex Director Fabrice Leggeri (Agence France-Presse 2016) is a way to open safe and legal routes into the EU. This would be 'a win-win situation' for all. Many asylum-seekers could find safety without risking their lives, and the EU could reassert more control over its borders without sacrificing its values' (Roth 2016).

Beyond all this, it seems necessary to engage in a global discussion about whether the distinction made in the 1951 Geneva Refugee Convention between valid reasons for asylum (personal threat through war and discrimination) and invalid reasons (economic needs) is still appropriate. In 1951, refugees mainly moved from eastern Europe to western Europe and the economic reasons were not as urgent as they are today in many parts of Africa and Asia. For those concerned, it makes no difference whether their lives are endangered by conflict or by malnutrition – the latter will probably become more urgent if climate change continues as at present. Though chances to find a new global agreement are tending towards zero, the EU, with its dominant trading policies and excessive use of global resources, has to assume its responsibility – of course, for the better, not for the worse (Kingsley 2016). In the end, a thorough revision of the global asylum system is needed. The EU's Asylum Procedures Directive could serve as a model.

In these days of heated populist debate at street demonstrations and in online forums, it is unlikely that there will be any fundamental change in EU migration practices. Leaders in Europe are in fear of losing decisive support from the people in their own countries, particularly since, with 51.9 % of the vote, the people in the UK expressed their will to leave the EU. Populists are in governmental positions in a number of EU member states and vocal opposition parties like the Front National in France, the FPÖ in Austria or the AfD in Germany are creating an atmosphere in which supportive decisions for immigrants seem more and more unattainable (Kennedy 2015). However, it is mandatory for responsible, considerate politicians and opinion-leaders these days not to enrich the irrational anti-immigration and pro-isolation discourse further; otherwise, the atmosphere in Europe will be increasingly poisoned, not by the immigrants, as Hungarian Prime Minister Victor Orbán said in July 2016 (Kroet 2016), but by people just like himself.

References

Agence France-Presse. 2016. More EU-bound Migrants Leaving from Egypt: EU Agency. Reliefweb. http://reliefweb.int/report/egypt/more-eu-bound-migrants-leaving-egypt-eu-agency. Accessed: 09 August 2016.

Alderman, Liz and John Kanter. 2016. Europe's Border Checks become Economic Choke Points. The New York Times. http://www.nytimes.com/2016/03/02/business/international/europes-new-border-controls-exact-a-cost.html. Accessed: 19 April 2016.

Austin, John Langshaw. 1962. How to do things with words. Oxford: Clarendon.

Avci, Esra Kaymak. 2016. Syria, Iraq excluded for readmission deal. Anadolu Agency. http://aa.com.tr/en/turkey/syria-iraq-excluded-for-readmission-deal/531311. Accessed: 09 August 2016.

Balzacq, Thierry. 2005. The Three Faces of Securitization: Political Agency, Audience and Context. European Journal of International Relations 11 (2): 171–201.

Balzacq, Thierry. 2010. Constructivism and Securitization Studies. In The Routledge Handbook of Security Studies, ed. Dunn Cavelty, Myriam and Mauer, Victor, 56–72. London/New York: Routledge.

Balzacq, Thierry. 2011. A Theory of Securitization: Origins, Core Assumptions, and Variants. In Securitization Theory: How Security Problems Emerge and Dissolve, ed. Balzacq, Thierry, 1–30. London: Routledge.

Balzacq, Thierry and Stefano Guzzini. 2015. Introduction: 'What Kind of Theory – if any – is Securitization? International Relations 29 (1): 97–102.

Balzacq, Thierry et al. 2015. 'Securitization' Revisited: Theory and Cases. *International Relations*. doi: 10.1177/0047117815596590.

BAMF. 2010. Annual Policy Report 2009. Federal Office for Migration and Refugees (BAMF). http://www.bamf.de/SharedDocs/Anlagen/EN/Publikationen/EMN/Politikberichte/emn-politikbericht-2009-germany.pdf?__blob=publicationFile. Accessed: 09 August 2016.

Banks, Martin. 2016. Brussels attacks demonstrate 'urgent need' for EU intelligence co-operation. The Parliament Magazine. https://www.theparliamentmagazine.eu/articles/news/brussels-attacks-demonstrate-urgent-need-eu-intelligence-co-operation. Accessed: 19 April 2016.

Belmonte, Martina. 2015. The EU Blue Card – is there a Need for a More Comprehensive Approach? IES Policy Brief 3. Brussels: Institute for European Studies. www.ies.be/files/3:2015%20Policy%20Brief-EN.pdf. Accessed: 14 November 2015.

Bigo, Didier. 1998. Sécurité et immigration: vers une gouvernementalité par l'inquiétude? Cultures & Conflits 31/32: 13–38.

Bigo, Didier. 2002. Security and Immigration: Towards a Critique of the Governmentality of Unease. Alternatives 27 (1): 63–92.

Bigo, Didier. 2008. Globalized (In)Security: the Field and the Ban-Opticon. In Terror, Insecurity and Liberty: Illiberal Practices of Liberal Regimes after 9/11, ed. Bigo, Didier and Anastassia Tsoukala, 10–48. New York: Routledge.

Bigo, Didier. 2011. Le "nexus" sécurité, frontier, immigration: programme et diagramme. Cultures & Conflits 84: 7–12.

Bigo, Didier. 2014. The (In)securitization Practices of the Three Universes of EU Border Control: Military/Navy – Border Guards/Police – Database Analysts. Security Dialogue 45 (3): 209–225.

Bigo, Didier et al. 2015. The EU Counter-Terrorism Policy Responses to the Attacks in Paris: Towards an EU Security and Liberty Agenda. CEPS Paper 81. Brussels: Centre for European Policy Studies. https://www.ceps.eu/system/files/LSE81 Counterterrorism.pdf. Accessed: 27 June 2016.

Bishop, D. Rachael. 2016. Our Mediterranean, our Survival. The New York Times. http://www.nytimes.com/2016/01/30/opinion/our-mediterranean-our-survival.html?emc=edit_ty_20160129&nl=opinion&nlid=54898013&_r=0. Accessed: 31 January 2016.

Boswell, Christina. 2006. Migration Control in Europe after 9/11: Explaining the Absence of Securitization. Journal of Common Market Studies 45 (3): 589–610.

Bundesregierung (2011) Illegale Einwanderung: Eine große Herausforderung für Europa, Magazin für Europa und Internationales, https://www.bundesregierung.de/Content/DE/Magazine/03MagazinEuropaInternationales/2011/08/Doorpage-08.html?context=Inhalt%2C0. Accessed: 24 October 2016.

Buzan, Berry et al. 1998. Security: A New Framework for Analysis. Boulder/London: Lynne Rienner.

Caillault, Clotilde. 2012. The Implementation of Coherent Migration Management through IOM Programs in Morocco. In The New Politics of International Mobility. Migration Management and its Discontents, ed. Martin Geiger and Antoine Pécoud, 133–154. Osnabrück: Institut für Migrationsforschung und Interkulturelle Studien.

Carrera, Sergio et al. 2013. The 'Arab Spring' and EU's Immigration Policy: A Critical Sociology on the Global Approach to Migration and Mobility. Washington: Middle East Institute, http://www.mei.edu/content/arab-spring-and-eus-immigration-policy-critical-sociology-global-approach-migration-and. Accessed: 15 April 2013.

Chebel d'Appollonia, Ariane. 2012. Frontiers of Fear: Immigration and Insecurity in the United States and Europe. Cornell: University Press.

Chryssogelos, Angelos-Stylianos. 2013. The Evolution of the 'Populist Potential' in European Politics: From New Right Radicalism to Anti-System Populism. European View 12 (1): 75–83.

Clandestino (2009) Size and Development of Irregular Migration to the EU. Counting the Uncountable: Data and Trends across Europe. Comparative Policy Brief October, http://irregular-migration.net//fileadmin/irregular-migration/dateien/4.Background_Information/4.2.Policy_Briefs_EN/ComparativePolicyBrief_SizeOfIrregularMigration_Clandestino_Nov09_2.pdf. Accessed: 24 October 2016.

Coleman, Nils. 2009. European Readmission Policy: Third Country Interests and Refugee Rights. Leiden: Brill.

Cuttitta, Paolo. 2007. The Changes in the Fight Against Illegal Immigration in the Euro-Mediterranean Area and in Euro-Mediterranean Relations. Genoa: University.

den Hertog, Leonhard. 2016. Fundamental Rights and the Extra-Territorialization of EU Border Policy: A Contradiction in Terms? In Foreigners, Refugees, or Minorities? Rethinking People in the Context of Border Controls and Visas, ed. Bigo, Didier et al., 205–226. Abingdon: Routledge.
Devisscher, Purdey. 2011. Legal Migration in the Relationship between the European Union and ACP Countries: The Absence of a True Global Approach Continues. European Journal of Migration and Law 13 (1): 53–94.
Düvell, Franck. 2011. Paths into Irregularity: The Legal and Political Construction of Irregular Migration. European Journal of Migration and Law 13 (3): 275–295.
Eisele, Katharina. 2013. Why Come Here if I Can Go There? Assessing the 'Attractiveness' of the EU's Blue Card Directive for 'Highly Qualified' Immigrants. CEPS Paper in Liberty and Security in Europe 60. Centre for European Policy Studies, https://www.ceps.eu/system/files/No%2060%20Eisele%20EU%20Blue%20Card%20Directive_0.pdf. Accessed: 25 April 2016.
European Commission. 2011. *Evaluation of EU Readmission Agreements*. Communication from the Commission to the European Parliament and the Council. COM(2011) 76 final. http://eur-lex.europa.eu/LexUriServ/LexUriServ.do?uri=COM:2011:0076:FIN:EN:PDF. Accessed: 09 August 2016.
European Commission. 2015a. The European Agenda on Security. Communication from the Commission to the European Parliament, the Council, the European Economic and Social Committee and the Committee of the Regions. COM(2015) 185 final. https://ec.europa.eu/anti-trafficking/sites/antitrafficking/files/eu_agenda_on_security_en.pdf Accessed: 28 June 2016.
European Commission. 2015b. A European Agenda on Migration. Communication from the Commission to the European Parliament, the Council, the European Economic and Social Committee and the Committee of the Regions. COM(2015) 240 final. http://ec.europa.eu/dgs/home-affairs/what-we-do/policies/european-agenda-migration/background-information/docs/communication_on_the_european_agenda_on_migration _en.pdf. Accessed: 14 June 2016.
European Commission. 2016a. Forth Report on Relocation and Resettlement. Communication from the Commission to the European Parliament, the European Council and the Council. COM(2016) 416 final. http://ec.europa.eu/dgs/home-affairs/what-we-do/policies/european-agenda-migration/proposal-implementation-package/docs/20160615/4th_report_on_relocation_and_resettlement_en.pdf. Accessed: 28 June 2016.
European Commission. 2016b. Communication from the Commission to the European Parliament and the Council on the State of Play of Implementation of the Priority Actions under the European Agenda on Migration. COM(2016) 85 final. http://ec.europa.eu/dgs/home-affairs/what-we-do/policies/european-agenda-migration/proposal-implementation-package/docs/managing_the_refugee_crisis_state_of_play _20160210_en.pdf. Accessed: 19 April 2016.
European Commission. 2016c. Stronger and Smarter Information Systems for Borders and Security. Communication from the Commission to the European Parliament and the Council. COM(2016) 205 final. Brussels: European Commission, http://www.eulisa.europa.eu/Newsroom/News/Documents/SB-EES/communi-

cation_on_stronger_and_smart_borders_20160406_en.pdf. Accessed: 24 October 2016.

Felbermayr, Gabriel et al. 2016. Trade Costs of Border Controls in the Schengen Area. Centre for Economic Policy Research. http://voxeu.org/article/trade-costs-border-controls-schengen-area. Accessed: 27 June 2016.

Fotiadis, Apostolis et al. 2016. Syrian Refugee Wins Appeal Against Forced Return to Turkey. The Guardian. https://www.theguardian.com/world/2016/may/20/syrian-refugee-wins-appeal-against-forced-return-to-turkey. Accessed: 28 June 2016.

Frontex. 2013. Annual Risk Analysis 2013. http://www.frontex.europa.eu/assets/Publications/Risk_Analysis/Annual_Risk_Analysis_2013.pdf. Accessed: 09 August 2016.

Frontex. 2016a. Annual Risk Analysis 2016. http://frontex.europa.eu/assets/Publications/Risk_Analysis/Annula_Risk_Analysis_2016.pdf. Accessed: 26 June 2016.

Frontex. 2016b. Central Med Remained Under Migratory Pressure in May. Frontex press statement. http://frontex.europa.eu/news/central-med-remained-under-migratory-pressure-in-may-9Wtxug. Accessed: 26 June 2016.

Frontex. 2016c. Number of migrants arriving in Greece dropped 90 % in April. Frontex press statement. http://frontex.europa.eu/news/number-of-migrants-arriving-in-greece-dropped-90-in-april-6e70Bw. Accessed: 28 June 2016.

García Andrade, Paula et al. 2015. EU Cooperation with Third Countries in the Field of Migration. Study for the LIBE Committee. http://www.europarl.europa.eu/RegData/etudes/STUD/2015/536469/IPOL_STU(2015)536469_EN.pdf. Accessed: 26 June 2016.

Giuffre, Mariagiulia. 2011. The European Union readmission policy after Lisbon. Interdisciplinary Political Studies 1, 7–19.

Grant, Stefanie. 2011. Recording and Identifying European Frontier Deaths. European Journal of Migration and Law 13 (2): 135–156.

Hansen, Lene. 2011. The Politics of Securitization and the Muhammad Cartoon Crisis: A Post-Structuralist Perspective. Security Dialogue 42 (4-5): 357–369.

Hayes, Ben and Mathias Vermeulen. 2012. Borderline – The EU's New Border Surveillance Initiatives. Assessing the Costs and Fundamental Rights Implications of EUROSUR and the "Smart Borders" Proposals. Heinrich Böll Foundation. https://www.boell.de/sites/default/files/DRV_120523_BORDERLINE_-_Border _Surveillance.pdf. Accessed: 09 August 2016.

Huggler, Justin. 2016. Austria Passes Emergency Law Allowing Asylum-Seekers to be Turned Away at the Border. Telegraph. http://www.telegraph.co.uk/news/2016/04/27/austria-passes-emergency-law-allowing-asylum-seekers-to-be-turne/. Accessed: 27 June 2016.

Huysmans, Jef. 2000. The European Union and the Securitization of Migration. Journal of Common Market Studies 38 (5): 751–777.

Kalantaryan, Sona and Iván Martin. 2015. Reforming the EU Blue Card as a Labour Migration Policy Tool? MPC Policy Brief 8. European University Institute. http://cadmus.eui.eu/handle/1814/35744. Accessed: 09 August 2016.

Kaplan, Michael. 2016. EU-Turkey Deal and Non-Syrian Refugees: How Afghans, Iraqis, Somalis, Others Could Be Hurt By Agreement. International Business Times. http://www.ibtimes.com/eu-turkey-deal-non-syrian-refugees-how-afghans-iraqis-somalis-others-could-be-hurt-2340449. Accessed: 04 May 2016.

Karakaya, Kerim. 2016. EU Deal with Turkey to Send Back Refugees Already on Thin Ice. Al-Monitor. http://www.al-monitor.com/pulse/originals/2016/03/turkey-syria-european-union-refugee-deal.html. Accessed: 04 May 2016.

Kasparek, Bernd and Fabian Wagner. 2012. Local Border Regimes or a Homogeneous External Border? The Case of the European Union's Border Agency Frontex. In The New Politics of International Mobility. Migration Management and its Discontents, ed. Geiger, Martin and Antoine Pécoud, 173–190. Osnabrück: Institut für Migrationsforschung und Interkulturelle Studien.

Kaunert, Christian and Sarah Léonard. 2012a. The Development of the EU Asylum Policy: Venue-Shopping in Perspective. Journal of European Public Policy 19 (9): 1396–1413.

Kaunert, Christian and Sarah Léonard. 2012b. The European Union Asylum Policy After the Lisbon Treaty and the Stockholm Programme: Towards Supranational Governance in a Common Area of Protection? Refugee Survey Quarterly 31 (4): 1–20.

Kaunert, Christian and Sarah Léonard. (forthcoming). Refugees, Security and the European Union. London: Routledge.

Kennedy, Dana. 2015. Can France's Far-Right Marine Le Pen Use Paris Attacks to Win Power? The Daily Beast. http://www.thedailybeast.com/articles/2015/11/15/france-s-far-right-boosted-by-attacks.html. Accessed: 09 August 2016.

Kingsley, Patrick. 2016. UN backlash against call to scale back Geneva convention on refugees. The Guardian. http://www.theguardian.com/world/2016/jan/06/un-backlash-against-call-to-scale-back-geneva-convention-on-refugees. Accessed: 25 April 2016.

Kroet, Cynthia. 2016. Victor Orbán: Migrants are 'a poison'. Politico. http://www.politico.eu/article/viktor-orban-migrants-are-a-poison-hungarian-prime-minister-europe-refugee-crisis. Accessed: 27 July 2016.

Léonard, Sarah. 2010. EU border security and migration into the European Union: FRONTEX and securitisation through practices. European Security 19 (2): 231–254.

Léonard, Sarah. 2015. Border controls as a dimension of the European Union's counter-terrorism policy: a critical assessment. Intelligence and National Security 30 (2-3): 306–332.

Limam, Mohamed and Raffaella Del Sarto. 2015. *Periphery under Pressure: Morocco, Tunisia and the European Union's Mobility Partnership on Migration*. EUI Working Papers, RSCAS 2015/75. European University Institute. http://cadmus.eui.eu/bitstream/handle/1814/37521/RSCAS_2015_75.pdf. Accessed: 16 June 2016.

Lucht, Hans. 2013. Pusher Stories: Ghanaian Connection Men and the Expansion of the EU's Border Regimes into Africa. In The Migration Industry and the Commercialization of International Migration, ed. Gammeltoft-Hansen, Thomas and Ninna Nyberg Sorensen, 190–214. Abingdon: Routledge.

Lupovici, Amir. 2014. The Limits of Securitization Theory: Observational Criticism and the Curious Absence of Israel. International Studies Review 16 (3): 390–410.

Maroukis, Thanos and Anna Triandafyllidou. 2013. Mobility Partnerships: A Convincing Tool for the EU's Global Approach to Migration? Notre Europe Policy Paper 76. Jacques Delors Institute. http://www.notre-europe.eu/media/mobility-parnerships-maroukistriandafyllidou-ne-jdi-feb13.pdf. Accessed: 09 August 2016.

Martin, Marie. 2012. Extension of Mobility Partnerships With Euro-Mediterranean Partners. Panorama. http://www.statewatch.org/news/2013/jan/mp-article.pdf. Accessed: 09 August 2016.

Mink, Júlia. 2012. EU Asylum Law and Human Rights Protection: Revisiting the Principle of Non-Refoulement and the Prohibition of Torture and Other Forms of Ill-Treatment. European Journal of Migration and Law 14 (2): 119–149.

Monar, Jörg. 2014. EU Internal Security Governance: The Case of Counter-Terrorism. European Security 23 (2): 195–209.

Neal, Andrew W. 2009. Securitizing and Risk at the EU Border: The Origins of FRONTEX, Journal of Common Market Studies 47 (2): 333–356.

Occhipinti, John. 2013. Availability by Stealth? EU Information-sharing in Transatlantic Perspective. In European Security, Terrorism and Intelligence: Tackling New Security Challenges in Europe, ed. Kaunert, Christian and Sarah Léonard, 143–184. Houndmills, Basingstoke: Palgrave Macmillan.

Panizzon, Marion. 2012. Readmission Agreements of the EU Member States: A Case for EU Subsidiarity or Dualism? Refugee Survey Quarterly 31 (4): 101–133.

Paul, Amanda and Demir Murat Seyrek. 2016. EU Visa-Liberalisation for Turks: Just around the Corner? EPC Commentary. European Policy Centre. http://www.epc.eu/documents/uploads/pub_6501_eu_visa-liberalisation_for_turks.pdf Accessed: 28 June 2016.

Pawlak, Patryk. 2012. The Unintentional Development of the EU's Security Governance Beyond Borders. European Foreign Affairs Review 17 (2 Special Issue): 87–107.

Pedersen, Morten Jarlbæk. 2015. The Intimate Relationship between Security, Effectiveness, and Legitimacy: A New Look at the Schengen Compensatory Measures. European Security 24 (4): 541–559.

Pop, Valentina. 2016. The EU-Turkey Migrants Deal. Wall Street Journal. http://blogs.wsj.com/briefly/2016/03/19/the-eu-turkey-migrants-deal-at-a-glance/. Accessed: 13 April 2016.

Rijpma, Jorrit and Mathias Vermeulen. 2015. EUROSUR: Saving Lives or Building Borders? European Security 24 (3): 454–472.

Roe, Paul. 2012. Is Securitization a 'Negative' Concept? Revisiting the Normative Debate Over Normal Versus Extraordinary Politics. Security Dialogue 43 (3): 249–266.

Roth, Kenneth. 2016. A Way for Europe to Remove Chaos from the Migration Crisis. Reuters Blog The Great Debate. http://blogs.reuters.com/great-debate/2016/01/31/a-way-for-europe-to-remove-chaos-from-the-migration-crisis/. Accessed: 25 April 2016.

Rosenblum, Marc R. 2010. Immigrant Legalization in the United States and European Union: Policy Goals and Program Design. MPI Policy Brief, http://www.migrationpolicy.org/research/immigrant-legalization-united-states-and-european-union. Accessed: 09 August 2016.

Rychnovská, Dagmar. 2014. Securitization and the Power of Threat Framing. Perspectives 22 (2): 9–31.

Schlaefli, Samuel. 2016. Migrationsforscher Kamel Dorai: "Niemand im Nahen Osten glaubt mehr an Europas Rolle als Hüter der Menschenrechte". Die Tageswoche. http://www.tageswoche.ch/de/2016_14/international/715515. Accessed: 26 June 2016.

Schumacher, Elizabeth. 2016. Report: Five times more attacks on refugee homes in Germany in 2015. Deutsche Welle. http://www.dw.com/en/report-five-times-more-attacks-on-refugee-homes-in-germany-in-2015/a-19011109. Accessed: 27 June 2016.

Seiffart, Oliver. 2012. The Development of the European Border Surveillance System (EUROSUR). In A Threat Against Europe? Security, Migration, and Integration, ed. Burgess, J. Peter and Serge Gutwirth, 133–152. Brussels: VUB Press.

Sözen, Ülkü Sezgi. 2015. EU-Turkey Readmission Agreement: Not a 'Carrot' but more a '?'. In Turkish Migration Conference. Selected Proceedings 2015, ed. Şeker, Güven et al., 53–66. London: Transnational Press.

Tardy, Thierry. 2015. Operation Sophia: Tackling the Refugee Crisis with Military Means. European Union Institute for Security Studies, http://www.iss.europa.eu/uploads/media/Brief_30_Operation_Sophia.pdf. Accessed: 17 June 2016.

Thielemann, Eiko and Daniel Schade. 2016. Buying into Myths: Free Movement of People and Immigration. The Political Quarterly 87 (2): 139–147.

Triandafyllidou, Anna and Maurizio Ambrosini. 2011. Irregular Immigration Control in Italy and Greece: Strong Fencing and Weak Gate-keeping Serving the Labour Market. European Journal of Migration and Law 13 (3): 251–273.

Trilling, David. 2015. Europe Could Solve the Migrant Crisis – if it wanted. The Guardian. http://www.theguardian.com/commentisfree/2015/jul/31/europe-migrant-crisis-political-choice-toxic-waste-sanctuary. Accessed: 24 April 2016.

UK House of Lords. 2016. Operation Sophia, the EU's naval mission in the Mediterranean: an impossible challenge. HL Paper 144. House of Lords, European Union Committee, http://www.publications.parliament.uk/pa/ld201516/ldselect/ldeucom/144/144.pdf. Accessed: 28 June 2016.

Völkel, Jan Claudius. 2014a. Money for Nothing, the Cricks for Free. Five Paradoxes in EU Migration Policy. Comparative Migration Studies 2 (2): 151–180.

Völkel, Jan Claudius. 2014b. More for More, Less for Less – More or Less: A Critique of the EU's Arab Spring Response à la Cinderella. European Foreign Affairs Review 19 (2): 263–282.

Völkel, Jan Claudius. 2016a. Why are so many people dying in the Mediterranean. Open Democracy. https://www.opendemocracy.net/can-europe-make-it/jan-v-lkel/what-stops-drowning-why-so-many-people-die-in-mediterranean. Accessed: 26 June 2016.

Völkel, Jan Claudius. 2016b. Livin' on the Edge: Irregular Migration in Egypt. Middle East Institute. http://www.mei.edu/content/map/livin%E2%80%99-edge-irregular-migration-egypt. Accessed: 12 April 2016.

Völkel, Jan Claudius. 2016c. Hiring Bullies as Bouncers. World Policy Blog. http://www.worldpolicy.org/blog/2016/03/23/hiring-bullies-bouncers. Accessed: 12 April 2016.

Wæver, Ole. 1995. Securitization and Desecuritization. In On Security, ed. Lipschutz, Ronnie D., 46–86. New York: Columbia University Press.

Wæver, Ole. 2015. The Theory Act: Responsibility and Exactitude as seen from Securitization. International Relations 29 (1): 121–127.

Weiner, Myron. 1992. Security, Stability, and International Migration. International Security 17 (3): 91–126.

Williams, Michael C. 2015. Securitization as Political Theory: The Politics of the Extraordinary. International Relations 29 (1): 114–120.

Droits de l'homme et migration dans les relations euro-méditerranéennes

Les principes européens ont sombré en Méditerranée

Catherine Teule

Résumé

Alors que l'on recense dans le monde 250 millions de migrants dont plus de 65 millions de réfugiés et déplacés[1], l'Union européenne semble avoir une seule obsession : ne s'attaquer aux racines de *« l'immigration »* que pour se replier à l'abri de ses frontières. Pour la poursuite de cet objectif, elle s'appuie sur la mise en œuvre de « partenariats » avec les pays tiers : ses voisins du partenariat euro-méditerranéen, mais aussi, plus en amont, les pays de la Corne de l'Afrique incités à enrayer les flux migratoires à leur source. De ces « partenaires », l'UE souhaite obtenir des facilités pour qu'ils réadmettent les migrants dans leurs pays d'origine ou de transit et elle tente de les associer à une politique de contrôle en « exportant » ses propres frontières. Outre la violation des

1 Selon la terminologie des organisations internationales, ces deux qualificatifs désignent des personnes qui ont été *contraintes* de quitter leur domicile pour échapper à un conflit armé, à la violence généralisée et à des violations des droits de l'homme. Voir UNHCR, Global trends – Forced displacements in 2015, http://www.unhcr.org/576408cd7.

En principe, on considère comme *« réfugiés »* les personnes ayant franchi les frontières pour trouver « refuge » dans un autre pays qui leur a accordé une protection internationale à la suite de leur demande d'asile ; les *« déplacés »* restent, en revanche, dans leur pays ou dans la région (on les qualifie souvent de « déplacés internes »). Selon le dernier rapport statistique du HCR, en 2015, sur les 65,3 millions de déplacements forcés, 21,3 étaient le fait de réfugiés ; 3,2 de demandeurs d'asile (en demande de protection internationale) ; 40,8 de déplacés internes. La forte augmentation de cette dernière catégorie, depuis quelques années, tient à la multiplication des conflits interétatiques. Ces déplacements forcés forment une part (croissante) de *la migration internationale* (250 millions de personnes en 2015).

Dans ce texte, le terme « migrants » est plus souvent utilisé, afin de recouvrir l'ensemble des différents motifs conduisant les étrangers aux frontières de l'UE. Le terme « réfugié » entend plus particulièrement désigner les personnes qui, comme les Syriens, fuient les zones de conflit, même si elles n'ont pas encore obtenu la protection internationale d'un pays.

droits des migrants, particulièrement celui de pouvoir quitter leur pays et de demander l'asile, cette instrumentalisation des pays tiers contribue à pousser ces personnes à chercher, encore et encore, les chemins les plus périlleux pour atteindre l'Europe. Au risque de faire de la Méditerranée la frontière la plus dangereuse de la planète.

1 Introduction

Sur une superficie d'environ 2,5 millions de kilomètres carrés – à peine 2 % de l'océan Atlantique –, la Méditerranée forme la frontière la plus mortifère de la planète : c'est là que, en 2015, se sont produites 70 % des morts ou disparitions de migrants du monde. Selon l'OIM (Organisation Internationale pour les Migrations), ce bilan macabre s'élèverait à 60 000 personnes en deux décennies (IOM 2016a), non compris les disparitions et décès au cours des trajets terrestres en amont. Ces drames humains ne doivent rien au hasard. Ils sont le fruit de près de 20 ans d'entêtement des politiques migratoires de l'Union européenne et de ses États membres dans une obsession hystérique de préservation sélective de leur territoire face au « risque migratoire ».

2 Des frontières de papiers aux armadas guerrières

« Communautarisée » depuis l'entrée en vigueur du traité d'Amsterdam (1999), « commune » depuis celui de Lisbonne (2008), la politique européenne en matière d'immigration et d'asile n'a, en effet, jamais réussi à s'émanciper des diktats des États membres. Ceux-là, pris dans un double mouvement d'expansion géographique vers l'Est et le Sud et d'une intégration politique mollement souhaitée se sont arc-boutés sur la défense de leur souveraineté nationale. Dans une course au moins-disant censée décourager l'immigration jugée « subie », les différents paquets législatifs des quinze dernières années (regroupement familial, asile, immigration de travail, retours, notamment) n'ont pu être élaborés que sur la base du plus petit dénominateur commun, peu garant des droits des migrants.

La lutte contre l'immigration irrégulière s'est, quant à elle, organisée autour de deux axes : d'une part, une politique malthusienne des visas de court séjour[2] soupçonnés de favoriser l'arrivée de demandeurs d'asile et le maintien sur le territoire

2 Dans certains cas, comme en France, cela couvre également les *visas de transit aéroportuaire* refusés pour éviter que, lors du changement d'avion, le bénéficiaire n'en profite pour rester sur le territoire de transit.

de migrants sans titre et dont, pour cette raison, sont exclus tous les pays africains et moyen-orientaux (Tubiana 2016) ; d'autre part, une fixation sur la sécurité physique des frontières extérieures, notamment à l'Est et au Sud de l'Europe élargie, justifiant la mise en place de Frontex[3] et la « bunkerisation » progressive de l'UE.

Cette dimension répressive ne se limite pas aux frontières géographiques de l'Europe. Elle est, en effet, explicitement déclinée dans toutes les démarches « partenariales » développées par l'UE avec ses voisins, que ce soit dans le cadre euro-méditerranéen (1995) ou la « Politique de voisinage » (PEV, 2004) et, plus généralement dans toute « la dimension extérieure » de la politique communautaire (Commission européenne 2002). Elle se traduit par une « exportation » des frontières européennes, jusqu'à former une enceinte de défense avancée au plus près des zones de départ des migrants. Dans la zone euro-méditerranéenne, la conséquence de près de 20 ans de cette politique européenne a été double.

3 Une concentration accrue des flux de migrants en Méditerranée

En premier lieu et paradoxalement, année après année, la fermeture des frontières, les contrôles aériens renforcés, la restriction de l'accès aux visas de court séjour, les limites opposées à la réunification familiale, les freins à la migration économique, etc. ont eu l'effet inverse de l'objectif recherché. En poussant les migrants à trouver des voies détournées pour parvenir sur le territoire de l'Union, ces mesures ont fait de la Méditerranée, en dépit de ses dangers mais avec ses dizaines de milliers de km de côtes et ses dizaines d'îles, la moins hermétique des frontières européennes. Une migration irrégulière s'y est donc organisée à partir des années 80, entretenue par l'existence d'un marché du travail informel dans nombre de pays européens (Fig. 1).

D'abord modérée (quelques dizaines de milliers de personnes par an) visant les côtes d'Italie, de Malte ou d'Espagne, elle a acquis une réalité plus précise aux yeux des Européens en février 2011, lors de l'arrivée de près de 30 000 Tunisiens[4], à Lampedusa (Teule 2011). À compter de 2014, l'extension des conflits au Moyen-Orient (Syrie, Libye, Irak), s'ajoutant aux déplacements de populations de la Corne de l'Afrique (Érythrée, Soudan, notamment) et d'Afghanistan, a produit une demande de protection internationale d'une ampleur inédite qui s'est traduite par

3 Agence européenne pour la gestion de la coopération opérationnelle aux frontières extérieures, créée en 2005. Voir Frontex, http://frontex.europa.eu/.

4 Surnommés « *harragas* » par la presse maghrébine, c'est-à-dire « ceux qui brûlent » (leurs papiers, les frontières), à savoir des migrants sans titre, sans visa et souvent jeunes.

Fig. 1 Entrées irrégulières par la mer en Grèce, Italie, Espagne et à Malte. 1998–2015 (Fargues 2016).

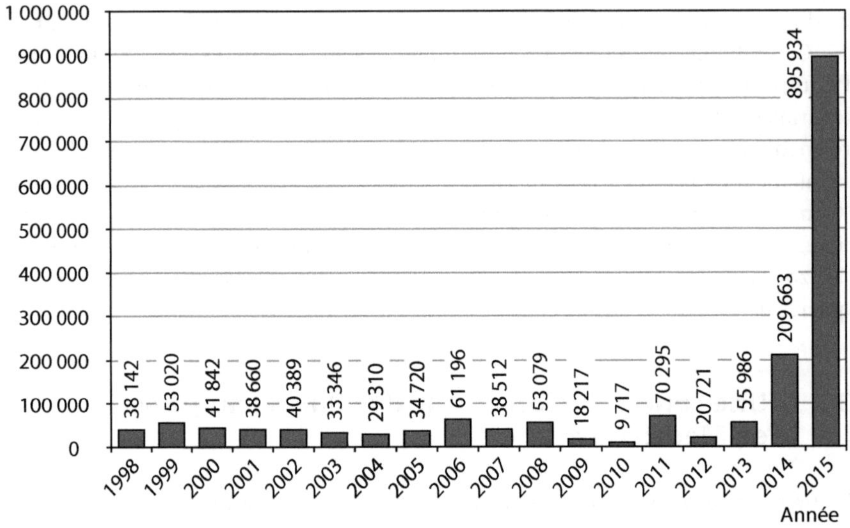

une migration « irrégulière »[5] tout aussi inédite : 108 000 arrivées en 2013 ; 276 000 en 2014 (European Commission 2015) ; 1,046 million en 2015, dont 96 % via la Méditerranée et à plus de 50 % d'origine syrienne (IOM 2015).

En deuxième lieu, jusqu'en 2014, la multiplication des interventions de Frontex, sous des noms divers (Hermès, Poseidon, Triton, Minerva, etc.), dans toutes les zones considérées comme menacées et le plus souvent avec l'appui d'États membres (Espagne) ou de pays tiers (Maroc, Libye), a souvent conduit à une baisse des arrivées directes dans lesdites zones. Mais, outre les critiques concernant les modes d'intervention de l'Agence et certaines violations manifestes des droits des migrants[6], dans leur globalité les flux ne se sont pas taris ; les chemins des migrants ont simplement changé et se sont allongés, à l'initiative des passeurs dont le fonds de commerce sait se diversifier à l'envi. (Fig. 2).

5 En fait, le qualificatif « irrégulier » n'est pas pertinent lorsqu'il concerne l'entrée sur un territoire national de personnes en recherche de protection internationale puisque « le demandeur d'asile » n'est pas tenu de disposer de documents pour franchir une frontière et que ce franchissement ne peut donc lui être interdit. V. art. 31 Convention de Genève du 28 juillet 1951.

6 Sur cette question, voir notamment : La Cimade 2016 et le site FRONTEXIT, http://www.frontexit.org/fr/.

Fig. 2 Transit Routes (IOM 2016b).

Du coup, les pays tiers jusqu'alors en relation directe avec l'UE (Maroc, Tunisie, Algérie, Libye, Syrie, Turquie, etc.) ont vu leur statut changer : de pays émetteurs d'une certaine émigration, ils sont aussi devenus pays de transit sur les routes entre l'Afrique continentale ou le Moyen-Orient et l'Europe. Certains même (Maroc, Turquie, Libye), bien malgré eux, sont devenus pays d'immigration, dans un cadre légal peu préparé. C'est donc, de leur côté, sur le fondement de relations de « partenariat » engagées depuis plusieurs années, que l'Europe cherche de nouveaux moyens de contenir les migrants en amont de la Méditerranée, voire au-delà, et recrute de nouveaux « garde-côtes » !

4 L'instrumentalisation des « partenariats »

Historiquement, c'est au Conseil européen de Tampere (1999), appuyé par celui de Séville (2002), qu'ont été posées les bases d'une intégration des questions d'asile et d'immigration dans « la dimension externe de l'action communautaire ». L'objectif était clairement énoncé : développer « une approche intégrée, globale et équilibrée visant à s'attaquer aux causes profondes de l'immigration illégale » et faire en sorte que « le partenariat avec les pays tiers concernés constitue un élément déterminant du succès de cette politique » (Commission européenne 2002, 42).

Le *« partenariat euro-méditerranéen »* issu du Processus de Barcelone (1995) était évidemment dans la cible[7]. Depuis, l'UE n'a eu de cesse d'élargir et d'affirmer des relations de cette nature : soit de façon multilatérale, notamment dans le *Processus de Rabat* (2006)[8], la *Stratégie de Dakar* (2011), le *Processus de Khartoum* (2014)[9] et le *Sommet de La Valette sur la migration* (2015) ; soit, dans une démarche bilatérale, avec le Maroc, la Tunisie, l'Égypte et la Jordanie en leur propo-

7 Le *Partenariat Euromed,* dit aussi Processus de Barcelone, a été institué en 1995 à Barcelone, à l'initiative de l'Union européenne (UE) et de douze autres États riverains de la mer Méditerranée (Algérie, Autorité palestinienne, Chypre, Égypte, Israël, Jordanie, Liban, Maroc, Malte, Syrie, Tunisie et Turquie). Depuis l'adhésion de Chypre et Malte à l'UE, Euromed rassemble, désormais, les 28 États membres de l'UE et dix États du sud de la Méditerranée. L'Albanie et la Mauritanie en sont membres depuis 2007. La Libye a un statut d'observateur depuis 1999 et prépare son intégration à moyen terme.

8 Le Processus de Rabat réunit, depuis 2006, près de 60 pays européens et africains de l'Afrique du Nord, de l'Ouest et du Centre ainsi que la Commission européenne (CE) et la Communauté Économique des États de l'Afrique de l'Ouest (CEDEAO) sur les enjeux migratoires.

9 Le 28 novembre 2014, les ministres des 28 États membres de l'UE et de plusieurs pays africains (Djibouti, Égypte, Érythrée, Éthiopie, Kenya, Somalie, Soudan, Soudan du Sud et Tunisie), ainsi que des représentants de l'Union européenne et de l'Union africaine ont adopté une déclaration visant à lancer l'« initiative sur la route migratoire UE-Corne de l'Afrique ».

sant des « *partenariats pour la mobilité* » (PPM) (Commission européenne 2007), à l'exemple de ceux qu'elle avait monté avec la Moldavie et le Cap-Vert en 2008.

On peut observer que, dans tous les textes issus de ces conférences ou sommets, dans tous les accords entre l'UE et les pays tiers, figurent des déclarations d'intention sur le respect des droits fondamentaux des migrants concernés. Mais on peut également remarquer que, quelle que soit la formulation retenue, cela n'entraine pas de véritable obligation pour les signataires et que, en définitive, l'objectif demeure étroitement centré sur les moyens nécessaires pour maintenir les migrants à distance et faciliter leur « reprise » par les pays d'où ils proviennent.

Ainsi, dans le texte cadrant les partenariats pour la mobilité et publié par la Commission en 2007, figurent les attentes européennes concernant notamment :

- « l'engagement (du pays tiers) de réadmettre effectivement ses propres ressortissants et d'apporter une coopération totale à leur identification ;
- l'engagement supplémentaire de réadmettre, dans des circonstances clairement définies, les ressortissants de pays tiers et les apatrides arrivés dans l'UE par le territoire du pays concerné, le cas échéant dans le cadre d'un accord de réadmission CE ;
  (…)
- des efforts en vue d'améliorer le contrôle aux frontières et/ou leur gestion, avec l'appui éventuel de la coopération opérationnelle avec les États membres et/ou FRONTEX ;
  (…)
- des mesures et des initiatives spécifiques pour lutter sérieusement contre le trafic de migrants et la traite d'êtres humains, dans le droit-fil de la convention du Conseil de l'Europe sur la lutte contre la traite des êtres humains (…) »

Étant précisé *in fine* que « ce type de mesures devra être mis en œuvre dans le strict respect des droits fondamentaux des personnes concernées, y compris les droits spécifiques des personnes susceptibles d'avoir besoin d'une protection international » (Ibid., 4–5, § II-B(1)).

La mise en œuvre de ces PPM, que ce soit avec le Maroc en 2013 ou la Tunisie en 2014, reproduisent les mêmes déséquilibres dans la hiérarchie des enjeux. C'est le constat qu'en faisait le Réseau Euro-méditerranéen des Droits de l'homme à l'occasion de la « déclaration conjointe » signée entre le Maroc, l'UE et neuf de ses États membres, le 7 juin 2013 :

> « Le Réseau constate que l'appel au renforcement et au déploiement d'instruments de lutte contre l'immigration irrégulière tient une place prépondérante parmi les propositions contenues dans la déclaration. Les parties s'engagent à signer, prochainement, un accord de réadmission au Maroc des ressortissants marocains ou d'État tiers, notam-

> ment les Subsahariens, en situation irrégulière dans l'UE et à établir un accord de travail entre le Maroc et l'agence européenne Frontex.
>
> Au vu de la situation prévalant au Maroc, un accord de réadmission comporterait de sérieux risques en termes de respect des droits des migrants et des réfugiés et les exposerait à des traitements inhumains et dégradants. En effet, les organisations de la société civile marocaine et le conseil national des droits de l'Homme ont largement dénoncé le sort des ressortissants subsahariens ‹ bloqués › au Maroc. La criminalisation de l'immigration irrégulière, inscrite dans la loi 02-03, l'absence de régime d'asile effectif et le climat xénophobe hostile aux migrants – allant jusqu'à causer la mort de nombreuses personnes ces dernières années –, sont autant de réalités que les parties ne peuvent pourtant pas ignorer.
>
> De plus, ces dispositifs de surveillance des frontières ont pour objectif d'empêcher les migrants et les réfugiés d'atteindre les frontières européennes. Loin de veiller aux besoins de protection, en particulier des plus vulnérables, ces mesures comportent en elles-mêmes des risques de violations par les États de leurs engagements internationaux et d'atteintes aux droits fondamentaux » (EuroMed Droits 2014).

Des réserves comparables se sont exprimées, à la suite de la « déclaration conjointe » signée entre l'UE et la Tunisie, le 3 mars 2014. Ce pays ne s'est toujours pas doté d'une législation sur l'asile lui permettant de respecter ses obligations internationales au regard de la Convention de Genève et de la Convention de l'OUA et les dispositions législatives sur le « délit d'émigration clandestine » n'ont toujours pas été abolies. Un tel contexte ne peut que rendre inquiétante la perspective de l'accord de réadmission que l'UE appelle obstinément de ses vœux[10] (voir *infra*).

La déclaration politique issue du Sommet de La Valette sur la migration de novembre 2015 tranche quelque peu sur cette conception européenne de « la mobilité ». Sans doute en raison des résistances exprimées par nombre de participants africains, elle pose d'emblée des exigences de respect des droits fondamentaux : « *Nous réaffirmons que nous sommes fermement résolus à respecter les obligations internationales et les droits de l'homme.* Le respect de la dignité des réfugiés et des migrants ainsi que la protection de leurs droits fondamentaux, quel que soit leur statut, demeureront notre priorité en permanence ». Et ce n'est que dans les 19 pages du programme d'action qui l'accompagne qu'apparaît l'engagement de « renforcer la *coopération afin de faciliter le retour et la réintégration durable des migrants irréguliers,* que ce soit en provenance des États membres de l'UE et pays associés ou des pays africains de transit et de destination » ou encore la décision

10 Voir : la déclaration commune de 10 associations : Partenariat de Mobilité entre la Tunisie et l'UE : l'externalisation des frontières européennes à marche forcée ; Tunis, Paris, Copenhague, Bruxelles, le 17 mars 2014, http://www.migreurop.org/IMG/pdf/cp_tunisie_fr-2.pdf.

d'apporter « un appui aux capacités nationales de contrôle des frontières terrestres, maritimes et aériennes ainsi qu'aux capacités de surveillance maritime aux fins de la prévention de la migration irrégulière, de la criminalité transfrontière et du terrorisme ainsi que du renforcement des opérations de recherche et de sauvetage » (Conseil européen 2015).

5 Réadmission v/s libéralisation des visas

Pour la Commission et les États membres, la réadmission par les pays d'origine ou de transit est jugée essentielle à l'efficacité de la politique européenne de retour[11]. C'est donc un point clé des négociations avec les pays tiers, dans le cadre d'un PPM ou directement, comme ce fut le cas avec la Turquie (2013). Dix-sept accords de ce type ont déjà été signés par l'UE et elle tente d'en faire de même avec l'Algérie, le Maroc et la Tunisie. A ces accords multilatéraux s'ajoutent des dizaines d'accords bilatéraux établis par les États membres (voir : Rekacewicz 2015).

Directement, cela facilite le renvoi de personnes interpellées en situation irrégulière (demandeurs d'asile déboutés ou migrants sans titre) vers les pays tiers signataires. La Commission propose même que ces pays détachent du personnel policier pour identifier leurs ressortissants « déboutés » présents dans les *hotspots* de Grèce et d'Italie. Indirectement, le fait de devoir « reprendre » ces migrants, et la crainte d'apparaître laxistes dans la lutte contre l'immigration irrégulière, est une incitation pour les pays tiers à mieux contrôler leurs frontières et à filtrer le transit des migrants et les sorties de leur territoire. L'UE met d'ailleurs à leur disposition des « officiers de liaison immigration » (OLI) ; détachés par les États membres, ils ont pour fonction « d'aider les autorités du pays hôte à éviter que les flux d'immigration illégale ne se forment sur leur territoire ou n'y transitent », sous diverses formes, dont la détection de faux documents ou le contrôle des documents des passagers, conjointement avec le personnel du pays concerné[12].

Pour les personnes, cette mise à distance juridique pratiquée par l'UE a un indéniable effet délétère, comme l'a souligné Nils Muiznieks, Commissaire aux droits de l'homme du Conseil de l'Europe : l'UE « conduit des pays tiers à modifier leur législation et leurs pratiques d'une manière qui risque d'entraîner des violations des droits de l'homme, notamment du droit de quitter un pays, de l'interdic-

11 Selon les estimations de la Commission européenne, en 2014 plus de 60 % des migrants en situation irrégulière ne quittaient pas le territoire européen après en avoir reçu l'ordre (Commission européenne 2015). Les chiffres publiés dans les derniers rapports de Frontex sont plus faibles (40 à 50 %), les bases statistiques étant sans doute différentes.

12 Règlement (CE) n° 377/2004 du Conseil du 19 février 2004 relatif à la création d'un réseau d'officiers de liaison « Immigration ».

tion des expulsions collectives et du droit de demander l'asile et d'en bénéficier » (Council of Europe, Commissioner for Human Rights 2013).

Outre un retour souvent « forcé » dans le pays d'origine ou de transit, par le jeu des accords en cascade que ce pays a lui-même passés avec ses voisins, les migrants peuvent, de proche en proche, se retrouver dans un pays qu'ils ont fui sans avoir pu faire valoir leur demande d'asile. Ainsi des risques de renvois encourus par des Afghans, Pakistanais, Bangladais, Africains renvoyés de Grèce vers la Turquie, dès la mise en œuvre de l'accord passé avec l'UE (Mützel 2016). Au Maroc, ils peuvent être placés en détention pour sortie illicite du territoire ; en Libye, la détention est le lot de tout migrant « irrégulier » ; partout, le retour dans le pays de transit se traduit par une relégation de sans-papiers, sans-droits, voire comme en Libye par des violences de la part de trafiquants, de bandes criminelles ou même de groupes armés.

Il faut donc insister, comme le font certaines ONGs et nombre de parlementaires européens, sur le fait qu'aucun accord de cette nature ne devrait être mis en œuvre sans consultation de la société civile des deux côtés de la Méditerranée et sans un suivi indépendant de ses conséquences (EuroMed Droits 2012).

Qui plus est, on peut juger que c'est un marché de dupes auquel l'UE engage les pays tiers. La contrepartie proposée est généralement « une facilitation des visas », mais qui concerne essentiellement la migration circulaire des acteurs économiques et non la suppression des visas de court séjour, ni l'ouverture de l'Europe à l'immigration étudiante ou familiale, pourtant jugées essentielles par ces pays. Les négociations actuellement engagées entre l'UE et la Tunisie témoignent de ce savant déséquilibre. Dans le texte d'annonce, la Commission précise en effet que, « s'agissant de l'accord visant à faciliter la délivrance de visas, les assouplissements pourraient porter par exemple sur l'allégement ou l'élimination, au moins pour quelques catégories de personnes, de certaines des obligations prévues par le Code Visa. En ce qui concerne l'accord sur la réadmission des migrants irréguliers, ce dernier devrait définir les procédures à suivre par les deux parties en vue de clarifier, de simplifier et d'accélérer la coopération dans ce domaine » (Commission européenne 2016b). C'est un bon exemple du décalage entre les aspirations des citoyens du pays tiers et les propositions de l'UE.

6 La mise hors-sol des frontières européennes

Par cette externalisation de sa gestion des flux migratoires à des pays qui ne sont pas tenus, par les conventions internationales ou la CEDH, aux mêmes normes de droit qu'elle-même, l'UE espère bien établir une première barrière limitant les arrivées de migrants sur son territoire, sans engager directement sa responsabilité au regard du respect de leurs droits. Depuis plusieurs années, des rapports d'ONGs montrent qu'il en est ainsi à la frontière marocaine de l'Espagne où l'accès aux enclaves de Ceuta et Melilla est entravé avec la coopération des gardes-frontières marocains[13]. En 2008, la signature d'un accord entre l'Italie et la Libye s'est traduite par l'interception et la reconduite systématique de centaines de migrants vers la Libye, avant que ces pratiques – assimilées à un refoulement – ne soient condamnées par la Cour européenne des droits de l'homme *(Hirsi et autres c. Italie)* (European Court of Human Rights 2012).

En termes plus directement opérationnels, les partenaires « voisins », comme le Maroc, sont également invités à contribuer à la surveillance des frontières et aux interceptions des embarcations repérées en mer. Certains d'entre eux bénéficient ainsi d'un « accord de travail » *(working arrangement)* avec Frontex pour former leurs personnels de répression *(capacity building project)* ou participent à des « opérations conjointes » en tant qu'observateur. Dans le cadre d'Eurosur, le « système européen de surveillance des frontières » lancé le 1er décembre 2013, les États européens peuvent également passer des accords de coopération bilatérale ou multilatérale avec ces mêmes pays tiers afin d'étoffer le système d'alerte précoce sur le départ des migrants.

Au large de la Libye, en revanche, c'est l'UE elle-même qui a pris les rênes de l'opération navale militaire EUNAVFOR MED (surnommée Sophia) lancée en juin 2015. L'objectif, nous dit-on, serait de « démanteler le modèle économique des réseaux de trafic de clandestins et de traites des êtres humains ». Mais, pour l'instant, Sophia demeure circonscrit aux eaux internationales ; les interceptions y touchent donc bien plus de migrants que de « passeurs » dont les « modèles » prennent forme sur le continent africain et non en mer. Au large de la Turquie, c'est l'OTAN qui a été appelé à la rescousse, en février 2016 en mer Égée, et surveille les eaux internationales et territoriales de la Grèce et de la Turquie.

Ces interceptions maritimes s'ajoutent à celles qui sont menées par Frontex. Et, dans tous les cas, se pose la question de la sécurité des migrants ainsi arraisonnés, celle du respect de leur droit à demander l'asile, celle du lieu vers lequel ils sont transférés … et celle de leur devenir.

7 Le maintien à distance des réfugiés

Dans un monde recensant 250 millions de migrants, dont 65 millions de personnes contraintes de fuir leur domicile ou leur pays, en raison de la guerre, des violations

13 Sur les renvois « à chaud » menés par l'Espagne, voir, notamment : Amnesty International 2015 et Jesuit Refugee Service (Espagne) 2016.

de leurs droits, de la mise en danger de leur vie ou de leur liberté, les manœuvres de l'UE qui s'évertue à financer des interceptions en mer et la clôture des côtes sud et est de la Méditerranée paraissent des armes de défense bien dérisoires. Entre la quasi-certitude de mourir dans un conflit, la perte de la liberté, les violences et le risque de disparaître en mer, les personnes ne font pas la balance. Les réfugiés, on l'a vu, continuent d'arriver en Europe et ils continueront de le faire, en payant plus cher les passeurs et en prenant plus de risques s'il le faut.

Aussi, ne pouvant vraiment stopper les arrivées, l'UE est de plus en plus tentée de bloquer les départs et d'organiser le maintien des migrants au plus loin du territoire. Et, pour cela, elle sait se montrer fort généreuse. Cette démarche, résumée sous « le concept de renforcement des capacités dans les régions prioritaires situées sur les principales routes migratoires »[14] vaut tant pour les personnes en recherche de protection que pour les migrants dits « économiques ». Elle n'est pas vraiment nouvelle dans la sémantique européenne puisque cet objectif figurait déjà dans les lignes du Processus de Khartoum adoptées en novembre 2014 ; mais l'on comprend que la Commission insiste car l'enjeu est de taille : la seule Afrique de l'Ouest compte plus de 8,4 millions de migrants internes !

Les États membres, n'hésitent d'ailleurs pas à appuyer dans ce sens, comme l'Italie qui dans un projet intitulé « Migration Compact » expose très clairement l'intérêt de réactiver « l'accord d'amitié » signé avec la Libye en 2008 et de développer, avec l'Afrique sub-saharienne, Soudan et Niger en particulier, des accords comparables à celui qui a été passé avec la Turquie (Governo italiano 2016). A La Valette, pour emporter l'adhésion de ses interlocuteurs africains, la Commission a promis un fonds de 1,8 milliard d'euros ; il doit être abondé d'un montant équivalent par les États membres dont certains, comme la France, participent au financement de centres de traitement des demandes d'asile en Afrique, comme à Agadez (Niger). A la Turquie, ce sont 3 milliards d'euros qui ont été promis à l'appui de l'accord « un pour un »[15]. Au printemps 2016, la Commission a proposé au Conseil et au Parlement européen que les moyens habituellement dévolus à l'aide au développement soient concentrés sur les objectifs migratoires, ce qui relève d'une éthique pour le moins surprenante.

14 European Council 2015.

15 Référence à l'accord signé, le 18 mars 2016, par l'UE et la Turquie pour « mettre fin à la migration irrégulière de la Turquie vers l'UE ». Outre le renvoi de « tous les nouveaux migrants en situation irrégulière qui partent de la Turquie pour gagner les îles grecques », le texte prévoit que « pour chaque Syrien renvoyé en Turquie au départ des îles grecques, un autre Syrien sera réinstallé de la Turquie vers l'UE ». Voir : Conseil européen 2016.

Il est vrai que la pratique n'est pas nouvelle. Elle est même intégrée dans le corpus législatif européen puisque la directive « qualification »[16], actuellement appliquée par les États membres, prévoit des réserves sur l'octroi du statut de réfugié à toute personne « susceptible de bénéficier d'une protection à l'intérieur de son pays contre les persécutions ou les atteintes graves dans une partie du pays d'origine ». Or ces zones de protection de « déplacés internes » sont, en partie, financées par le programme ECHO de l'UE et la Commission insiste pour que les États membres y contribuent plus activement, par exemple en Jordanie, au Liban ou en Irak.

Au terme de cet état des lieux, force est d'observer que, à la violence mafieuse des passeurs et des trafiquants, aux risques létaux du désert ou de la mer, l'Union européenne ajoute une violence institutionnelle, source de maltraitances juridique et humaine indignes, souvent même attentatoires au droit à la vie et à la liberté de tout être humain. Elle se dédouane en instrumentalisant particulièrement les partenaires euro-méditerranéens.

On aurait aimé que l'UE et ses membres prennent acte de la nouvelle configuration d'une migration en recherche de protection internationale et décident d'en prendre leur part au lieu de s'en protéger. La réforme récente du système d'asile commun (2013–2015), comme l'existence d'une directive sur la protection temporaire (2001) justement conçue pour faire face à des situations d'afflux, leur en donnaient les moyens. Mais les États membres ne l'ont pas entendu ainsi. On peut légitimement craindre que les réformes annoncées de la législation européenne de l'asile n'en portent la trace (AEDH 2016).

Références

Amnesty International. 2015. Peurs et barbelés. La stratégie de l'Europe pour tenir les réfugiés à distance. https://www.amnesty.org/fr/documents/euro3/2544/2015/fr/. Accessed : 19th October 2016.

AEDH (Association européenne pour la défense des droits de l'Homme). 2013. Pourquoi l'AEDH s'oppose à la signature d'accords de réadmission de l'Union européenne (Note d'analyse). http://www.aedh.eu/plugins/fckeditor/userfiles/file/Communiqu%C3%A9s/R%C3%A9admission%20AEDH%20note%20d'analyse%2010_2013%20FR.pdf. Accessed : 19th October 2016.

16 Directive 2011/95/UE du 13 décembre 2011 précisant les conditions que doivent remplir les ressortissants des pays tiers ou les apatrides pour pouvoir bénéficier d'une protection internationale.

AEDH (Association européenne pour la Défense des Droits de l'Homme). 2016. Coercition et exclusion ne font pas une politique d'asile équitable. http://www.aedh.eu/Coercition-et-exclusion-ne-font,3346.html. Accessed : 20th October 2016.

Balleix, Corinne. 2013. La politique migratoire de l'Union européenne. Collection Réflexe Europe. Paris : La Documentation française.

Balleix, Corinne. 2015. La politique européenne d'immigration et d'asile. Toute l'Europe. http://www.touteleurope.eu/les-politiques-europeennes/immigration-et-asile.html. Accessed : 19th October 2016.

Cochetel, Vincent. 2015. Politique d'asile en Europe : comment répondre aux défis venant de la Méditerranée ? Question d'Europe n°365, 7 septembre 2015. http://www.robert-schuman.eu/fr/doc/questions-d-europe/qe-365-fr.pdf. Accessed : 19th October 2016.

Cogolati, Samuel, Nele Verlinden and Pierre Schmitt. 2015. Les migrants en Méditerranée : La protection des droits de l'homme. Étude pour le Parlement européen. http://www.europarl.europa.eu/RegData/etudes/STUD/2015/535005/EXPO_STU(2015)535005_FR.pdf. Accessed : 19th October 2016.

Clochard, Olivier and Nicolas Lambert. 2015. L'évolution d'un régime. Mort aux frontières et contrôles migratoires en mer Méditerranée. In Migrations en Méditerranée, eds. Schmoll, Camille, Hélène Thiollet and Catherine Wihtol de Wenden. Paris : CNRS Editions.

Council of Europe, Commissioner for Human Rights. 2013. The right to leave a country. http://www.coe.int/t/commissioner/source/prems/prems150813_GBR_1700_TheRightToLeaveACountry_web.pdf. Accessed : 19th October 2016.

EuroMed Droits. 2012. Partenariats pour la mobilité avec la Tunisie et le Maroc : des garanties concernant le respect des droits doivent être préalables à tout accord. http://euromedrights.org/fr/publication/partenariats-pour-la-mobilite-avec-la-tunisie-et-le-maroc-des-garanties-concernant-le-respect-des-droits-doivent-etre-prealables-a-tout-accord/. Accessed : 19th October 2016.

EuroMed Droits. 2014. Document d'analyse du Partenariat de Mobilité signé entre le Royaume du Maroc, l'Union Européenne et neuf États membres. http://euromedrights.org/fr/publication/document-danalyse-du-partenariat-de-mobilite-signe-entre-le-royaume-du-maroc-lue-et-neuf-etats-membres/. Accessed : 19th October 2016.

European Court of Human Rights. 2012. Arrêt Hirsi Jamaa et autres c. Italie – Grande Chambre Cour européenne des droits de l'Homme, 23 février 2012 – http://hudoc.echr.coe.int/eng#{«fulltext»:[«Arrêt Hirsi Jamaa et autres»],«itemid»:[«001-109230»]}. Accessed : 12th October 2016.

Fargues, Philippe. 2016. Un million de migrants arrivés sans visa en Europe en 2015 : Qui sont-ils ? INED Population et Sociétés n° 532.

Fargues, Philippe and Hervé Le Bras. 2009. Migrants et migrations dans le bassin de la Méditerranée. LesNotes IPEMED n°1. http://www.ipemed.coop/adminIpemed/media/fich_article/1315940113_LesNotesIPEMED_1_migrantsetmigrations.pdf. Accessed : 19th October 2016.

Governo italiano. 2016. Migration Compact, Contribution to an EU strategy for external action on migration. www.governo.it/sites/governo.it/files/immigrazione_0.pdf. Accessed : 20th October 2016.

IOM (International Organization for Migration). 2015. Mixed Migration Flows in the Mediterranean and Beyond. http://doe.iom.int/docs/Flows%20Compilation%202015% 20Overview.pdf./. Accessed : 19th October 2016.

IOM. 2016a. Fatal Journeys Volume 2 : Identification and tracing of dead and missing migrants. https://publications.iom.int/books/fatal-journeys-volume-2-identification-and-tracing-dead-and-missing-migrants. Accessed : 19th October 2016.

IOM. 2016b. Transit Routes. http://migration.iom.int/europe/. Accessed : 24th October 2016.

Jesuit Refugee Service (Espagne). 2016. Sin protección en la frontera. Derechos humanos en la frontera Sur : entre Nador y Melilla. Infosj. https://infosj.es/noticias-sj/4489-sin-proteccion-en-la-frontera-sur-entre-nador-y-melilla. Accessed : 20th October 2016.

La Cimade. 2016. Frontières européennes. Défense d'entrer ? http://www.lacimade.org/wp-content/uploads/2016/06/La_Cimade_FrontieresUE_pl.pdf. Accessed : 19th October 2016.

Mützel, Daniel. 2016. Ankara accusée d'expulser illégalement des Afghans. EurActiv. https://www.euractiv.fr/section/l-europe-dans-le-monde/news/ankara-accused-of-forcibly-repatriating-at-risk-afghans/. Accessed : 20th October 2016.

Parizot, Cédric. 2015. Les murs en Méditerranée. Antiatlas des frontières. http://www.antiatlas.net/blog/2015/12/17/les-murs-en-mediterranee/. Accessed : 19th October 2016.

Rekacewicz, Philippe. 2015. Cartographie : L'Europe des accords de réadmission. In Contenir les migrants au plus loin des frontières européennes… jusqu'à les rendre invisibles, Teule, Catherine. Vivre ensemble n° 155. http://asile.ch/2015/12/27/28833/. Accessed : 19th October 2016.

REMI (Revue européenne des migrations internationales). 2015. Migrations au Maghreb et au Moyen-Orient : le temps des révolutions 2015/3-4 (Vol. 31). Université de Poitiers.

Ritaine, Evelyne. 2012. La fabrique politique d'une frontière européenne en Méditerranée. Le « jeu du mistigri » entre les Etats et l'Union. Etudes du CERI n°186. http://enigmur.hypotheses.org/3595. Accessed : 19th October 2016.

Rodier, Claire. 2010. Frontex, l'agence tout risque. Plein droit 4/2010 (n° 87). www.cairn.info/revue-plein-droit-2010-4-page-8.htm. Accessed : 19th October 2016.

Teule, Catherine. 2011. Face aux migrants tunisiens, une Europe bornée. Hommes & Libertés n°154. http://www.ldh-france.org/IMG/pdf/H_L154_Actualite_2._Face_aux_migrants_tunisiens_une_Europe_bornee_.pdf. Accessed : 19th October 2016.

Tubiana, Michel. 2016. La politique européenne des visas de court séjour. Après-Demain n°39, Juillet 2016.

UNHCR (United Nations High Commissioner for Refugees). 2016. Global Trends – Forced Displacements in 2015. http://www.unhcr.org/576408cd7. Accessed : 19th October 2016.

Wihtol de Wenden, Catherine. 2009. L'Europe, un continent d'immigration malgré lui. Études 3/2009 (Tome 410). www.cairn.info/revue-etudes-2009-3-page-317.htm. Accessed : 19th October 2016.

Union Européenne

Comité Économique et Social européen. 2013. L'immigration irrégulière par voie maritime dans la zone euro-méditerranéenne. REX/375 EESC-2013-2533. http://www.eesc.europa.eu/?i=portal.fr.rex-opinions.28785. Accessed : 19th October 2016.

Commission européenne. 2002. Intégrer les questions liées aux migrations dans les relations de l'Union européenne avec les pays tiers. COM(2002) 703 final.

Commission européenne. 2007. Communication (…) relative aux migrations circulaires et aux partenariats pour la mobilité entre l'Union européenne et les pays tiers. COM(2007) 248 final. http://eur-lex.europa.eu/legal-content/FR/TXT/PDF/?uri=CELEX:52007 DC0248&from=FR. Accessed : 19th October 2016.

Commission européenne. 2015. Plan d'action de l'UE en matière de retour. COM(2015) 453 final. http://ec.europa.eu/dgs/home-affairs/what-we-do/policies/european-agenda-migration/background-information/docs/effective_return_policy_fr.pdf. Accessed : 19th October 2016.

Commission européenne. 2016a. Communication relative à la mise en place d'un nouveau cadre de partenariat avec les pays tiers dans le cadre de l'Agenda européen en matière de migration. COM(2016) 385 final. http://eur-lex.europa.eu/legal-content/fr/ALL/?uri=CELEX%3A52016DC 0385. Accessed : 19th October 2016.

Commission européenne. 2016b. L'UE et la Tunisie commencent des négociations en vue de faciliter la délivrance de visas et la réadmission. Communiqué de presse. http://europa.eu/rapid/press-release_IP-16-3394_fr.htm. Accessed : 20th October 2016.

Conseil européen. 2015. Sommet de La Valette sur la migration, 11–12 Novembre 2015 – Plan d'action & Déclaration politique. http://www.consilium.europa.eu/press-releases-pdf/2015/11/40802204984_fr.pdf. Accessed : 19th October 2016.

Conseil européen. 2016. Déclaration UE-Turquie. Communiqué de presse. http://www.consilium.europa.eu/fr/press/press-releases/2016/03/18-eu-turkey-statement/. Accessed : 20th October 2016.

European Commission. 2015. Questions and Answers : Smuggling of Migrants in Europe and the EU response. MEMO/15/3261.

European Council. 2015. Valletta Summit on Migration, Plan d'action. http://www.consilium.europa.eu/fr/meetings/international-summit/2015/11/ACTION-PLAN-FR-%282%29_pdf/. Accessed : 20th October 2016.

Germany's integration debate: Migration as a societal challenge

Ambivalent Germany

How to deal with migration, Muslims and democracy

Naika Foroutan

Abstract

In 2001 Germany positioned itself for the first time as a country of immigration – that's almost 50 years after the first German-Turkish "guest worker" contracts were signed. This act of recognition changed the political and legal landscape as demands for political, social and cultural rights suddenly became legitimate. Society responded both in support and rejection for these new demands, creating a cleaveage between pro- and anti-diversity positionings. This ambivalence becomes particularly apparent when discussing the situation of Muslims in Germany: Grounded with empirical data this paper shows how the implementation of minority rights is cognitively accepted, while rejected and disapproved of in connection with Muslims in Germany.

1 Transformation of Germany into a country of immigration

According to the latest press releases of the Federal Statistical Office, net immigration in Germany in 2015 totalled 1,139,000 people (Statistisches Bundesamt 2016b). That is the largest number of immigrants to enter the country in the past 20 years, since the Asylum Compromise of 1993. The compromise placed tough restrictions on immigration, with the result that the immigration rate significantly decreased in subsequent years. In 2008 and 2009, Germany experienced negative net migration, thus making Germany a de facto emigration country (Bundesamt für Migration und Flüchtlinge 2016, 14). However, first the financial and then the euro crisis both led to increased numbers of immigrants entering Germany from 2010 onwards. At the same time, German industry has publicly addressed the demographic change occurring in Germany and the country's need for immigration. In 2015, 17.1 million people with a migration background[1] lived in Germany, comprising 21 % of the German population. Of these, the majority (9.3 million) held German citizenship, while 7.8 million were nationals of other countries (Statistisches Bundesamt, 2016c). A quarter of people with a migration background are Muslim; of them, around half possess German citizenship. The majority of people with a migration background living in Germany stem from another European country; in the last five years, this portion of the population has grown significantly as a result of the financial and economic crises. In 2014, almost three quarters of all immigrants (73.8 %) came to Germany from another European country (ibid., 15). Even in 2015, 58 % of the immigration influx to Germany was from within Europe (Statistisches Bundesamt, 2016b).

These numbers prove that Germany is a country of immigration that has been shaped by significant demographic changes as well as by increasing cultural, ethnic, religious and national diversity. The mingling of people with and without a migration background in the workplace, the family and in everyday life – which fosters the establishment of personal alliances: partnerships, marriages, daughters-in-law and sons-in-law, parents-in-law, children and friends – leads to the fact that this migration background is a lived reality for more people than only the migrants themselves, and that the migrant experience therefore is relevant to more people (Foroutan et al. 2014, 38).

Considering that 17 million people (that is approx. 20 % of the population) in Germany have a migration background, we can say that whilst including family relations (which also include family members without a migration background) almost 35 % of total population is directly or indirectly affected by the category migration background. It thus becomes increasingly difficult to use migration as a dividing line for different groups of society, as the migration experience is a social reality for so many (ibid.). German society's self-perception is increasingly moving beyond the migration aspect and on to negotiating social positioning, rights and self-concepts in relation to equality of opportunity: migration and immigration are politically recognised as constitutional elements of society, competing norms and values are being negotiated in a variety of ways, alliances are being developed based on attitudes on diversity, and rejection of right-wing ideologies are formulated regardless of the fact whether one has a migration background or not. At the same time, plural societies are witnessing the growth of visibly antagonistic positions, and right-wing populist discourse with strong xenophobic and

1 Migration background is a commonly used term in Germany to describe individuals who themselves, or at least one parent have moved to Germany after 1949. The term was introduced by the German Federal Statistical Office in 2005.

particularly anti-Muslim rhetoric is gaining an ever stronger foothold in mainstream society (Decker, Kiess and Brähler 2014).These ambivalences are affecting German society during its transformation into a plural society shaped by immigration and emigration flows, a society that increasingly recognises its migration reality as fixed and is now ready to find a new self-description that moves beyond the migration aspect.

For decades, from the guest worker recruitment treaties in 1955 up until the switch to a red–green government in 1998, the German government rejected to position itself as a country of immigration. However, since the early 2000s, official political documents[2] have used the term 'country of immigration' to describe Germany. The social sciences, seeking to underscore not only the political but also the social change that has resulted from this situation, also use the term 'immigration society' (Bade 2013) or 'migration society' (Broden and Mecheril 2007).

The numbers show that there have repeatedly been peaks and troughs in the immigration flow to Germany over the last 25 years. If we examine the years 1991 and 1992, we notice a very strong increase in immigration, with a migration surplus of about 800,000 people in 1992[3] (Bundesamt für Migration und Flüchtlinge 2016, 14). Looking at the years 2008 and 2009, it is noticeable that Germany practically became a country of emigration, as the number of emigrants exceeded the number of immigrants by about 80,000 (ibid.). The question of whether or not Germany is a country of immigration was a hotly debated topic during those years, even though it had been officially politically established in the documents of the Süssmuth Committee that Germany was indeed a country of immigration (Unabhängige Kommission "Zuwanderung" 2001).

While the numbers of immigrants barely changed through the official recognition, the narrative certainly did. The new narrative of Germany as a country of immigration was accompanied by many legal changes. The reformed German citizenship law replaced what was known as *jus sanguinis,* the blood-based law of nationality that had existed since 1913, which allowed only those who had German ancestors to become German citizens. With the reform of this law in 2001, it became possible to obtain German citizenship based on other criteria that did

---

2 In September 2000 the Independent Commission of Immigration officially declared that Germany is a country of immigration. This Commission was led by Rita Süssmuth (CDU) and the final report was presented to the Federal Minister of the Interior Otto Schilly (SPD) in July 2001. This report contained recommendations for future immigration policy and is seen as an official, legal and political recognition of being a country of immigration (Unabhängige Kommission "Zuwanderung" 2001).

3 These large numbers are linked to the violent break-up of the former Yugoslavia as well as the transformation processes in Eastern Europe which led to intensified migration movements in the 1990s (Bundesamt für Migration und Flüchtlinge, 2005).

not include being of German descent. This was a massive change to the narrative of national identity and is in line with modern concepts of citizenship that allow someone to obtain a national identity document without having been born in the country or having ancestors from that country. Furthermore, Germany also implemented a new immigration law as well as laws enabling the recognition of international qualifications and dual citizenship. These changes were ushered in with the help of a new guiding principle – that of 'Germany is a country of immigration'.

The most recent statistics on immigration in Germany, for the year 2015, show that Germany had an extremely high net total of immigrants of 1,139,000 that year. After the mentioned significant emigration of 2008 and 2009, Germany experienced increased immigration once again after the financial crisis of 2008, caused mainly by immigration from other EU countries. In 2014, 60 % of newly arrived immigrants in Germany stemmed from other EU member states (Bundesamt für Migration und Flüchtlinge 2016, 15). In 2015 as well, the majority of immigrants came from the European Union (45 %). If the 13 % of immigrants from other European countries outside the EU are counted in, even in the big refugee year nearly 60 % of the immigrants came from Europe (Statistisches Bundesamt, 2016b).

What was the real impact of the increased immigration in 2014? Compared to the other countries the increased immigration in Germany represented a significant hike in raw immigration. But in how far did this increase mean an administrative burden to the *Länder* and in how far did it actually change the population size? The *Länder* such as Saarland, Sachsen-Anhalt and Thuringia experienced a decrease in their populations despite this rise in immigration to Germany; among all the *Länder*, Berlin experienced the relatively greatest population increase, though still rather moderate at an increase of 1.4 %; and the *Länder* with the next highest rates of immigration, namely Hamburg, Hessen and Baden-Württemberg, experienced immigration rates of just under one per cent. In light of the perceptions and the narrative of foreignisation in Germany, it is important to put the population increase into perspective by pointing to this value of one per cent.

The Federal Statistical Office in Germany published its initial estimates for 2015 at the beginning of 2016. Specifically, it published numbers based on what is known as the EASY Registration System, used to carry out initial registrations of asylum seekers; these numbers are then passed on to the Federal Office for Migration and Refugees. These numbers pointed to an initial registration rate of almost 2 million, although it is to be expected that this number probably includes double and triple registrations of some of the same people. As a result, the estimates provided by the Federal Statistical Office state that, taking into consideration the number of people who left the country last year, net immigration in Germany in 2015 numbered about 1.1 million (Statistisches Bundesamt 2016a).

Net migration for 2015 exceeds the standing record total from the year 1992, when about 800,000 immigrants entered Germany. However, it is not an unusually high level of net migration as the numbers for 1992 were similar. In 1992, Germany was experiencing a much more difficult economic and structural situation than it has today, characterised by a phase of rising unemployment, the structural and emotional challenges of reunification, and a time of intense social unrest throughout the country, especially later on in Rostock-Lichtenhagen, Solingen and Mölln[4] as a result of increasing racism and xenophobia.

I will conclude the empirical part of this article by asking how Germany has changed and how it is now represented in its demography. Who is German, who is still a migrant? A foreigner is someone who doesn't hold a German passport. In that sense foreigner is an easily defineable category. Yet we know that in our daily discourse conventions, 'foreigner' can easily be used to describe someone who simply looks different, even if that person holds a German passport. For example, when we talk about pupils in Germany, we have what is known as the Option Regulation, i.e. dual citizenship. Pupils who start primary school in Germany hold German passports. There is a minimal last percentage category of pupils at German primary schools who do not hold German citizenship, for example the children of diplomats or stateless Palestinian children. Thus in essence, there are no longer any foreign children in German schools. All of them have German passports. And yet the idea that they are foreign is still part of our daily speech, in our stories, even if it is well-intended, such as when a teacher says 'my German and my foreign children'. The realisation that Germanness has very diverse elements has not yet become part of mainstream perception.

2 Attitudes towards Muslims in Germany

Since the September 11 attacks and the subsequent proclamation of the 'war on terror', the image of Muslims as terrorists, archaic warriors or anachronistic religious believers has subsequently trickled out of international relations debates and entered the national *Diskurs-Raum* (public debate) in Germany.

This was especially evident throughout the debate that was carried out in 2010/2011 by the *Bundesbank's* executive board member and former Berlin state finance minister Thilo Sarrazin. His controversial book *Deutschland schafft sich ab*

4 In the 1990s racist-motivated acts of violence against asylum seekers and people with a migration background in general increased strongly in Germany. Rostock-Lichtenhagen, Solingen and Mölln saw arson attacks committed by neo-Nazis which resulted in many injured people and even deaths (Bundeszentrale für politische Bildung 2013).

('Germany Does Away with Itself') concludes that Muslims are less intelligent because of their cultural ties, that they prefer to live off the state rather than work, and that they have too many children – while well-educated native Germans are having too few. This book sold more than one million copies and became a bestseller in 2010.

Common attributes and associations that are being linked with Muslims in Germany are 'fanatic', 'backwards', 'intolerant' or 'undemocratic', as a study by the German Institute for Human Rights found (Bielefeldt 2007, 4–5). The study also describes how 21.4 % of Germans think that 'Muslim immigration to Germany should be stopped'. When asked whether 'Muslim culture fits into our Western world', three out of four respondents answered negatively (ibid). Islam and being Muslim are being perceived as something in strong contrast to being German. In the public eye, a five-year period of widespread accusations after 9/11 turned 'the Muslims' into a group with low internal group differentiation and a security issue. Moreover, it led to remarkable alienation and estrangement between the constructed Muslim community and the majority non-Muslim society.

A recent study conducted by the Friedrich Ebert Foundation, a foundation linked to the German Social Democratic Party (SPD), entitled 'Intolerance, Prejudice and Discrimination: A European Report' analysed anti-democratic attitudes in eight European countries. From a comparative perspective it found that 'Europeans are largely united in their rejection of Muslims and Islam. The significantly most widespread anti-Muslim attitudes are found in Germany, Hungary, Italy and Poland, closely followed by France, Great Britain and the Netherlands' (Zick, Küpper and Hövermann 2012, 63). Almost *half* of all Germans said that there are too many Muslims living in the country – even though they make up only 5 % of the population – and that they are too demanding and that their religion is intolerant (ibid., 61).

A long-term study conducted by the University of Münster investigating the 'Perception and Acceptance of Religious Diversity' in a comparative analysis found that Germany has a worse relationship to non-Christian religions than other European countries like Denmark, France, the Netherlands or Portugal. When asked: 'How is your personal attitude towards the members of the following religious groups?', 62.2 % of surveyed Germans living in the former East German *Länder* and 57.7 % living in the former West German *Länder* answered 'negative' or 'extremely negative' concerning Islam (Denmark 35.6 %, France 36.7 %, the Netherlands 35.9 %, Portugal 33.5 %) (Pollack 2010, 5). Germans also answered significantly more negative than people in other countries when asked about Hinduism, Buddhism or Judaism. When the same study referred to positive attributions, nearly one third of the Dutch (32.6 %) associated Islam with peace and 44.9 % with solidarity, while in Germany positive attributions of peace and solidarity towards

Islam were only given by 6.6 % (former East German states) and 8.1 % (former West German states) of the German population (Danish (25.9 %/37.6 %), French (13.6 %/31.9 %), Portuguese (19.8 %/27.4 %)) (ibid., 6).

These biased attitudes are sometimes expressed violently or aggressively: there have been several attacks on mosques, people perceived to be Arab or Muslim have been threatened, organisations receive daily hate mails and anti-Muslim Internet blogs have received growing attention (Shooman 2014).

Moreover, on a socio-economic level, people with a Muslim migration background are less likely to be hired or even invited to a job interview when their name doesn't sound 'German' enough (SVR 2014), they have a harder time finding an apartment for the same reasons, and children with a 'migration background' are less likely to receive a teacher's recommendation for continuing higher education (Jürges and Schneider 2006).

3 Narrative exclusion

Having shown that anti-Muslim sentiments are being broadly examined and researched in Germany, I would like to exemplify the outgrouping of Muslims from national identity with an empirical analysis conducted by our research team at the Berlin Institute for Integration and Migration Research (BIM). National identity serves as a cohesive trigger to construct an emotional 'we'. Being placed outside this collective 'we' can mean being being excluded from political, social and cultural participation as well as legal representation. Being placed outside the collective identity seems even to allow denying minorities (in this case Muslims) fundamental constitutional rights, which is a sign of anti-democratic attitudes.

The empirical data presented here stem from a nationwide representative telephone survey with 8,270 German-speaking participants aged 16 and above, conducted between 24 September 2013 and 15 April 2014. In one survey experiment, respondents were presented with a variety of statements in which Muslims were compared with a collective 'we' that respondents were able to define for themselves in a follow-up question. Two of these statements contained two stereotypes that corresponded to the core stereotypes related to violence and educational aspiration as established in the Sarrazin debate ('Muslims are more aggressive than we are', 'Muslim parents have the same educational aspirations as we do'). The respondents were asked to state whether they agreed or disagreed with these statements. The follow-up question was, 'Who did you actually have in mind when using the word "we"?', and was asked openly. The experiment thereby fulfilled two purposes: on the one hand, the goal was to measure stereotypical attitudes towards

Muslims, and on the other hand, we wanted to test a hypothesis with previously established discurses, namely one that states that Muslims are not included within the stated 'we', and therefore are not perceived as part of the German narrative (Foroutan et al. 2014).

3.1 Stereotypical narrative of aggression and lack of educational aspirations

From research on prejudices and stereotypes, we know that a so-called 'outgroup' always has significance for the 'ingroup' (Tajfel and Turner 1986; Brewer and Brown 1998). The notions about Muslims that exist in Germany tell us something about the self-perception, fears and projections of the non-Muslim population (Attia 2007). These references change over time and the ideas ascribed to those who are perceived as 'others' change along with them. Whereas 'the others' were deemed unpunctual, dirty and lazy – characteristics to describe guest workers in the 1960s (Hunn 2005) – Germans understood themselves as punctual, clean and hardworking. Today we describe German identity as democratic, tolerant and enlightened, while 'the other' is seen as anti-democratic, intolerant and in need to undergo enlightenment. These ascriptions are often associated with Islam and Muslims (Weidner 2011). These exclusionary value discourses are flanked by stereotypical narratives that often re-interpret and establish socialisation factors as traits and mentalities and code them as fundamental aggressive tendencies or a genetic lack of educational aspiration, and then ascribe these characteristics to the culture, ethnicity, religion or nationality of the group in question.

Some 26.5 % of survey respondents agreed with the statement 'Muslims are more aggressive than we are', while 64.2 % disagreed with it (see Fig. 1). These results show that the majority of respondents rejected the claim that Muslims are aggressive. Nevertheless over a quarter connects being Muslim with an aggression potential.

On educational aspirations of Muslims, most repondents (55.2 %) agreed that 'Muslim parents have the same educational aspirations as we do', 30 % disagreed on that, and 15 % said they wouldn't know. We can conclude from this that little more than half of respondents assume that the topic of education finds equal resonance among Muslim families as in their own. The responses to this statement reflect the strong perspective among Germans that Muslim families are not as interested in education issues as non-Muslims are. However, over the last few years, it has repeatedly been empirically proven that the educational aspirations particularly of Muslim parents in Germany are very high, which coincides with the results of sociological research regarding immigrants' desire for upward mobility.

Figure 1 Exclusion from a national collective

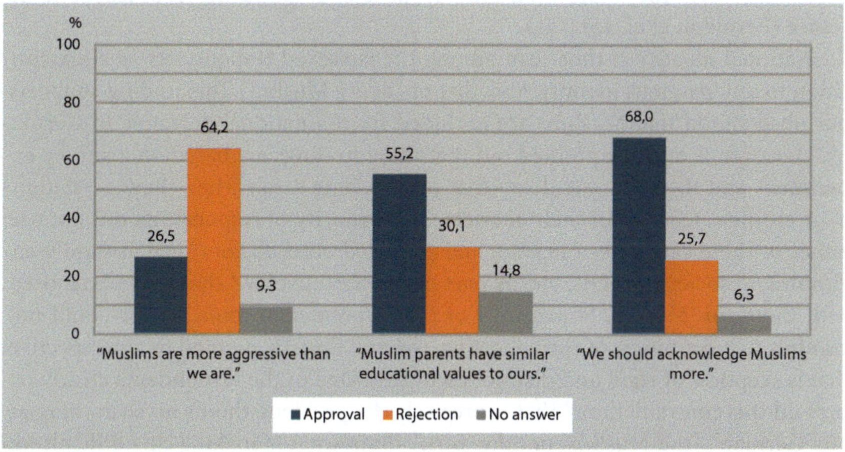

Source: Foroutan et al. 2014, 30.

More interesting than the results of these two statements is the interpretation of a hidden experiment covered in these two statements. Both statements had the words "we/us" in them while "othering" Muslims. Interestingly enough only 74 respondents out of the total 8,215 respondents explicitly criticized the question format. This shows how the narrative in German identity for many does not include Muslims as part of a German collective.

The *us–them* dichotomy sketched above represents an experimental part of the research question, as respondents were subsequently given the opportunity to further explain their concept of the 'we' mentioned in the statements, by being asked by the interviewers: *Who did you actually have in mind when using the word 'we'?*

As this question was designed for open-ended answers, a broad spectrum of responses was collected and subsequently coded and categorised to derive statistical data: 37.6 % of respondents of respondents described the 'ingroup' "we" with "we Germans", "the German population" or "Germany" (ibid., 32). Such answers can be seen as markers of narrative exclusion, as they imply that 'German' and 'Muslim' are mutually exclusive categories – as if there were no German Muslims and no Muslim Germans. In fact, 45 % of the four million Muslims living in Germany are German citizens (Haug, Müssig and Stichs 2009, 80).

People could have answered differently. For example, they could have said: *'By saying "Muslims are more aggressive than we" are, I meant more aggressive than us, the Christians.'* Or they could have said: *'I meant us, the non-Muslims.'* This would have been a more logical conclusion as Christians and Muslims are both religious groups; however they were used only by 5.8 % of respondents in at least one instance (Foroutan et al. 2014, 32).

National identity is thus seen among the surveyed respondents as a juxtaposition to any religious identity, also that of "being Muslim". This finding supports our observation that Muslims are excluded from a national narrative in Germany. However, it must be pointed out that these findings are based on a survey experiment and that it is not clear what respondents mean when they use national or ethnic categories in their answers. The majority of respondents did not use either of these categories (48.6 %), and provided other factors such as family environment, society, friends, etc. as part of the narrative 'we' that they juxtaposed with the term 'Muslim'. Some 9.3 % of the respondents would not or could not commit to a definition of the collective 'we' and thereby pointed to a perspective that is sceptical of rigid and distinct identities. One of the respondents clearly expressed this contradiction: 'That is precisely the problem: there's no such thing as "the German", "the Muslim" or "the Turk", that's what is making this difficult for me' (ibid.).

3.2 The ambivalences of being German

Furthermore, in our survey we asked respondents what being German means to them and which criteria are important to the population when it comes to being German. We noted that almost 100 % of respondents answered, 'Being able to speak German'. A very high number, 80 %, said, 'Holding German citizenship' (see Fig. 2).

These are two very unequivocal items that form part of a modern citizenship law. It is recognised that it is possible to *become* German, and that this requires speaking the language and holding German citizenship. At the same time, respondents moderated this expectation, with only 40 % agreeing on that: 'It is not enough to be able to speak German; one must be able to speak it without an accent'. In reality, this probably does not refer to dialects, but rather the fact that even small errors in one's spoken German allow listeners to determine that the speaker has not spent his or her entire life in Germany. Making tiny mistakes when it comes to articles allows one to hear that it is a difficult and complicated language and that it is sometimes not possible to learn to perfection.

What was of great interest to us when we posed the question about how to deal with minorities was the fact that about 40 % of respondents said that being German required giving up wearing a headscarf (ibid.). This is an ambivalence that I have previously pointed out. On the one hand, there is obviously a high cognitive

Figure 2 Conditions of belonging

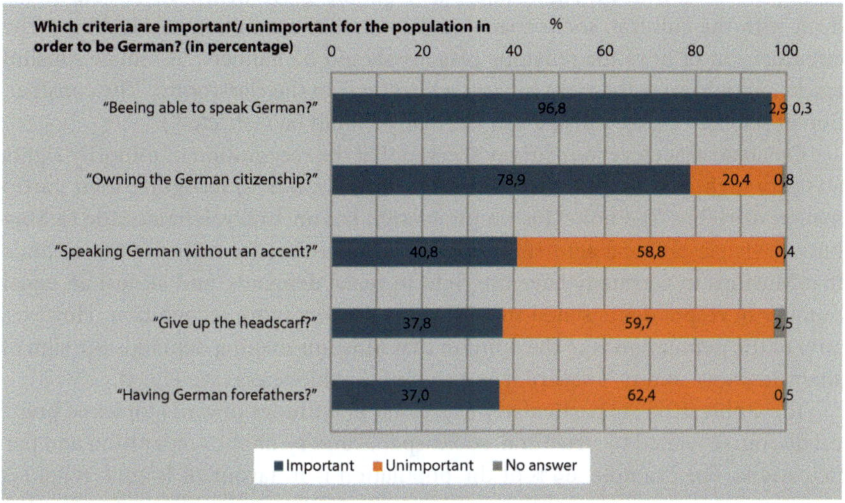

Source: Foroutan et al. 2014, 25–26.

awareness of the fact that this country has changed, that citizenship has changed, that the country has become more diverse and that being German also implies looking different or having a different sounding name. Despite all of this, it is not enough to be able to speak German and to hold German citizenship; if one wears a headscarf, then approximately 40 % of the population believes that you cannot be German. Another 37 % are of the opinion that being German really does require having German ancestors (ibid.).

3.3 Acceptance of equal rights of minorities

This outgrouping of Muslims from the collective community can also be observed in some controversial debates about the cultural, socio-spatial and symbolic recognition of religious diversity. Discussions about circumcision, mosque construction and the headscarf, which we are using here to exemplify the topics of cultural, socio-spatial and symbolic recognition have repeatedly shaped the political discourse over the last few years and illustrate the restrictions of religious rights with which Muslims are confronted in Germany. How is the cultural, socio-spatial and symbolic recognition of Muslims regarded by the population in Germany?

We surveyed our respondents on their political attitudes on Muslims while asking items on Muslim rights and participation in Germany. Three statements dealt with the cultural, socio-spatial and symbolic recognition of Muslims ('The circumcision of boys for religious reasons should be banned'; 'A female Muslim teacher should have the right to wear a headscarf in the classroom'; 'The construction of publicly visible mosques in Germany should be restricted').

On an abstract level our survey showed that the recognition of minority rights was very high, but on the concrete level there was a lack to recognize their participation or rights. The non-Muslim population has an ambivalent attitude to Muslims as visible political actors: on the one hand, a decisive majority (67 %) finds that Muslims in Germany have the right to make demands, and almost an equal number of respondents stated that Muslims deserve more recognition. However, 20 % of the population is of the opinion that Muslims making demands is a sign of shamelessness, and 17 % regard it as a sign of thanklessness (see Fig. 3).

The ambivalence is particularly expressed in attitudes towards topics of political discourse related to structural, socio-spatial and symbolic recognition and participations. For example, 69 % of the population is in favour of Islamic religious instruction in schools, but at the same time, 60 % of respondents want to ban the religion-based circumcision of boys. Meanwhile, almost half of all Germans (49 %) believe that female Muslim teachers should not be allowed to wear headscarves in class, and 42 % would like to restrict the construction of mosques (see Fig. 4).

There seems to be an obvious lack of knowledge on fundamental rights in Germany such as the Article 4 of the German constitution which guarantees religious freedom, the freedom to practice one's religion and the right to build places of worship, as well as not to be impeded in one's right to practice one's religion. This debate continues to stay up to date and takes on new dynamics every time. Currently we are discussing the introcution of a law on a binding "integration contract" for immigrants in which they are forced to agree to fundamental German values. A large portion of the population is of the opinion that such a law should be introduced. But the question is whether we can really achieve progress if we regard integration merely as an obligation on the part of minorities while neglecting to ask what role the majority society should play in the integration process. Instead of a one-way integration it is possible to think about a collective integration that everyone in the society signs as it is is everyone's duty to adhere to fundmental core rights of the German constitution.

Figure 3 Cognitive acceptance I

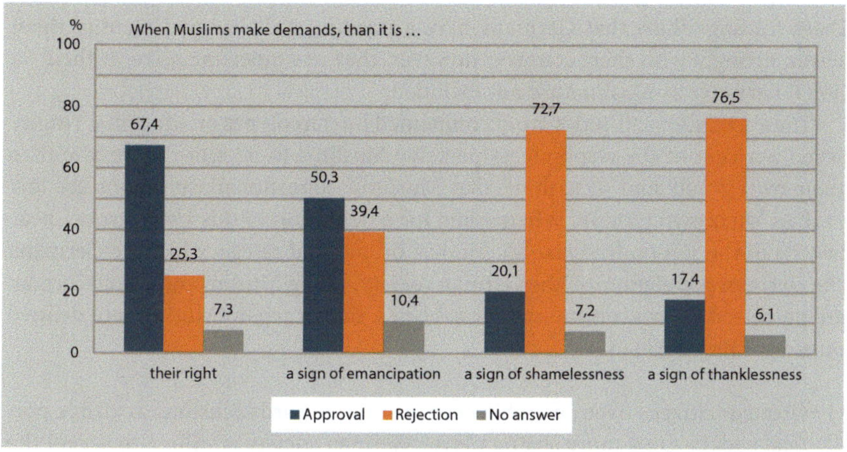

Source: Foroutan et al. 2014, 34.

Figure 4 Cognitive acceptance II

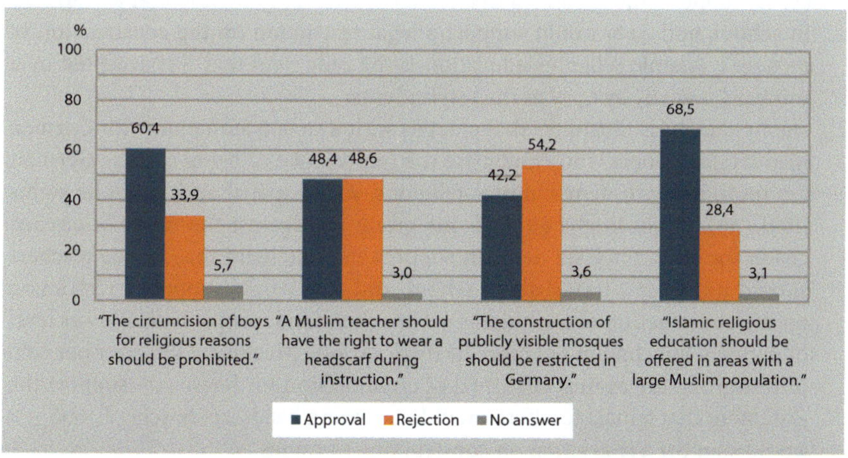

Source: Foroutan et al. 2014, 34–35.

4 Conclusion

These findings show that Germans have a positive self-view and identify themselves strongly with their country; however, they are quiet exclusive in their national narrative as Muslims are not included.

These excluding attitudes are accompanied by stereotypes on Muslims. Twenty-seven per cent of the respondents perceive Muslims to be more aggressive than 'their own group' and 30 % think that Muslims' educational aspirations are lower than 'their own group's'. When asked for a definition of this 'own- group', nearly 40 % of the respondents use an ethnical or national category like 'we Germans', 'the German population' or 'the German society'. Being Muslim and being German are perceived as two contradictory categories. In this regard Muslims are defined outside of the 'German we'.

1) German citizens have an ambivalent position towards Muslims as visible political agents. On a more abstract level, German society is willing to accept the participation rights of Muslims, but on more concrete levels, crucial rights are rejected: a majority of the population (67 %) accepts the right of Muslims to claim rights in Germany, but simultaneously 60 % of the respondents refuse to accept the ritual of circumcision for boys. Nearly every second respondent (48 %) supports the statement that female teachers should not wear a headscarf in school, and 42 % would support a legal restriction on the construction of mosques. Islamic religious education is the only item that was accepted by a minority, namely by 69 % of the respondents.
2) The first analysis illustrates that citizens with a strong affiliation with German identity, i.e. people who emphasise the importance of being seen as German, are more likely to deny cultural-religious, social-spatial and symbolic rights (ibid., 36). Accordingly, 68 % of this group are against the ritual of circumcision for boys. Fifty-six per cent support the statement that female teachers should not wear a headscarf in school, and 55 % would support a restriction on the construction of mosques. On the other hand, people with a lower level of national attachment are more likely to include Muslims. Fifty-four per cent of this group are against the ritual of circumcision for boys, 43 % support the statement that female teachers should not wear a headscarf in school, and 35 % would support a restriction on constructing mosques.
3) We can summarise by saying that the willingness to exclude Muslims from the collective German narrative refers not only to discursive, identity and emotional positions, but also to the fundamental question of accepting the democratic rights of minorities: practicing one's religion and constructing places of worship are – with specific restrictions – fundamental civil rights. Negative at-

titudes do not necessarily lead to action, but the 75 attacks on mosques and 1,031 attacks on refugees and their shelters in 2015 (Meisner, Tretbar and Keilholz 2016) must be seen not only as clear criminal acts but also as a lack of basic knowledge about democracy. Heterogeneous societies shaped by migration discourses must therefore more thoroughly educate their populations about democratic principles if they want right-wing populism to be stopped.

References

Attia, Iman. 2007. Orient- und IslamBilder. Interdisziplinäre Beiträge zu Orientalismus und antimuslimischem Rassismus. Münster: Unrast.

Bade, Klaus. 2013. Kritik und Gewalt. Sarrazin-Debatte, 'Islamkritik' und Terror in der Einwanderungsgesellschaft. Schwalbach: Wochenschau Verlag.

Bielefeldt, Heiner. 2007. Das Islambild in Deutschland. Zum öffentlichen Umgang mit der Angst vor dem Islam. Second edition. Berlin: Deutsches Institut für Menschenrechte.

Brewer, Marilyn and Rupert Brown. 1998. Intergroup relations. In The handbook of social psychology, Eds. Daniel Todd Gilbert and Susan T. Fiske, 554–594, Vol. 2, fourth edition. Boston, MA: McGraw Hill.

Broden, Anne and Paul Mecheril. 2007. Migrationsgesellschaftliche Re-Präsentationen: Eine Einführung. In Re-Präsentationen: Dynamiken der Migrationsgesellschaft, Eds. Anne Broden and Paul Mecheril, 7–28. Düsseldorf: IDA-NRW.

Bundesamt für Migration und Flüchtlinge. 2005. Migration, Asyl und Integration in Zahlen. 14. Auflage. Nürnberg: Bundesamt für Migration und Flüchtlinge.

Bundesamt für Migration und Flüchtlinge. 2016. Migrationsbericht des Bundesamtes für Migration und Flüchtlinge im Auftrag der Bundesregierung. Migrationsbericht 2014. Nürnberg: Bundesamt für Migration und Flüchtlinge.

Bundeszentrale für politische Bildung. 2013. 20 Jahre Brandanschlag in Solingen. http://www.bpb.de/politik/hintergrund-aktuell/161980/brandanschlag-in-solingen-28-05-2013. Accessed: 15 July 2016.

Decker, Oliver, Johannes Kiess and Elmar Brähler. 2014. Die stabilisierte Mitte. Rechtsextreme Einstellungen in Deutschland 2014. Leipzig: Universität Leizpig.

Foroutan, Naika, Coskun Canan, Sina Arnold, Benjamin Schwarze, Steffen Beigang and Dorina Kalkum. 2014. Deutschland postmigrantisch I: Gesellschaft, Religion, Identität. Erste Ergebnisse. Berlin: Humboldt-Universität zu Berlin.

Haug, Sonja, Stephanie Müssig and Anja Stichs. 2009. Muslim Life in Germany: A Study Conducted on Behalf of the German Conference on Islam. Nürnberg: Bundesamt für Migration und Flüchtlinge.

Hunn, Katrin. 2005. "Nächstes Jahr kehren wir zurück…". Die Geschichte der türkischen "Gastarbeiter" in der Bundesrepublik. Göttingen: Wallstein Verlag.

Jürges, Hendrik and Kerstin Schneider. 2006. Age at school entry and teachers' recommendations for secondary school track choice in Germany. http://www.

vwl.uni-freiburg.de/iwipol/faculty_seminar/age_at_school_entry.pdf. Accessed: 15 July 2016.

Meisner, Matthias, Christian Tretbar and Christine Keilholz. 2016. Dresden und die "neue Qualität der Gewalt". http://www.tagesspiegel.de/politik/anschlaege-auf-moschee-und-kongresszentrum-dresden-und-die-neue-qualitaet-der-gewalt/14609440.html. Accessed: 28 September 2016.

Pollack, Detlef. 2010. Studie "Wahrnehmung und Akzeptanz religiöser Vielfalt". http://www.uni-muenster.de/imperia/md/content/religion_und_politik/aktuelles/2010/12_2010/studie_wahrnehmung_und_akzeptanz_religioeser_vielfalt.pdf. Accessed: 15 July 2016.

Sachverständigenrat deutscher Stiftungen für Integration und Migration (SVR). 2014. Diskriminierung am Ausbildungsmarkt. Ausmaß, Ursachen und Handlungsperspektiven. Berlin: SVR.

Shooman, Yasemin. 2014. "...weil ihre Kultur so ist" Narrative des antimuslimischen Rassismus. Bielefeld: Transcript.

Statistisches Bundesamt. 2016a. Nettozuwanderung von Ausländerinnen und Ausländern im Jahr 2015 bei 1,1 Millionen. Press release No. 105, 21 March 2016.

Statistisches Bundesamt. 2016b. 2015: Höchststände bei Zuwanderung und Wanderungsüberschuss in Deutschland. Press release No. 246. 14 July 2016.

Statistisches Bundesamt. 2016c. Bevölkerung mit Migrationshintergrund auf Rekordniveau. Press release No. 327, 16 September 2016.

Tajfel, Henri and John C. Turner. 1986. The Social Identity Theory of Intergroup Behavior. In Psychology of Intergroup Relations, Eds. Stephen Worchel and William G. Austin, 7–24, second edition. Chicago: Nelson-Hall.

Unabhängige Kommission "Zuwanderung". 2001. Zuwanderung gestalten. Integration fördern. Bericht der Unabhängigen Kommission "Zuwanderung". Berlin: Bundesministerium des Innern.

Weidner, Stefan. 2011: Aufbruch in die Vernunft. Islamdebatten und die islamische Welt zwischen 9/11 und den arabischen Revolutionen. Bonn. Dietz Verlag.

Zick, Andreas, Beate Küpper and Andreas Hövermann. 2011. Intolerance, Prejudice and Discrimination. A European Report. Berlin: Friedrich-Ebert-Stiftung.

Reassessing the opinion–policy gap

How PEGIDA and the AfD relate to German immigration policies[1]

Hannes Schammann

Abstract

The rising numbers of asylum seekers have revitalized the debate on immigration and cultural diversity in Germany. On the one hand, a substantial amount of volunteers lived the notion of Germany as a "welcoming society". On the other hand, movements like PEGIDA, the "Patriotic Europeans Against the Islamization of the Occident", and political parties like the AfD, the "Alternative for Germany", have entered the stage. They do not only stand for a right-wing populism that is well-known all over Europe but also for an attitude which Groß and Hövermann (2014) name "marktförmiger Extremismus" (economic extremism). For some scholars of migration politics, the rise of PEGIDA and AfD is just another proof of the so-called opinion-policy gap hypothesis in migration studies. Gary Freeman (1995) famously argued that there is a gap between public opinion, which is constantly calling for restrictive immigration policies, and factual immigration policies in Western democracies, which are becoming more expansive over time. This contribution will reflect on the positions and demands of PEGIDA and the AfD against the backdrop of the opinion-policy gap hypothesis. It will do so by analyzing the alleged gap between PEGIDA/AfD and factual policies in three main arenas of the immigration debate: identity, security, and economy (Rosenblum/Cornelius 2012). It will argue that the gap shows different characteristics depending on the respective arena.

1 A previous version of this paper was published in German: Schammann, Hannes. 2015. PEGIDA und die deutsche Migrationspolitik. Ein Beitrag zur Differenzierung des Opinion-Policy Gap in der Migrationsforschung. Zeitschrift für Politikwissenschaft 25 (3), 309–334.

1 Introduction

A central topic of immigration research in political science is the investigation of contradictions found in the formulation and implementation of immigration policies. Gary Freeman (1995) formulated the widely accepted hypothesis that immigration policies in liberal democracies are characterised by a persistent opposition between more liberal policies and significantly more restrictive attitudes of the population. Even though this so-called opinion–policy gap has recently been called into question (Bonjour 2011; Ellermann 2006; Morales et al. 2015; Scholz 2012), it continues to dominate immigration research in such a way that it has been labelled the 'Iron Law' (Bonjour 2011: 111).

Faith in the opinion–policy gap hypothesis has led many to interpret the strengthening of parties such as 'Alternative for Germany' (*Alternative für Deutschland* [AfD]) or the phenomena of large-scale demonstrations by 'Patriotic Europeans Against the Islamisation of the West (Occident)' (*Patriotische Europäer gegen die Islamisierung des Abendlandes* [PEGIDA]) as the reaction of a 'restrictive population' to 'liberal policymaking'. Klaus Bade, for instance, concludes that German immigration policy 'has, in recent years, rushed ahead of public perception in seven-league boots' (Bade 2015: 20).

This contribution challenges this claim and subjects the opinion–policy gap to a critical investigation using PEGIDA and the AfD as case studies. First it will present the debate surrounding the opinion–policy gap hypothesis in immigration research. The paper will then classify the core demands made by PEGIDA and the AfD within the institutional context of German immigration policy, while particularly taking into account the central aspects of every immigration debate: identity, security and economy (Rosenblum and Cornelius 2012). Finally, it will propose a differentiated dimensioning of the opinion–policy gap in immigration policy.

2 The opinion–policy gap with immigration research in political science

Addressing the contradictions in national immigration policies has been a significant component of immigration research in political science since the early 1990s. Numerous studies have since addressed the empirically established discrepancies between public opinion, proclaimed policies and the actual effect. Some of the most influential works have been submitted by Hollifield (1992a, 1992b), Cornelius et al. (1994) and Freeman (1995). In particular, Gary Freeman (1995) developed and established the so-called opinion–policy gap hypothesis. It refers to the observation that immigration policies in liberal democracies are at all times and under all circumstances significantly more liberal and expansive than desired by the general public (Freeman 1995). According to Freeman, there are two primary reasons for this opinion–policy gap: firstly, a 'constraint discourse over immigration' (Freeman 1995: 883); the constraint discourse ensures that positions which are too far away from the fundamental values of liberal democracy are excluded from policy formulation. Secondly, while immigration is clearly advantageous for some groups (employers, among others) its disadvantages are diffuse and difficult to apportion to a specific group (Freeman 1995: 885). Freeman concludes that only a small, but well-organised number of interest groups seek an expansive immigration policy while a larger, but less effectively organised public strives for a restrictive immigration policy.

Although Freeman sees a more open conflict in European countries regarding immigration policy than in classic immigration countries (the United States, Canada, Australia, New Zealand), ultimately, the opinion–policy gap is occurring between two sides whose relationship remains undetermined. Freeman himself refers to this weak link later on and notes that a differentiated observation could necessitate a revision of his hypothesis: 'Disaggregating public opinion according to specific aspects of immigration policy may undermine generalizations about a gap between public opinion and policy' (Freeman and Tendler 2012: 325).

The opinion–policy gap hypothesis has taken a triumphant stance in immigration research and is considered by some as probably the only 'universal truth about immigration policy' (Rosenblum and Cornelius 2012: 246). Saskia Bonjour (2011: 111) critically asserts that it has attained the status of an 'Iron Law', rendering further research on the existence and quality of the opinion–policy gap unnecessary. With the intention of reinvigorating critical analysis, several authors emphasise that the gulf between public opinion and political decision is not as clear as previously thought. Firstly, the different natures of public debates and political decision-making processes which allow a difference in content to appear bigger than it really is should be taken into account (Castles 2004; Kolb 2004). Secondly, restrictive tendencies are also noted among political decision-makers and administrations (Eule 2014; Lahav 2004). Thirdly, and conversely, the attitude of the population is not only restrictive – it also exhibits noticeable liberal tendencies (Bonjour 2011; Ellermann 2006).

The scepticism generated by the absoluteness of the opinion–policy gap is also shared by Morales et al. (2015), who, over a period of 15 years, have been investigating the relationship between public opinion and immigration policy in seven European nation states[2]. The results show that for just three nations (the Nether-

2 Belgium, Ireland, the Netherlands, Austria, Switzerland, Spain, United Kingdom (UK).

lands, Austria, Spain) there is a clear opinion–policy gap, while in two cases (UK, Ireland) there is even opinion–policy congruence.

Scholz (2012) concludes in her investigation of the influence of political ideas on immigration policy in Germany and France that stakeholders in political debates '[must] establish a congruence between the presented interpretations of immigration and the overriding spirit within society' (ibid.: 305). She argues that 'the gap is less of a "before-after phenomenon" but rather a phenomenon inherent in immigration policy' (ibid.: 310) which connects the population with the political decision-making system. Bonjour adopts a similar position; in her examination of Dutch policy on family reunion she claims, '[i]mportantly, the immaterial values that shape policy makers' decisions are more often than not values that resonate broadly in society as a whole: the tone of the public debate, rather than invariably tending toward restriction, may therefore very well push toward expansive entry policies' (Bonjour 2011: 112).

It is a significant achievement by the authors mentioned above to have challenged the status of the opinion–policy gap as an 'Iron Law'. Yet, the theoretical foundations which could re-dimension the opinion–policy gap have still to materialise. To date, the articulated sense of scepticism has manifested itself against the absoluteness of Freeman's hypothesis along with the call for greater differentiation (including Lahav and Guiraudon 2006: 207). What is needed is some further conceptual clarity.

But how can this best be achieved? The relation between public opinion and immigration policies must be specified and looked at in greater detail. The study by Rosenblum and Cornelius (2012) is helpful here; it identifies three overarching core topics structuring the debates surrounding the broad direction of immigration policies[3]. The first core topic revolves around identity. It represents a discussion on cultural differences and national identity – a discussion which is 'less concrete but more intensely felt' (ibid.: 248). It reflects an emotional conflict regarding the prerequisites of belonging. The discussion focuses mainly on the compatibility of migrant ethnicity and religion with the welcoming nation. The second topic structuring policy formulation is driven by security questions (e.g. how immigration endangers the national security of the welcoming country), a discussion which is located on the threshold between domestic and foreign affairs (ibid.: 250 et seq.). It deals with issues such as how a balance is to be struck between humanitarian obligations and the interests of national security. The third core topic concerns economic aspects. The discussions focus mostly on how immigration can be

3 The term immigration policy is also understood here and in the following as integration policy in line with Rosenblum and Cornelius (2012).

shaped efficiently, how its net gains can be maximised and, in doing so, how equitable distribution can be achieved (ibid.: 247 et seq.).

3 Case studies: PEGIDA and AfD

In the search for a case study in which these three core aspects (identity, security and economy) are represented by 'disorganised' opinion as suggested by Freeman (1995: 886), attention quickly turns to the large-scale demonstrations held by PEGIDA in several cities in Germany, which shaped public discussion on immigration policy from October 2014 until approximately January 2015. The movement initially started as the Facebook group 'Peaceful Europeans against the Islamisation of the West (Occident)' *('Friedliche Europäer gegen die Islamisierung des Abendlandes')* (Geiges et al. 2015: 11). Some days later, the group replaced 'peaceful' with 'patriotic' and took the name PEGIDA on the first of its 'evening walks' – always held on Mondays, alluding to the so-called Monday demonstrations against the government of the German Democratic Republic in the years 1989 and 1990. For the first of those walks on 20 October 2014 in Dresden, PEGIDA mobilised approximately 300 people. This number increased by the end of the year to approximately 15,000 participants in Dresden. Demonstrations were also held in other German cities (including Cologne, Hanover and Leipzig) from December 2014 onwards; these aligned themselves with PEGIDA but in the majority of cases were only able to gather a few hundred people.[4] The demonstrations reached their peak on 12 January 2015, directly after the Islamist terrorist attacks on the Parisian satirical publication Charlie Hebdo, when between 17,000 and 25,000 participants were counted in Dresden during the rally (Vorländer et al. 2015: 9 et seq.). Following the cancellation of the demonstration in Dresden on 19 January 2015 due to a terror alert, the movement lost significant momentum (Geiges et al. 2015: 18 et seq.). But at its peak, PEGIDA was able to mobilise members of the public from the political middle ground, in addition to overtly right-wing extremists (Rucht et al. 2015: 19). Even in the spring of 2016, a representative survey discovered that over 40 % of the German population agreed with at least some of PEGIDA's demands (Decker et al. 2016).

An informed look at the results of the protest and movement research (especially Rucht et al. 2015) as well as the positional papers by PEGIDA (2014, 2015) shows

4 However, the grouping 'Hooligans against Salafis' ('Hooligans gegen Salafisten' [HoGeSa]) had previously been able to mobilise several thousand people in Cologne and Hanover. Content and staff-related overlaps with PEGIDA have been proven even when HoGeSa distanced itself considerably from PEGIDA in January 2015 (Geiges et al. 2015: 22 et seq.).

that all three topic areas identified by Rosenblum and Cornelius were touched upon by PEGIDA: even the name of the movement reflects the fear of 'foreign infiltration', coupled with fear stemming from a loss of national identity. The warning of criminal activity by foreigners, together with an increased awareness of security, is clearly noticeable. However, PEGIDA also states the demand for a more efficient immigration policy, for example in line with immigration legislation found in Canada or Australia (further details in section 4). These positions are amalgamated in the description of Islam as a danger for the nation and nation state (identity), for life and limb (security) and for growth and prosperity (economy).

The political party AfD, which was founded in 2013, picked up PEGIDA's rhetoric. It warned against the infiltration of foreign cultures and articulated its scepticism towards supranational solutions on immigration from both economic and national security perspectives. The AfD, being a party, cannot be classified as a 'disorganised public'. Nevertheless, the electoral successes in four federal states (Baden-Württemberg: 15.1 %, Rhineland-Palatinate: 12.6 %, Saxony-Anhalt: 24.3 %, Mecklenburg-West Pomerania: 20.8 %) show that the AfD reflects demands and positions held by a significant share of the German population.

Through their presence in the three central topic areas, the AfD and PEGIDA provide the possibility of a conceptual advancement of the envisioned differentiation of the opinion–policy gap by Freeman and Tendler (2012: 325) along the lines of specific aspects of immigration policy. Therefore, they can serve as a starting point for a differentiated description of the relation between a position perceived to be significantly restrictive, and the de facto immigration policy. Although the empirical results of the analysis remain limited to both phenomena, the resulting conceptual insight can help trigger a re-dimensioning of the opinion–policy gap.

4 PEGIDA, AfD and German immigration policy

In this section, a comparison will be made between the demands officially stated by the AfD and PEGIDA with regard to the topics of identity, security and economy and the direction of German immigration policy. Both the specific policies – these being on the accommodation of Islam or on nationality – and historical developments and organisational aspects will be considered.

a) Immigration policy as identity policy

The most prominent immigration policy narrative from PEGIDA is the 'Islamisation of the West', and with it a foreign infiltration by an – allegedly so culturally and religiously opposed – other (Rucht et al. 2015: 29 et seq.). Placards at their demonstrations clearly display Islamophobic slogans such as 'Hate, Violence, Koran' or 'Islam = Carcinoma' (ibid.: 43). The denigration of Islam as a foreign or threatening concept is mirrored by a desire surveyed in 81 % of those people interviewed by Rucht and colleagues for a strengthening of the country's own national sentiment (ibid.: 28). In the official statements, particularly in the comprehensive 19-point 'Position Paper of PEGIDA' (PEGIDA 2014) and the 'Dresden theses' (PEGIDA 2015), Islam plays a subordinated role. However, the 'protection of our Christian-Jewish Western culture' (PEGIDA 2014)[5] is also demanded here. This leads to immigration policy being conceived first and foremost as an identity policy.

Directly after its establishment, when the AfD was influenced by individuals and positions stemming from a nationalist conservative current (Bebnowski 2015), it maintained only cautious, identity policy-related positions and shaped itself as more of an anti-Euro party. However, in the course of an immigration influx to Germany during 2015, and in its dealings with the demonstrations held by PEGIDA, the AfD adopted increasingly similar positions. It subsequently began articulating a national identity policy and issued a warning against the foreign infiltration of Germany by Islam (Häusler 2016).

Identity policy is a multifaceted term which has been appropriated by various academic disciplines with different objectives. From the perspective of immigration policy it refers to a policy of belonging and with that, in particular, to the right of citizenship (inter alia Hollifield 1992b: 585). It has also witnessed the development of an extensive collection of research literature.[6] Rogers Brubaker (1992) had long had a significant influence on the debate; in his analysis of naturalisation legislation in Germany and France, he refers to path dependencies which can be traced back to the 19th century. While he identifies a Republican ideal for centralist France, he diagnoses an ethnic–cultural understanding of national identity for the German 'national community' *('Volksgemeinschaft').* This thesis has endured for as long as the relatively strict *jus sanguinis* (principle of descent) has applied to the attainment of citizenship in Germany. With the introduction of an ever increasing number of elements from *jus soli,* the principle of birthright citizenship, and a simplified process of naturalisation from 1999 onwards, the culturalist argumentation put forward by Brubaker became exposed to growing criticism. Susanne Worbs (2014: 52, 100) ascertains that no overarching, consensual understanding of

5 In the so-called 'Dresden theses' (PEGIDA 2015) the adjective 'Christian-Jewish' is left out. Observers see this as an opening for the right-wing, anti-Semitic scene (Benneckenstein 2015). The paper otherwise contains very few new positions.

6 See inter alia Hansen (2000); Hansen and Weil (2002); Kymlicka (2003); Soysal (1994); Naujoks (2014); Joppke (2010); Hagedorn (2001); Thränhardt (2008).

citizenship can be diagnosed for Germany. Instead, it is possible to speak of perpetually conflicting views whose majorities have changed in the course of time.

The debate surrounding a German or European *Leitkultur* ('leading culture' or 'guiding culture') is located within this context, which was initiated by Bassam Tibi (1996) and only brought into the public and political sphere in the year 2000. Tabloid papers, the parliament and scientific articles all discussed in equal measure to what extent in what ways the majority society could demand immigrants to adapt to its way of life (Oberndörfer 2001; Lammert 2006; Nowak 2006). From 2006 onwards, this discussion was closely linked with the development of citizenship tests in the federal states, in which the prerequisites of citizenship could be forged into the form of specific knowledge questions. The spectrum stretched from questions regarding a bourgeois canon in the state of Hesse – 'The German artist Caspar David Friedrich painted a landscape of the Baltic island of Rügen in one of his most famous works. What is the motif of this painting?'[7] – through to a test of ethos in Baden-Württemberg where, for example, attitudes to 'honour killings' required an explanation during discussion.[8]

The search for the indisputable and test-appropriate contents of a German *Leitkultur* was subsequently coordinated by the Federal Ministry of the Interior, which led to a sobering survey on the establishment and functioning of the political system in Germany and a corresponding naturalisation course.[9] Agreement was then reached on a minimal consensus which linked the concept of belonging to knowledge of the German language and a basic understanding of the political system. It was the proponents of a republican understanding of citizenship who were victorious in the end. But the discussion had only been settled temporarily. The established camps reformed themselves in the debate surrounding dual citizenship: while the proponents of a more republican model of citizenship favoured dual nationality, opponents highlighted possible conflicts of loyalty (Worbs 2014: 142). Given that the dual passport then advanced to become an election theme during the German parliamentary elections in 2013 (ibid.: 37), the positioning of parties with regard to this question was both transparent and electable.

The nature of debate became particularly explosive regarding identity and belonging due to repeated references to an alleged incompatibility between a 'West-

7 Schrey, Martina. 2008. Baden-Württemberg bleibt bei Gesinnungsfragen. Spiegel Online. http://www.spiegel.de/politik/deutschland/einbuergerungstests-baden-wuerttemberg-bleibt-bei-gesinnungsfragen-a-557688.html. Accessed: 12th October 2016.

8 See 100 Fragen aus Hessen 2006 zum Einbürgerungstest. Susannealbers.de http://www.susannealbers.de/06wissen-100fragen-01.html. Accessed: 12 October 2016.

9 Bundesamt für Migration und Flüchtlinge. 2012. Der Einbürgerungstest. http://www.bamf.de/DE/Einbuergerung/WasEinbuergerungstest/waseinbuergerungstest.html?nn=1362952. Accessed: 12 October 2016.

ern' and 'Islamic' culture, as had been previously formulated by Huntington (1997). Numerous popular academic and, in part, populist publications presented the presence of Islam and of Muslims as a threat. This was most evident in the writing and statements made by the politician and economist Thilo Sarrazin, in which Islam was the subject of 'ethnicisation', and in which it was suggested that there is a link between intelligence and religious affiliation (detailed in Bade 2013). Simultaneous efforts by the federal and state governments to approach Islamic organisations stood in direct contrast to such statements. Then-Federal Minister of the Interior Wolfgang Schäuble initiated the German Islam Conference in 2006 in the midst of discussions surrounding *'Leitkultur'* and naturalisation (Tezcan 2013). Similar Islam Conferences were also held at *Länder* level in the following years. At the time of the PEGIDA demonstrations, the institutional localisation of Islam in the Federal Republic's political and legal system was already well advanced: the states of Bremen and Hamburg had already signed so-called 'state agreements' with Islamic organisations and the states of Hesse and Hamburg had even granted an organisation the status of a corporation under public law (detailed in Spielhaus and Herzog 2015).

It can hardly be argued that discussions concerning Islam and German citizenship law were conducted in back rooms in a form of conspiratorial clientelism, within the meaning of Freeman (1995) – on the contrary, hardly any discussion concerning German immigration policy has been (and is) held so publicly, loudly and continuously. PEGIDA therefore cannot assert that parties and politicians have failed to acknowledge 'restrictive' attitudes. PEGIDA's demand for the protection of national identity – and the propagation of an 'occidental culture' as an alternative concept to the Islamic 'Orient' – is therefore to be seen as more of an effort to reignite an otherwise lost debate. The politicians of established parties and media representatives have reacted to this attempt with an overwhelming rejection. There is an overriding tendency to want to file away the vexatious topic of a *Leitkultur.* Angela Merkel's long-awaited acknowledgement that Islam is a part of modern Germany is perhaps the most poignant example of this.[10]

With regard to aspects relating to identity policy, the conclusion can be drawn that there is a significant distance between the AfD and PEGIDA on the one hand and policy regulations and measures on the other. Klaus Bade's expression 'seven-league boots' (2015: 20), with which politics has rushed ahead of large parts of the population, appears appropriate here – in particular as he implies that the opinion–policy gap does not exist a priori in questions of belonging, but rather only came into being as a result of changes to immigration policy objectives.

10 See Zeit Online. 2015. 'Der Islam gehört zu Deutschland'. http://www.zeit.de/politik/deutschland/2015-01/angela-merkel-islam-deutschland-wulff. Accessed: 12th October 2016.

b) Immigration policy as security policy

In contrast to political parties and the media, the police enjoy a high degree of trust among PEGIDA demonstrators (Rucht et al. 2015: 25), but also among society as a whole (Decker et al. 2016: 60). The fear of 'foreign infiltration' is linked with the call for a stronger security apparatus both by PEGIDA and the AfD. This is particularly noticeable in the increased demands that the police be better equipped, and that there be a zero tolerance policy towards foreigners (PEGIDA 2014, 2015). In its 2016 manifesto the AfD argues along these lines in 'Unchecked mass immigration brings with it increased criminality' (AfD 2016: 64). The AfD's demand that 'the protection of citizens against immigration-related criminality should be given top priority' (ibid.: 65) is based on this. The second dominant immigration policy narrative from PEGIDA and AfD is that immigration policy must necessarily be a security policy.

These are by no means pioneering efforts by PEGIDA and AfD. Horvath (2014: 58–62) highlights that, in principle, immigration policy bears security policy characteristics which are 'structurally anchored' (ibid.: 62). It is therefore not surprising that German immigration and integration policies are – like immigration policies in almost any country – shaped by a strong discourse regarding security (Baumann 2009; Klusmeyer and Papademetriou 2009). By and large, the focus is 'either on controlling illegal immigration or on the prevention of Islamic terrorism' (Baumann 2009: 1). The former became popular following the high number of asylum seeker applications at the beginning of the 1990s, the latter following the attacks on 11 September 2001. Within the respective contexts, terms such as 'floods of asylum seekers' (Jäger 2014: 13) or 'sleepers' (14) perpetuated both a 'burden topos' (Wengeler 2003: 303) and a 'danger topos' (ibid.: 306), which had already been observed since the 1960s (ibid.: 368).

However, the focus on security concerns in Germany has not only been a long-standing tradition in media and political debates; it is also deeply embedded institutionally. In the first 20 years after the end of the Second World War it was primarily the local police forces who were responsible for dealing with questions concerning foreign nationals residing in Germany.[11] This was still regulated by the Police Act for Foreign Nationals *(Ausländerpolizeiverordnung)* enacted in 1938 during the Third Reich. The legal connection of immigration and criminality was transformed into a more generalist interlacing of immigration and security with

11 This assignment even applied in the former German Democratic Republic (GDR) until 1990. The separate consideration of the GDR is necessary when wishing to investigate the more intense uptake in demonstrations in East Germany. A significant proportion of developments witnessed here is attributable to the time after 1990.

the adoption of the Aliens Act *(Ausländergesetz)* of 1965: responsibility at the local and regional level was transferred to the immigration offices, which, for their part, are frequently assigned to the municipal public order offices *(Ordnungsämter)*. At the federal level, immigration policy was brought under the control of the Federal Ministry of the Interior (BMI).[12] Even the German Islam Conference, which since 2006 acts as a central dialogue forum between state and Muslim organisations in Germany, has been organised under the responsibility of the BMI.

In addition to questions concerning immigration and Islam, the Federal Ministry of the Interior is also responsible for public security, combating terrorism, disaster control and general administrative matters. The consequence of this linking up of tasks at a subordinated level is that immigration and security authorities reside in the same location. These are primarily the Federal Police *(Bundespolizei)*, the Federal Criminal Police Office *(Bundeskriminalamt)*, the Federal Office for the Protection of the Constitution *(Bundesamt für Verfassungsschutz)* and, last but not least, the Federal Office for Migration and Refugees (*Bundesamt für Migration und Flüchtlinge*, BAMF), which, in addition to assessing asylum applications and implementing federal integration measures, also bears responsibility for the Central Register of Foreign Nationals. All subordinated to the Federal Ministry of the Interior, these authorities can cooperate more easily than if they were subordinated to different ministries. It should also not be underestimated that the switching of posts for employees between authorities within a ministry's preserve is easier. Thus, the interlinking of security and immigration policy is expanded to an individual employee level, making it a part of everyday working life.

Against this backdrop it is no surprise that the federal government repeatedly reacts with understanding to demands for an ever stronger focus on security in relation to questions concerning immigration and Islam. Interior Minister Thomas de Maizière acknowledged, for example, during the PEGIDA demonstrations in 2014 that the fears being articulated were comprehensible: 'For how many more years will 200,000 asylum seekers be making their way to Germany? Are there terrorists among them? [...] These are legitimate questions. We take them seriously.'[13] An opinion–policy gap within the meaning of diametrically opposed objectives between politics and PEGIDA can only be inferred with great difficulty. However, it can be said that a difference remains in the assessment of the necessary re-

12 The strong role played by the Federal Ministry of the Interior in immigration policy corresponds to the status quo in the majority of EU countries (European Migration Network 2010: 12). Even though there should be no comparison of perspective at this point, it can however be maintained that Germany does not represent an exception to the rule.

13 See Peters, Freia and Martin Lutz. 2014. De Maizière will Pegida-Hetze mit Fakten kontern. Welt. http://www.welt.de/politik/deutschland/article135308170/De-Maiziere-will-PEGIDA-Hetze-mit-Fakten-kontern.html. Accessed: 12th October 2016.

sources for the common objective. From the viewpoint of PEGIDA and the AfD, German immigration policy would have to follow the chosen path for national security with even more consistency.

c) Immigration policy as economic policy

PEGIDA and AfD articulate numerous resentments against immigrants. But they cannot be accused of a fundamental agitation towards all forms of immigration, as they speak fervently in favour of controlled and market-oriented immigration 'based on the role models of Switzerland, Australia, Canada or South Africa' (PEGIDA 2014). The AfD states: 'Qualified immigrants with a high degree of willingness to integrate are welcome in the job market' (AfD 2016: 62). They also have no fundamental objections against asylum for those who have suffered political persecution, but do, however, desire a faster and, above all, more efficient assessment by the Federal Office for Migration and Refugees (BAMF) (Rucht et al. 2015: 21 et seq., 40). Immigration must not burden the German state, but rather must 'serve Germany's interests as a welfare state, as a nation of economy and culture' (AfD 2016: 62) by way of 'qualitative immigration' (PEGIDA 2015). Thus, for AfD and PEGIDA immigration policy is primarily economic policy.

This utilitarian stance is in no way outstanding. Throughout the history of German immigration policy, economic considerations have played a major role in policy decisions. For example, the so-called 'guest worker' policy after the Second World War was a one-sided view of the job-market-relevant potential shown by the immigrants. Any deficits among these people which should have been met with integration measures were ignored (Bade 2005: 218). The exploitable immigrant skills were also at the centre of the failed 'Green Card' initiative for IT specialists (Kolb 2004) or the dismantling of legislative barriers to immigration for highly qualified professionals in recent years.

In contrast to labour migration, the German discourse on humanitarian immigration and, above all, asylum seekers was based on other premises in previous decades. It was characterised by an almost complete absence of focus on potential in legislative foundations, political debates and administrative acts. Possible contributions by refugees to the German employment market played no role at all; instead, through Article 16 and subsequently Article 16a in the German Constitution *(Grundgesetz)*, there was an exclusive focus on the need for protection by the asylum applicant: 'Those who have suffered political persecution shall receive asylum'. Even the laws of the Geneva Convention are aligned exclusively with the applicant's deficits, just like the obstacles to deportation which can lead to subsidiary protection – from ill health to the inability to ensure one's safety in the country of origin.

German immigration policy is, thus, traditionally characterised by a categorical division into useful work immigration and the deficits of refugees. This is further manifested that a 'track change' from an asylum application procedure to a residence permit for commercial purposes is fundamentally not possible. However, evidence of a discourse entanglement has been noted for some time. For example, the then-president of the BAMF, Manfred Schmidt, argued in favour of a skills assessment for asylum seekers.[14] For this reason, in 2013 the BAMF started a joint project with the Federal Labour Office *(Bundesagentur für Arbeit)* which envisaged, among other things, a skills test to run parallel to the asylum application procedure for asylum seekers (initially only for those with a high degree of probability of attaining refugee status).[15] Statements by other stakeholders have followed a similar direction. For example, the president of the Association of German Chambers of Commerce and Industry (*Deutscher Industrie- und Handelskammertag* [DIHK]), Eric Schweitzer, from 2014 onwards repeatedly demanded residence permits for those asylum seekers who could be successfully integrated into the economy, in particular apprentices.[16] As a consequence, the 'Integration Law' in the summer of 2016 promises residence permits to those asylum seekers who have successfully started an apprenticeship – regardless of whether they are granted asylum or not.

Such demands and activities reflect that utility-oriented selection mechanisms appear as increasingly legitimate instruments in what was originally a purely humanitarian asylum application procedure. In the relevant publications this allegedly pragmatic policy approach is repeatedly linked with the term 'migration management', which, in the opinions of numerous authors, is increasingly influencing the immigration policy of liberal democracies (Buckel et al. 2014; Geiger and Pécoud 2012). Even though the approach is by no means new, Germany's determined adherence to it does signal a veritable turnaround: while German immigration and integration policy has remained 'strangely unclear' for several decades (Castro Varela 2008: 86), because it fears adopting clear positions on desirable and, above all, undesirable immigrants, it now appears that a clear direction is being established. Anyone who is of economic utility is welcome. In contrast to the recruitment of guest workers, the distinction between useful and less useful immigrants is being made on an increasingly individualised basis, and irrespective of

14 See Lau, Miriam. 2015. 'Wir wollen euch haben'. Zeit Online. http://www.zeit.de/2015/06/migration-manfred-schmidt-gegen-einwanderungsgesetz. Accessed: 12 October 2016.

15 See Bundesamt für Migration und Flüchtlinge. 2014. 'Jeder Mensch hat Potenzial'. http://www.bamf.de/SharedDocs/Meldungen/DE/2014/20140403-mensch-potenzial.html. Accessed: 12 October 2016.

16 See Deutscher Industrie- und Handelskammertag. 2014. Schweitzer Integrationsgipfel. http://www.dihk.de/presse/meldungen/2014-12-01-schweitzer-integrationsgipfel. Accessed: 30 March 2015.

the primary motive for immigration. Consequently, Germany is moving significantly closer to classic immigration countries such as the United States, Canada, New Zealand and Australia.

How does this development align with the demands made by the AfD and PEGIDA? An alignment with classical immigration countries and an increase in the efficiency of asylum application procedures are core demands of both parties. An opinion–policy gap does not apply here. In reality they reproduce an emergent discourse, thus advancing a reorientation of German immigration policy together with companies and civil society organisations. Even those scientific contributions to the debate made by proclaimed proponents of a liberal immigration policy frequently emphasise the potential and monetary gains to be had from immigration (inter alia Bonin 2014).

5 Attempt at a differentiated dimensioning and conclusion

The objective of this contribution was to convey a differentiated look at the opinion–policy gap in immigration policy introduced by Freeman (1995). The AfD and PEGIDA were selected as case studies for the critical observation, initiated by Freeman himself, of the hypothesis, as both embody the contrasting elements of 'liberal policy' and 'restrictive population' particularly well. They also articulate their positions regarding the three central topic areas of the immigration debate: identity, security and economy. By comparing the demands on immigration policy in the areas in question, three tentative manifestations of the relationship between politics and (partial) public opinion can be determined for now.

Firstly, the analysis has shown that German identity policy has in fact 'rushed ahead [of a part of the population] in seven-league boots' (Bade 2015: 20). The policy shift here stems from the political decision-making system and is either (still) not or only partially supported by the public. The resulting opinion–policy gap is by no means *a priori* and all-encompassing, but rather describes the different speeds of change. In order to describe more appropriately the relationship between a population 'left behind' and the policy, it is proposed that reference is made to a policy–opinion lag, i.e. a delayed acceptance of a shift in immigration policy by a section of the population.

Secondly, it is evident that the call for a security-oriented immigration policy continues to be firmly fixed in the institutional apparatus of the Federal Republic. Accordingly, the most prominent reactions of the federal government can be found in an almost caring appeasement: an appreciation of those fears is expressed, while reassuring that all necessary measures have been undertaken to resolve the problem. If there was a divide between AfD/PEGIDA and policy, this could be most appropriately described as an intensity gap, this being the differing assessment of a challenge's intensity and the measures required. In contrast to the policy–opinion lag it is not about a fundamental realignment but rather the enhanced intensity of the measures. Moreover, the demand for a policy shift with the intensity gap originates from the protesting population. The government is the protector of the status quo.

Thirdly and finally, the utility-oriented view of the AfD and PEGIDA is also clearly visible in current immigration policy measures and debates. This has the effect that the corresponding demands are not even called into question by the proclaimed opponents of the movement. PEGIDA is not a straggler here as in questions of identity policy, nor is it an admonisher as with security orientation; it is rather a supporter of an emergent discourse. Rather than being an opinion–policy gap, this is a simultaneous shift of public opinion and policies – a phenomenon that could be described in line with Morales et al. (2015) as opinion–policy congruence.

Here, the proposed dimensioning describing the relationship between immigration policy and population is certainly not conclusive. It does, however, permit a differentiated observation of the opinion–policy gap and explains which political reaction follows which demand by the population: a policy–opinion lag provokes disapproving warnings through politics. An intensity gap is accompanied by proclamations of understanding and instruction and could lead to measures of symbolic policy. Opinion–policy congruence ultimately ensures the willingness to engage seriously with the demands of the movement in one aspect. Self- and external perception as a protest against formulated immigration policy is built, above all, around the first two forms. But only its anchoring in the third establishes the rationale of a movement and its appearance in broader debates.

Thus, this contribution speaks to those who emphasise that the opinion–policy gap in immigration policy is by no means as straightforward as assumed by many. Furthermore, the investigation has made it clear that the gap should by no means proceed along the lines of a divide between 'liberal' and 'restrictive'; instead, it should consider that different relations between 'public opinion' and 'policy' could lead to different sub-policies as assumed by Freeman and Tendler (2012: 325). Although the analysis of two quite closely interlinked case studies only permits limited generalisation, it could also be assumed that the relation between public opinion and policy depends on the underlying debate arena. This could warrant an assessment of whether, for example, with regard to security policy an intensity gap exists comprising several cases and states, and whether there is a policy–opinion gap in identity policy. But even if this assumption is not shared, these findings could also be of interest for diverse research efforts, for example with political culture research. Even media and political debates could become far more targeted through the qualified designation of specific 'building blocks', which are the subject of disagreement between a section of the population and de facto immigration policy. A return to a differentiated observation of the opinion–policy gap is thus recommended for both immigration research and politics.

References

Alternative für Deutschland. 2016. *Programm für Deutschland*. Stuttgart.

Bade, Klaus J. 2005. Nachholende Integrationspolitik. *Zeitschrift für Ausländerrecht und Ausländerpolitik* 25 (7), 217–222.

Bade, Klaus J. 2013. *Kritik und Gewalt. Sarrazin-Debatte, "Islamkritik" und Terror in der Einwanderungsgesellschaft*. Schwalbach am Taunus: Wochenschau Verlag.

Bade, Klaus J. 2015. Integration ist keine Einbahnstraße. Worauf wir uns einstellen müssen, wenn Einwanderung und Integration gelingen sollen. *Rotary Magazin* (2/2015), 18–21.

Baumann, Mechthild. 2009. *Migration und Sicherheit*. Bonn.

Bebnowski, David. 2015. *Die Alternative für Deutschland. Aufstieg und gesellschaftliche Repräsentanz einer rechten populistischen Partei*. Wiesbaden: Springer VS.

Benneckenstein, Felix. 2015. 'Dresdner Thesen': PEGIDA radikalisiert sich nun auch schriftlich. netz-gegen-nazis.de. http://www.netz-gegen-nazis.de/artikel/%E2%80%9Edresdner-thesen%E2%80%9C-pegida-radikalisierung-nun-auch-auf-dem-papier-10066. Accessed: 12 October 2016.

Bonin, Holger. 2014. *Der Beitrag von Ausländern und künftiger Zuwanderung zum deutschen Staatshaushalt*. Gütersloh: Bertelsmann.

Bonjour, Saskia. 2011. The Power and Morals of Policy Makers: Reassessing the Control Gap Debate. *International Migration Review* 45 (1), 89–122.

Boswell, Christina. 2007. Theorizing Migration Policy: Is There a Third Way? *International Migration Review* 41 (1), 75–100.

Brubaker, Rogers. 1992: *Citizenship and Nationhood in France and Germany*. Cambridge: Harvard University Press.

Buckel, Sonja, Fabian Georgi, John Kannankulam and Jens Wissel. 2014: *Hegemonieprojekte im Kampf über die Migrationspolitik und Europäische Integration In Kämpfe um Migrationspolitik*, ed. Forschungsgruppe "Staatsprojekt Europa". Bielefeld, 61–84.

Bundesamt für Migration und Flüchtlinge. 2012. Der Einbürgerungstest. http://www.bamf.de/DE/Einbuergerung/WasEinbuergerungstest/waseinbuergerungstest.html?nn=1362952. Accessed: 12 October 2016.

Bundesamt für Migration und Flüchtlinge. 2014. "Jeder Mensch hat Potenzial". http://www.bamf.de/SharedDocs/Meldungen/DE/2014/20140403-mensch-potenzial.html. Accessed: 12 October 2016.

Castles, Stephen. 2004: The Factors That Make and Unmake Migration Policies. International Migration Review 38 (3). http://www.jstor.org/stable/27645419. Accessed: 12 October 2016.

Castro Varela, María do Mar. 2008. Was heißt hier Integration? Integrationsdiskurse und Integrationsregime. In *Alle anders – alle gleich?*, ed. Landeshauptstadt München, Sozialreferat, Stelle für interkulturelle Arbeit, 77–88.

Cornelius, Wayne A./Martin, Philip L. and James F. Hollifield. 1994: Introduction: The Ambivalent Quest for Immigration Control. In *Controlling Immigration*, eds. Cornelius, Wayne A., Takeyuki Tsuda, Philip L. Martin and James F. Hollifield, 3–41. Stanford: University Press.

Decker, Oliver, Johannes Kiess and Elmar Brähler (eds.). 2016. *Die enthemmte Mitte. Autoritäre und rechtsextreme Einstellung in Deutschland/Die Leipziger Mitte-Studie 2016*. Gießen: Psychosozial Verlag.

Deutscher Industrie- und Handelskammertag. 2014. Schweitzer Integrationsgipfel. http://www.dihk.de/presse/meldungen/2014-12-01-schweitzer-integrationsgipfel. Accessed: 30 March 2015.

Ellermann, Antje. 2006: Street-level Democracy: How Immigration Bureaucrats Manage Public Opinions. In *Special Issue on Immigration Policy in Europe: The Politics of Control*, eds. Virginie Guiraudon and Gallya Lahav, 293–309. London, New York: Routledge.

European Migration Network. 2010: *Organisation of Asylum and Migration Policies in the EU Member States.*

Eule, Tobias G. 2014: *Inside Immigration Law. Migration Management and Policy Application in Germany*. Farnham: Ashgate.

Freeman, Gary P. 1995: Modes of Immigration Politics in Liberal Democratic States. *International Migration Review* 29 (4), 881–902.

Freeman, Gary P. and Stuart M. Tendler. 2012: Interest Group Politics and Immigration Policy, *In The Oxford Handbook of the Politics of International Migration*, eds. Rosenblum, Marc R. and Daniel J. Tichenor, 324–344. Oxford/New York: University Press.

Geiger, Martin and Antoine Pécoud (eds.) 2012: *The New Politics of International Mobility. Migration Management and its Discontents*. Osnabrück.

Geiges, Lars, Stine Marg and Franz Walter. 2015: *Pegida. Die schmutzige Seite der Zivilgesellschaft?* Bielefeld.

Hagedorn, Heike. 2001. *Wer darf Mitglied werden? Einbürgerung in Deutschland und Frankreich im Vergleich*. Opladen: Leske + Budrich.

Hansen, Randall. 2000. *Citizenship and immigration in Post-War Britain. The institutional origins of a multicultural nation*. Oxford/New York: University Press.

Hansen, Randall and Patrick Weil. 2002. *Dual Nationality, Social Rights, and Federal Citizenship in the U.S. and Europe. The Reinvention of Citizenship*. New York: Berghahn.

Häusler, Alexander. 2016: Einleitung. In *Die Alternative für Deutschland*, ed. Häusler, Alexander, 1–3. Wiesbaden: Springer VS.

Hollifield, James F. 1992a. *Immigrants, Markets, and States. The Political Economy of Postwar Europe*. Cambridge: Harvard University Press.

Hollifield, James F. 1992b. Migration and International Relations: Cooperation and Control in the European Community. *International Migration Review* 26 (2), 568–595.

Horvath, Kenneth. 2014. *Die Logik der Entrechtung. Sicherheits- und Nutzendiskurse im österreichischen Migrationsregime*. Wien: University Press.

Huntington, Samuel P. 1997: *The Clash of Civilizations and the Remaking of World Order*. New York.

Jäger, Margarete. 2014. Skandal und doch normal. Zu den Verschiebungen und Kontinuitäten rassistischer Deutungsmuster im deutschen Einwanderungsdiskurs. *Überblick* 20 (2), 10–18.

Joppke, Christian. 2010. *Citizenship and Immigration*. Cambridge: Polity.

Klusmeyer, Douglas B. and Demetrios G. Papademetriou. 2009. *Immigration Policy in the Federal Republic of Germany. Negotiating Membership and Remaking the Nation*. New York: Berghahn.

Kolb, Holger. 2004. *Einwanderung zwischen wohlverstandenem Eigeninteresse und symbolischer Politik. Das Beispiel der deutschen "Green Card"*. Münster: LIT Verlag.

Körs, Anna. 2015. Die Hamburger Staatsverträge mit Muslimen und Aleviten im Spiegel der Bevölkerungsmeinung. Zur Notwendigkeit gesellschaftlichen Dialogs. In *Impulse für die Migrationsgesellschaft*, eds. Dirim, İnci, Ingrid Gogolin, Dagmar Knorr, Marianne Krüger-Potratz, Drorit Lengyel, Hans H. Reich, Wolfram Weiße, 209–224. Münster, New York: Waxmann.

Kymlicka, Will. 2003. *Multicultural citizenship. A liberal theory of minority rights*. Oxford: Clarendon Press.

Lahav, Gallya. 2004. *Immigration and politics in the new Europe. Reinventing borders*. Cambridge/New York: University Press.

Lahav, Gallya/Guiraudon, Virginie, 2006: Actors and Venues in Immigration Control: Closing the Gap between Political Demands and Policy Outcomes, in: Virginie Guiraudon/Gallya Lahav (Hrsg.), *Special Issue on Immigration Policy in Europe: The Politics of Control*, London, New York, 201–223.

Lammert, Norbert (ed.). 2006. *Verfassung, Patriotismus, Leitkultur. Was unsere Gesellschaft zusammenhält*. Hamburg: Hoffmann und Campe Verlag.

Lau, Miriam. 2015. "Wir wollen euch haben". Zeit Online. http://www.zeit.de/2015/06/migration-manfred-schmidt-gegen-einwanderungsgesetz. Accessed: 12 October 2016.

Morales, Laura, Jean-Benoit Pilet and Didier Ruedin. 2015. The Gap between Public Preferences and Policies on Immigration: A Comparative Examination of the Effect of Politicization on Policy Congruence (Pre-Print). *Journal of Ethnic and Migration Studies* (accepted).

Naujoks, Daniel. 2014. The securitization of dual citizenship. National security concerns and the making of the Overseas Citizenship of India. *Diaspora Studies*, 1–19.

Nowak, Jürgen. 2006. *Leitkultur und Parallelgesellschaft. Argumente wider einen deutschen Mythos*. Frankfurt am Main: Brandes & Apsel.

Oberndörfer, Dieter. 2001. Leitkultur und Berliner Republik. Die Hausordnung der multikulturellen Gesellschaft Deutschlands ist das Grundgesetz. *Aus Politik und Zeitgeschichte* (1-2/2001), 27–30.

PEGIDA. 2014: Positionspapier der PEGIDA. www.lvz-online.de/f-Download-d-file.html?id=2942. Accessed: 9 April 2015.

PEGIDA. 2015. Dresdner Thesen. Gemeinsam für Deutschland!, https://legida.eu/images/legida/Dresdner_Thesen_15_02.pdf. Accessed: 12 October 2016.

Peters, Freia and Martin Lutz. 2014. De Maizière will Pegida-Hetze mit Fakten kontern. Welt. http://www.welt.de/politik/deutschland/article135308170/De-Maiziere-will-PEGIDA-Hetze-mit-Fakten-kontern.html. Accessed: 12 October 2016.

Rosenblum, Marc R. and Wayne A. Cornelius. 2012. Dimensions of Immigration Policy. In *The Oxford Handbook of the Politics of International Migration,* eds. Rosenblum, Marc R., and Daniel J. Tichenor, 245–273. Oxford/New York: University Press.

Rucht, Dieter, Priska Daphi, Piotr Kocyba, Michael Neuber, Jochen Roose, Franziska Scholl and Moritz Sommer. 2015. *Protestforschung am Limit. Eine soziologische Annäherung an Pegida*. Berlin: Wissenschaftszentrum für Sozialforschung.

Scholz, Antonia. 2012. *Migrationspolitik zwischen moralischem Anspruch und strategischem Kalkül. Der Einfluss politischer Ideen in Deutschland und Frankreich.* Wiesbaden: Springer VS.

Schrey, Martina. 2008. Baden-Württemberg bleibt bei Gesinnungsfragen. Spiegel Online. http://www.spiegel.de/politik/deutschland/einbuergerungstests-baden-wuerttemberg-bleibt-bei-gesinnungsfragen-a-557688.html. Accessed: 12 October 2016.

Soysal, Yasemin Nuhoğlu. 1994: *Limits of Citizenship. Migrants and postnational membership in Europe.* Chicago: University Press.

Spielhaus, Riem and Martin Herzog. 2015. *Die rechtliche Anerkennung des Islams in Deutschland. Ein Gutachten für die Friedrich-Ebert-Stiftung.* Berlin: Friedrich-Ebert-Stiftung.

Tezcan, Levent. 2013. Das strittige Kollektiv im Kontext eines Repräsentationsregimes. Kontroversen auf der Deutschen Islam Konferenz (2006–2009). In *Die Integrationsdebatte zwischen Assimilation und Diversität,* eds. Ezli, Özkan, Andreas Langenohl, Valentin Rauer and Claudia M. Voigtmann, 159–181. Bielefeld: transcript.

Thränhardt, Dietrich. 2008. *Einbürgerung. Rahmenbedingungen, Motive und Perspektiven des Erwerbs der deutschen Staatsangehörigkeit.* Bonn: Friedrich-Ebert-Stiftung.

Tibi, Bassam. 1996. Multikultureller Werte-Relativismus und Werte-Verlust. Demokratie zwischen Werte-Beliebigkeit und pluralistischem Werte-Konsens. *Aus Politik und Zeitgeschichte* (52-53/1996), 27–36.

Vorländer, Hans, Maik Herold and Steven Schäller. 2015: *Wer geht zu PEGIDA und warum? Eine empirische Untersuchung von PEGIDA-Demonstranten in Dresden.* Dresden: Zentrum für Verfassungs- und Demokratieforsschung.

Wengeler, Martin. 2003. *Topos und Diskurs. Begründung einer argumentationsanalytischen Methode und ihre Anwendung auf den Migrationsdiskurs (1960–1985)*. Tübingen.

Worbs, Susanne. 2014: *Bürger auf Zeit. Die Wahl der Staatsangehörigkeit im Kontext der deutschen Optionsregelung*. Nürnberg: Bundesamt für Migration und Flüchtlinge.

Zeit Online. 2015. "Der Islam gehört zu Deutschland". http://www.zeit.de/politik/deutschland/2015-01/angela-merkel-islam-deutschland-wulff. Accessed: 12 October 2016.

'I am not a racist, but …'

The phenomenon of hate comments on refugees in Germany and how to deal with them

Jana Sinram

Abstract

The so-called refugee crisis of 2015 has changed the volume and content of hate comments on social media and the comments sections of German broadcasters and newspapers. 'I'm not a racist, but …' – with this phrase usually being followed by a racist remark, a prejudiced statement or an accusation against media or politicians, it has created a toxic atmosphere that poses a huge barrier for the successful integration of refugees in Germany. The domestic intelligence service noted in its latest report that there was a 'complete disappearance of inhibitions' in social networks, with refugees, politicians and volunteers being dehumanised and threatened. This essay looks at the phenomenon of hate comments more closely and discusses how media and society should deal with it. How does it affect the relationship between the political establishment, the media and the people? What should journalists and social media such as Facebook and Twitter do? And when should legal authorities step in?

'I'm not a racist, but …'. 'You ought to be able to say that …'. At the height of the so-called refugee crisis in the late summer and autumn of 2015, there were hardly any articles on the topic in German media that did not trigger at least one or two user comments beginning with one of these phrases. Both were typically followed by either a racist remark on refugees in general, immigrants or Muslims, a prejudiced statement on Islam or an accusation that the media were not telling the truth about what was really going on. Typically, a lot of commentators used the term 'Lügenpresse', a term that was utilised by the Nazis in the 1930s to discredit the free press and that translates into 'liar press'. Many of them would ask why the media were 'concealing' certain facts about refugees coming to Germany or other

European countries, like refugees supposedly abusing women, stealing or being terrorists that were just waiting to strike in German cities. A lot of users on social media were referring to themselves as 'besorgte Bürger' – a term that translates into English as 'concerned citizens'. These concerned citizens were claiming to be worried about German culture and German values that were endangered as millions of 'Islamist' refugees 'flood' the country like a tsunami. There were hysterical debates about refugees misbehaving in public swimming pools, about burkinis and headscarves, and about male refugees refusing to take food from female volunteers. Certain right-wing news sites created hashtags with portmanteau words such as #rapefugees or #krimigranten – the latter being an equivalent to the English hashtag #crimigrants. Thousands of Twitter users retweeted pictures of beaten up women, girls and seniors claiming they had been attacked by refugees or other Muslim immigrants.

The situation left journalists wondering how to react to the overwhelming volume of remarks in the comments sections and the emails received about articles on migration. Should prejudiced comments be ignored or was it better to delete them? Where was the line to be drawn between freedom of expression and unacceptable hatred? And what was the right way to cover the new mass phenomenon?

All of this peaked in January 2016 after hundreds of woman reported sexual assaults by groups of men supposedly from North Africa in the city centre of Cologne on New Year's Eve. To this day, it is not completely clear what happened. There have been more than a thousand complaints, most of them about sexual attacks and theft. Most of the offenders that could be identified were from Morocco and Algeria, plus some from Iraq, Syria and Germany (Reker 2016). There have been a few lawsuits and the state parliament of North Rhine-Westphalia has formed a commission of inquiry to investigate, amongst other things, the role of the police. In the weeks and months following the events in Cologne, commentators switched to an 'I told you so' attitude, blaming both those who had welcomed arriving refugees the year before – ridiculing them as 'welcome-clappers' *(Willkommensklatscher)* – as well as the established politicians and parties who were accused of being 'national traitors' *(Volksverräter)*. In the focus of attention was chancellor Angela Merkel, who commentators held responsible for a refugee policy that had enabled 1.1 million asylum seekers to cross into Germany in 2015. 'Ms Merkel, what did you do with our beautiful and once safe country?', asked one of the more polite users on Facebook after the axe attack by a young asylum seeker in a regional train near Würzburg in July 2016, before the motive behind the terrible act was even clear. One of the less polite citizens had in October 2015 been carrying a gallows construction bearing the names of Merkel and vice-chancellor Sigmar Gabriel at a demonstration of the right-wing populist political movement Pegida ('Patriotic Europeans against the Islamisation of the West') in Dresden.

So what exactly qualifies a remark as a 'hate comment'? The definition is not an easy one as the boundaries are blurred. In general, any remark that complies with elements such as insult, harassment or sedition is a hate comment. However, this can also be the case for statements that are more diffused. I would argue that any comment that is suitable to normalise racism and xenophobia qualifies as a hate comment. Although this is not a completely new phenomenon – some journalists with a non-German background have been receiving hate mail or even death threats on quite a regular basis for some years now (Hür 2015)[1] – both the sheer volume and the content of comments have changed. They have now, so it seems, become so normal that people do not mind using their real name in comments sections or on Facebook even when leaving highly racist or anti-Semitic remarks or threats. To give an example: in April 2015, the New Right[2] politician Tatjana Festerling posted a report by the public broadcaster *Deutschlandfunk* on her Facebook page, making abusive remarks about the broadcaster's correspondent to the federal state of Saxony, who in the report was covering a Pegida demonstration attended by the Dutch populist politician Geert Wilders. A man, later identified to be a welfare recipient and father of four children, commented on Festerling's post by posting a picture of a man holding a gun and demanding 'kill that bitch'. The correspondent reported him and he was later convicted for insult by a court in Dresden, which imposed a fine (Deutschlandfunk 2016).

So what are the problems arising from hate speech? This question was addressed by Germany's domestic security agency, the Federal Office for the Protection of the Constitution *(Bundesverfassungsschutz)*, in its annual report of 2015. The authors pointed out that the increasing numbers of refugees and the public discourse had resulted in a steady increase of people who were sceptical or hostile, going as far as claiming that the government had lost control. The report noted that Pegida and other social movements were giving xenophobic attitudes a scope, and thus helping right-wing extremism out of its isolation. Extremists were using social networks for their propaganda, to recruit new followers and agitate against refugees. 'With a complete disappearance of inhibitions, refugees as well as politicians and volunteers are dehumanized and threatened' (Bundesministerium des Innern 2016, p. 62). With strategies like that, social networks play, according to

1 Some of them have formed the group 'Hate poetry' and read hate mail they receive live on stage to confront prejudice head-on (Hür 2015).

2 New Right is a term that is used in several countries to describe right-wing groups that explicitly do not want to be associated with the 'old' National Socialism and argue on more intellectual terms.

the report, an important role in radicalising individuals in real life: many of them form groups in virtual environments to later meet and take action against refugee centres or other targets (ibid., p. 42, 61).

Even though the most extreme comments are to be found on the New Right movement's websites or in their Facebook groups, the mainstream media in Germany (and many other European countries) all have to deal with hate comments. There are certain topics that cannot be posted online without attracting prejudiced or racist remarks. This applies to any report on refugees, immigration, integration or Islam as well as news items and commentaries on terror attacks, Pegida demonstrations and the right-wing populist party *Alternative für Deutschland* (AfD). Nowadays, noticeably even articles that have absolutely nothing to do with any of the cited topics are used by certain users and so-called trolls to comment on the 'refugee crisis' and Islam.

So what can be done against hate speech? First of all, it has to be clear that if commentators call for violence against others, they should be prosecuted by the law enforcement authorities. The same goes for posts that are in other ways chargeable in Germany, such as 'incitement of the masses' *(Volksverhetzung)*. The conviction of the man insulting a *Deutschlandfunk* correspondent serves as a case in point, making clear that threats are not tolerated by society, even if they are made in a virtual environment – and so is the fact that the Federal Criminal Police Office in mid-July 2016 conducted the first nationwide police raids against 60 people linked to hate comments. According to the agency, the aim was to counter the growing verbal radicalism on the Internet and related offences (Zeit Online 2016). The raid, again, sent an important signal that hate speech is not tolerated. The European Union has also started to deal with hate speech. It has created working groups to organise so-called 'counter-speech' and to target hate speech and terrorist propaganda, for example the Internet Referral Unit (IRU), associated with the European law enforcement agency Europol (Otto et al. 2016).

Secondly, social media companies such as Facebook or Twitter should react and delete racist comments and other conspicuous content pointed out to them. That applies to any comment that is liable to promote violence or xenophobia in society. The two companies as well as YouTube and Microsoft, together with the European Commission, put forward a Code of Conduct on illegal online hate speech in late May 2016. They acknowledged that 'the spread of illegal hate speech online not only negatively affects the groups or individuals that it targets, it also negatively impacts those who speak out for freedom, tolerance and non-discrimination in our open societies and has a chilling effect on the democratic discourse on online platforms' and promised a 'continued development of internal procedures and staff training to guarantee that they review the majority of valid notifications for removal of illegal hate speech in less than 24 hours and remove or disable access to such content, if necessary' (European Commission 2016). However, media, politicians and NGOs in Germany criticised the Code of Conduct as being too soft. They argued that the companies did not have to change their existing procedures to fulfil the Code of Conduct and doubted that it would change anything at all (Kühl 2016; Reinbold 2016). Another argument was that Facebook and others were much too slow when someone reported hate speech and that the wording of the Code of Conduct was too vague to change that – a point that I would agree with regarding the rather unambitious goal that social media companies should review not all but only the *majority* of valid notifications for removal of illegal hate speech within 24 hours.

Thirdly, the media have a responsibility of their own to deal with all those comments that are not chargeable but that nevertheless spread prejudice against refugees and other minorities on their own websites and social media pages. They should moderate and engage in discussions and, if necessary, delete hate comments. This poses, however, a huge challenge for most newspapers, broadcasters and online platforms as almost none of them has the resources and staff that would be needed to deal with hundreds of commentators criticising refugees, politicians and journalists or insulting other users. Even if they had, it is highly questionable whether this moderation would make a difference, as most of those who leave hate comments and accuse politicians and journalists seem not at all interested in debating; instead, they prefer to continue spreading poison.

So should this be a reason to give up and let hate commentators win? Certainly not. There are other, different ways to deal with the phenomenon. *Spiegel Online,* for example, has chosen to disable comments under most articles related to the refugee crisis. This decision ensures that xenophobic comments cannot be spread on the website, but the step also carries the risk of justifying the right-wing populist accusation that the mainstream media are not listening to the people and, thus, are a *Lügenpresse.* Plus, this practice is not possible on social media such as Facebook. There, at least the unlawful remarks should be deleted. But, under all circumstances, journalists have to continue to report on the situation of refugees in Germany and other European countries. They have to continue to address topics such as Pegida and the AfD, and if AfD members represent anti-Semitic or racist theories, this has to be called what it is: anti-Semitism and racism. A few German journalists stand out through a tough stance against hate speech. Anja Reschke of public service broadcaster *NDR,* for instance, called the Germans in a widely shared TV commentary to start an 'insurgence of the decent' against racist hate speech (Gemmer 2015). Dunja Hayali, a journalist with Iraqi parents and working for the public service television broadcaster *ZDF,* engaged with hate messages she received on her Facebook page. 'This is Germany?', she asked, for example, and then stated: 'This is unworthy and embarrassing' (Gasteiger 2015).

According to the scholar Micha Brumlik, the phrase 'I'm not a racist, but …' stands for the ideology of the New Right and the Identitarian movement[3], whose members claim not to be racists, but instead to be committed to their regional, national and cultural provenance (Brumlik 2016, pp. 81–92; Wüllenkemper 2016). A lot of commentators using this phrase would, however, not even consider themselves part of the Identitarian movement. It has been adopted by all sorts of people who have sympathies for Pegida or the AfD or who are at least afraid of refugees and want the German borders to be closed. Thus, the phenomenon of hate comments has also revealed a crisis between the political establishment, the media and the people. A lot of Germans do not trust the 'established' politicians or the mainstream media to be 'on their side' any more. It is, therefore, a good idea if the media address the reservations and make the work of their journalists as transparent as possible. How are decisions to publish or not to publish made? Where do news editors get their information? Do government officials call broadcasters such as *Deutschlandfunk* and request them to report in a certain way? No, actually, they don't.

But, to be clear: hate comments and racist remarks on refugees are far from being a media problem. They create a toxic atmosphere, lower the threshold for violence and therefore create a huge barrier for the successful integration of refugees. The phenomenon should therefore be addressed not only by the media but also by politicians and civil society at large. The goal must be to re-establish communication in a more polite kind of way to enable a real and productive discussion on how to deal with one of the biggest challenges of our time.

References

Brumlik, Micha. 2016. Das alte Denken der neuen Rechten. Mit Heidegger und Evola gegen die offene Gesellschaft. Blätter für deutsche und internationale Politik 3: 81–92.

Bundesministerium des Innern. 2016. Verfassungsschutzbericht 2015. https://www.verfassungsschutz.de/embed/vsbericht-2015.pdf. Accessed: 22 July 2016.

Deutschlandfunk. 2016. In eigener Sache: Facebook-Hetzer muss Geldstrafe zahlen. Deutschlandfunk. http://www.deutschlandfunk.de/in-eigener-sache-facebook-hetzer-muss-geldstrafe-zahlen.1818.de.html?dram:article_id=358477. Accessed: 22 July 2016.

3 The Identitarian movement is a socio-political movement that originally started in France. 'Identitarians' in Germany and Austria argue that every ethnos has its right to live, but only in its own living space.

European Commission. 2016. Press release: European Commission and IT Companies announce Code of Conduct on illegal online hate speech. http://europa.eu/rapid/press-release_IP-16-1937_en.html. Accessed: 22 July 2016.

Gasteiger, Carolin. 2015. Dunja Hayali gegen Fremdenhass: Aber was??? Süddeutsche Zeitung Online. http://www.sueddeutsche.de/medien/dunja-hayali-gegen-fremdenhass-aber-was-1.2626673. Accessed: 22 July 2016.

Gemmer, Monika. 2015. Anja Reschke und die Hater. Frankfurter Rundschau Online. http://www.fr-online.de/digital/ard-tagesthemen-kommentar-anja-reschke-und-die-hater,1472406,31400110.html. Accessed: 22 July 2016.

Henriette Reker. 2016. Vielleicht habe ich den Frauen zu wenig Trost gespendet. Zeit Online. http://www.zeit.de/zeit-magazin/2016-06/henriette-reker-armlaenge-aeusserung-fehler. Accessed: 11 September 2016.

Hür, Kemal. 2015. Hate poetry: Journalisten lesen Hassbriefe vor. Deutschlandfunk. http://www.deutschlandfunk.de/hate-poetry-journalisten-lesen-hassbriefe-vor.862.de.html?dram:article_id=312157. Accessed: 11 September 2016.

Kühl, Eike. 2016. Zuckerbrote gegen Hass im Netz. Zeit Online. http://www.zeit.de/digital/internet/2016-06/hasskommentare-eu-selbstverpflichtung-facebook-google. Accessed: 22 July 2016.

Otto, Thomas, Steiner, Falk and Peter Welchering. 2016. Der schwierige Kampf gegen islamistische Propaganda. Deutschlandfunk. http://www.deutschlandfunk.de/bei-facebook-twitter-und-co-der-schwierige-kampf-gegen.724.de.html?dram:article_id=361946. Accessed: 22 August 2016.

Reinbold, Fabian. 2016. Hasskommentare im Netz: Berlin hadert mit Brüssels Facebook-Kodex. Spiegel-Online. http://www.spiegel.de/netzwelt/netzpolitik/facebook-berlin-hadert-mit-bruessels-hatespeech-kodex-a-1095197.html. Accessed: 22 July 2016.

Wüllenkemper, Cornelius. 2016. Die "Neue Rechte" und ihre Argumente: "Ich bin kein Rassist, aber…". Deutschlandfunk. http://www.deutschlandfunk.de/die-neue-rechte-und-ihre-argumente-ich-bin-kein-rassist-aber.691.de.html?dram:article_id=359919. Accessed: 22 July 2016.

Zeit Online. 2016. Bundeskriminalamt: Razzien wegen Hasskommentaren im Netz. Zeit Online. http://www.zeit.de/politik/deutschland/2016-07/bundeskriminalamt-razzia-hetze-im-internet-hass-kommentare#comments. Accessed: 22 July 2016.

[illegible] 2016. [illegible] [illegible]

[illegible] [illegible]

Emotions matter

Fear and (non-)empathy in German reactions to the "refugee crisis"[1]

Annette Jünemann

Abstract

Against the backdrop of Germany's welcome culture on the one hand and rising xenophobia on the other, this article explores the impact of emotions on German reactions to the "refugee crisis". While volunteers in support of refugees were driven by feelings of compassion motivating them to offer their help, many other people felt fear motivating them to harshly reject the admission of refugees. What distinguishes the first group from the second seems to be the capability to identify and empathise with the refugees. Since the emotion of fear is at the very core of xenophobia, counteracting xenophobic attitudes demands the acquisition of a better understanding of the interplay between fear and the ability to empathize. Insights from cognitive psychology explain why empathy with someone perceived as a threat can only develop under very specific conditions. To create these conditions, it is important to reach out to everyone who, for whatever reason, holds xenophobic views. Given that people with deviant opinions – including xenophobia – often join the same peer-groups like families and circles of friends and colleagues, this article suggests that people actively involved in the support of refugees could create the necessary environment for empathy to develop and ideally function as an antidote against xenophobia.

1 I am extremely thankful for the constructive, stimulating, and empathic (!) critique of Nicolas Fromm and Nikolas Scherer, who both contributed a lot to the genesis of this article.

1 Introduction

In the summer of 2015, an ever-growing number of refugees fleeing from the Syrian civil war and other places of distress set off to seek refuge in the EU, provoking what was later called the "refugee crisis". Although it is actually a humanitarian crisis for the refugees because they are the ones in deprivation, their collective move also triggered a major political crisis in Europe, disuniting the EU and many of its member states, including Germany, the country on which this article focuses. Europe's crisis became acute in early September 2015 when Germany announced that it would temporarily open its borders for refugees.[2] Chancellor Merkel's unilateral decision resulted in a heated debate, turning Europe's latent dispute on migration into an open conflict. Her famous phrase "wir schaffen das"[3], which was originally meant to encourage German people to cope with an extraordinary humanitarian challenge, divided public opinion into two almost antagonistic camps: those who sympathize with refugees and those who starkly reject them. Although it was most probably a spontaneous reaction to the humanitarian crisis, Merkel's contested decision to open the borders stands for the general conviction that Europe – and Germany – have a moral obligation to share the burden of accommodating refugees. This fundamental idea of a universal humanitarianism is at the heart of all political controversies because in the eyes of the critics, it endangers the security and wellbeing of the European people or, to be more precise, the wellbeing of the respective home countries. It is noteworthy that there is a staggering lack of solidarity not only with the refugees, but also among EU member states, which refuse to share burdens and responsibilities.[4] It is not easy to remain neutral in such an antagonistic debate, also as an academic. In fact, this article is not at all neutral, but sympathizes strongly with the idea of universal humanitarianism.[5] Nevertheless, instead of deepening the discursive rift any further, this article aims at building bridges. Today's heated debates on the "refugee crisis" do not seem to lead anywhere. On the contrary, their dichotomy is counterproductive and overtly grist on the mills of xenophobic extremists such as the right-wing so-

2 For details on the deploring situation of refugees who got trapped in Hungary preceding Germany's decision to open the borders, see the report of "bordermonitoring-eu", a registered German non-profit organization: Bordermonitoring-eu. 2015. Of Hope. Hungary and the long Summer of Migration. http://bordermonitoring.eu/ungarn/2015/09/of-hope-en/. Accessed: 28th October 2016.

3 This phrase can be translated literally as "we will manage", but in analogy to Obama's famous phrase from his election campaign, also as "yes we can".

4 For a critical assessment of Dublin III, the cornerstone of the Common European Asylum System, see Fratzke 2015.

5 Not to be equated or confused with Germany's *current* and increasingly restrictive management of the "refugee crisis".

cial movement PEGIDA or Germany's new populist party, the slightly less radical AfD.[6] Although both are resolute protagonists in the migration discourse, this article does not focus on them, but on the many people in Germany and elsewhere who are xenophobic in the original sense of the word: "fear of that which is perceived to be foreign or strange" (Chumacov et al. 2014, 496). If we want a productive debate on the so-called refugee crisis, we have to take their fears seriously, though without giving in to their distorted logic of inclusion and exclusion that all too often transforms fear into rejection or even hate.

2 The emotional (re-)turn in International Relations

Fear is an emotion, and taking fear seriously means acknowledging that emotions are decisive analytical factors in International Relations (IR). This perspective is still contested in mainstream IR, even though many scholars have recently started to emphasize the role of emotions in international politics, claiming that emotions such as shame, fear or hope, released by humiliation, threat or solidarity, offer better explanations for political decision-making than rational calculation.[7] Their works mark the beginning of what is today labelled as an "emotional turn". It started with a critical reading of the history of ideas, going back to the age of enlightenment when liberalism introduced the principle of reason into political theorizing. Liberal ideas paved the way to the overcoming of theological legitimations of political power and social disparity. However, liberal thought also had the negative side effect of excluding emotions as an analytical factor from further theory building. The image of utilitarian actors who consciously take decisions based on reason dominated political theories for a long time, especially in the young field of IR, which only emerged after World War I. In vast contrast to this image, however, emotions are at least *implicitly* included in most rational choice approaches, as Simon Koschut points out: Hans Morgenthau, the most important representative of classical realism, admitted that emotions co-determine the balance of power; Neo-realist Kenneth Waltz identified fear as the root cause for the security dilemma, and Institutionalist Robert Keohane referred to empathy as a precondition for trust and cooperation (Koschut 2015, 3). Until the 1960s, emotions were at most addressed with a negative bias, reviving 19th-century images of the "angry mob" and "primitive crowd" (Godwin et al. 2000, 66). It was a few more years be-

6 For details on PEGIDA and AfD, see the article by Hannes Schammann in this edited volume.

7 For an overview of relevant literature on the "emotional turn" see Schieder and Spindler 2014, 9f.

fore emotions were explicitly identified as analytical factors, for example in Robert Jervis' analysis of perceptions and misperceptions in foreign policies (Jervis 1976). When research on social movements started in the 1980s, emotions were still addressed with a prevalent negative and also gendered normative bias. According to a feminist critique, reason was – and still is – all too often framed as a male attribute associated with strength, whereas emotions were framed as a female attribute associated with weakness (Bargetz and Sauer 2010). As a result, rationality and emotion often have been – and still are – perceived as antagonistic and hierarchical concepts, disguising their interplay when people judge a situation. "Emotions and cognitions do not exist in dichotomy or discontinuity, except in our scholarship." (Crawford 2014, 537) It is the merit of constructivist perspectives that have helped to overcome this artificial dichotomy, arguing that emotions are socially constructed cognitive evaluations (Koschut 2015, 4). Today, there is growing consensus among scholars that emotions are shaped by society and therefore not only an individual and private phenomenon, but also and foremost a collective one, intertwined with pre-existing social, cultural, and political contexts (Hutchison and Bleiker 2014, 499). The following study is embedded in this theoretical perspective, which – against the backdrop of its genesis – should be labelled as an emotional re-turn.

It was an extremely emotional situation when trains crammed with refugees arrived in Germany in early September 2015. Political observers were surprised that so many Germans from all walks of life rushed to the stations to welcome them and to offer help. What started as a rather spontaneous and humanitarian gesture evolved into a more structured effort to support refugees. A loose network of local initiatives developed, with people working together with the churches, the Red Cross, other welfare organisations and established NGOs supportive of refugees.[8] Without being experts on the countries the refugees came from or on the EU's debated migration regime, many of the newly born activists started to help by implementing a very simple charity approach. The emergence of this broad movement is amazing against the background of the Islamophobic discourse in Germany[9], especially since the terror attacks of 9/11. In this discourse, "the Muslim" is portrayed – in line with orientalist traditions (Said 1978)[10] – as an almost vital threat to "the West" and Western norms and values, whatever they may be. Nev-

8 One of the established and highly professional NGOs supporting refugees is Pro Asyl, founded in 1986 as a national platform with regional branches in every *Bundesland,* the so called *Flüchtlingsräte:* https://www.proasyl.de. Accessed: 16th November 2016.

9 For details on the exclusion of Muslims from the collective German narrative, see the article by Naika Foroutan in this edited volume as well as Hahn 2006.

10 Said was the first to systematically analyze Western (mis-)perceptions of the "Orient" from a critical post-colonial perspective.

ertheless, when confronted with the bedraggled refugees, local activists did not see them as the hazardous Islamists they had been warned of, but simply as "poor boys in need", as one of the helpers put it.[11] This very simple formulation is not self-evident, because it stands for the recognition of the refugees as fellow people in the overarching human "we" group, opening the door for identification and empathy. Thus, Germany's welcome culture seems to confirm Neta Crawford's argument that empathy overrides fear and could therefore function like an antidote against xenophobia (Crawford 2014). This argument, however, also works the other way round: Yes, empathy can override fear, but, at the same time, fear is one of the most decisive factors hindering people to empathize. I hold that the relation between fear and (non-)empathy is much more ambiguous and can just as well result in a vicious circle producing and reproducing xenophobia. After all, many people in Germany do not empathize with refugees, harshly rejecting them and referring to manifold risks their admission would entail. The aim of this article is to determine the conditions under which empathy can develop and what it takes to unfold the productive power Crawford ascribes to it. To do so, it is necessary to gain a better understanding of the complex interplay between (non-)empathy, fear and xenophobia.

To start with, Section 2 elaborates on the notion of empathy, which is not an emotion itself, but – in a nutshell – the capability to share the emotions of others. While in-group empathy is an almost natural social practice, out-group empathy is much more difficult to achieve, especially when the "other" is perceived as a threat. Section 3 deepens the analysis with regard to the notion of fear, the most archaic yet complex emotion we have. Fear is both a physical and a cognitive reaction to what is perceived as a threat, whereby the latter is at least in part socially constructed. Drawing on the literature of cognitive psychology, Section 4 explores the challenges to countering xenophobia in a socially constructed climate of fear. The fifth and final section deals with how to overcome these challenges, presenting suggestions on how to pave the way for empathy to disrupt the fatal logic of inclusion and exclusion which is at the core of xenophobia.

3 Empathy: How to empathize with the threatening other

Empathy itself is not an emotion, but the capability to affectively share and cognitively understand the emotions of others, including the capability to understand

11 This article is informed by the results of participant observation conducted in a small community near Hamburg that started in January 2015.

how others might understand one's own behaviour. Empathy comprises "1) an awareness of the distinction between the self and the other; 2) the ability to take the perspective of the other; and 3) the ability to regulate one's own emotions to avoid being overwhelmed with what the other person is feeling and by one's own affective response to the other person" (Segal 2011, 267). Since empathy usually paves the way for sympathy because it helps a better understanding to be acquired of someone's judgements and decisions, "empathy" and "sympathy" are notions that are often used synonymously in common speech. Such simplifications, however, result in a misleading romanticization of the concept, ignoring the fact that empathy can also be utilized to manipulate another person for reasons that are not necessarily altruistic. Whereas empathy in the context of behavioural therapy is certainly in the interest of the person concerned, this is not the case in the context of marketing or criminological profiling, as both practices draw on empathy. "... empathic engagement can distance as much as it connects, exclude as much as it humanizes, fix as much as it transforms and oppress as much as it frees." (Pedwell 2014, 190) Thus, empathy is not a normative concept in itself, but needs specific pre-conditions to unfold benevolent qualities.

Humans have an anthropological disposition to emphasize with others that is later shaped through processes of socialisation, starting in early childhood.[12] Over the years, the capability to emphasize can either de- or increase. This depends on manifold positive or negative context factors. Neglected children find it much more difficult to develop an empathic personality than children who grow up in a trustful and attentive environment (Bauer 2014). Since empathy is sensitive to external influence, shortfalls in early childhood can later be compensated to a certain extent through training with psychological and/or pedagogical means, such as role games. Being empathic is not only beneficial for individuals; it is also a decisive social skill for the functioning of a community, internally strengthening social cohesion and externally facilitating mutual trust and cooperation. However, the internal dimension is much easier to accomplish than the external one because in-group empathy functions slightly differently to out-group empathy.

In-group empathy is deeply ingrained in the human body as a precondition for survival. Ideally, it starts within the family and among close friends who surround a child when it is growing up. As the circle of people surrounding the child widens, these people become more and more heterogeneous, delivering a sort of natural training in empathy for the child and later the adult. As long as they belong more or less to the same social and/or cultural environment, empathizing with

12 Research on empathy is genuinely interdisciplinary because the concept was initially analyzed and defined from the perspectives of social and cognitive psychology and neuroscience.

them suffices for people to draw conclusions based on themselves. "Humans find it easier to feel empathy and to develop empathic understanding with those they are close to and the deeper the connections, the greater the empathy." (Crawford 2014, 541) There is even neurological proof of this phenomenon. When humans observe people who are similar to them experiencing pain, they develop measureable biological activities that are missing when the observed people are dissimilar to them (ibid., 542). Affective deficits vis-à-vis the different "other" can only be compensated through a cognitive understanding of the other's situation. Due to the divergent social and/or cultural background, however, concluding from one's own perspective can be misleading. The question of how to adequately interpret the living conditions of other people and the emotions these might raise is anything but self-evident, especially when the social, cultural and political contexts diverge as much as they do with regard to refugees in this case study. Moreover, grasping the difficulties of out-group empathy also requires group-level emotions to be taken into consideration. Jonathan Mercer holds that group emotion "can be stronger than, and different from, emotion experienced as an individual because group members share, validate, and police each other's feelings." (Mercer 2014, 515) Group emotions go with identity and, perhaps even more, with the fear of identity loss, as is the case in the current "refugee crisis".

4 Fear and fear entrepreneurs in the discourse on refugees

Fear is one of the most archaic emotions we have and thus deeply engrained in our bodies. The ability to immediately recognize a vital threat was, and perhaps still is, essential for the survival of mankind. The bodily component refers to physical reactions to a 'threat recognition' e.g. accelerated heart-beating or the reflex to flee or fight. At the same time, however, fear is a reaction that draws on our *knowledge* about the *perceived* threat. This cognitive component of fear refers to the cognitive act of recognizing something as a threat. This 'threat recognition' is based on our accumulated knowledge – that is, on our experiences. Consequently, to recognize something as a threat is at least in part socially constructed.[13] The dividing line between the bodily and the cognitive dimensions of fear might not be as clear-cut as constructivist theorizing suggests.[14] Today, we no longer have to cope with sabretooth tigers that perhaps triggered instinctive threat reactions; our social en-

13 On the socially constructed fear of migrants see in extenso Blanc 2011.

14 For the complex interplay between physical and cognitive dimensions within emotions see Wolf 2012, 607.

vironment and, with it, our evaluations and judgments on what is threatening or not have thus become much more complex. With regard to the "refugee crisis", it is becoming obvious that threat perception is anything but natural: Migration can be understood as the movement of people which is, by itself, a neutral event. This event, however, can be interpreted in a positive or negative way. It is the socially acquired knowledge, gathered from broader public discourses and private conversations and encounters, that determines how people approach migrants. "The physical feeling of fear triggered by the perception of threat is universal, but the threat perception itself is culturally and socially determined." (Blanc 2011, 9)

The fact that individuals rarely develop opinions and beliefs in isolation, but develop their evaluations in the context of collective discourse, links the emotional (re-)turn to the preceding linguistic turn. This nexus is well illustrated by the concept of securitization. In a nutshell, the concept claims that there are no objective threats waiting to be discovered, but only *socially* constructed threats. An issue becomes a security issue if an actor convinces his audience that it must be interpreted as security-relevant. Once an issue is "securitized", that is to say, transformed into a security issue, it allows extraordinary measures to be taken (Buzan et al. 1998). Successful securitization depends neither on a single actor nor on socially particular elevated actors (e.g. a statesman). If the threat construction is widely accepted socially, not to say hegemonic, it is possible to speak of what Emmanuelle Blanc describes as a "fear climate". Those who participate in the production of a "fear climate" by word and deed are, again in her words, "fear entrepreneurs" (Blanc 2011, 11). In our case study, these can be politicians, social movements like PEGIDA, media, social media, but also ordinary people in their everyday conversations and encounters. A fear climate develops when the perception of threat is manifold and dominant. The first factor can be clearly identified in the German discourse on the "refugee crisis" because the securitization of refugees[15] – that is, their portrayal as threats – is threefold, referring to fears of physical, economic and societal insecurity.[16] In contrast to that, the second factor, domination, is contested due to a strong counter-discourse, which will be discussed later.

Prominent features of the securitizing discourse on refugees are narratives that merge the issue of migration with the issue of terrorism, addressing the fear of physical insecurity (Götsch 2016). The fact that terror attacks have been committed by people who came to Germany disguised as refugees is misused in these narratives to put all refugees under general suspicion of being terrorists. Another example that also serves to trigger fears of physical infringement is the discourse

15 In securitizing discourses on migration the notions of a migrant, a Muslim and a refugee are used almost synonymously.

16 The securitization of migration is nothing new. For an overview, see also Baumann 2009.

which arose after the events in New Year's Eve in 2015 in Cologne. During that night, hundreds of people, most of them with North African backgrounds, collectively harassed and in some cases even raped women and girls. In the aftermath, however, these events were discursively turned against *all* refugees, the result being that all of them were denounced as potential rapists and thus as a vital threat to the sexual integrity of (German) women. The narrative of the potential rapists re-produces racist and culturalist stereotypes claiming sexual aggressiveness to be an essential attribute of Arab and Muslim males.

Generalizing is another typical strategy in the production of enemy images[17] that can be observed in narratives drawing on economic fears, which are produced through two contradicting narratives: The first one depicts refugees as "Sozialschmarotzer" (cadgers living on social services), claiming that *they* only come to Germany to profit from *our* social welfare regime without being willing to work. The other narrative claims that refugees are a burden on society because *they* take away *our* jobs. Together, the two narratives make it impossible for refugees to act appropriately because they are accused of being rivals either on the job market or in the social services. In consequence, the argument goes, only the very few "real" refugees should be allowed to stay, whereas the masses of economic refugees ("Wirtschaftsflüchtlinge") should be deported.

What is especially antagonizing is the effect of those narratives that target refugees as a threat to identity, addressing fears of societal insecurity. Here, immigration is depicted as a challenge to the popular concept of an ethnically and/or religiously homogenous identity. Despite the empirical reality that Germany is already a multi-cultural society due not only to ethnic and religious heterogeneity but also to the existence of manifold sub-cultures, the narrative claims that there is one overarching *Leitkultur* (leading culture) that everyone shares and that is incompatible with the proclaimed culture of Muslims, the religion held by the majority of refugees. According to this narrative, culture is something static and essential that is related to ethnic and/or religious origin. It is telling that nobody has so far been able to define the so-called *Leitkultur* precisely; it is sufficient to mention it again and again to depict refugees as a vital threat to "German" identity. The securitizing discourse on refugees is based on what Edward Said coined as "othering"[18], that is, the construction of identity through the construction of a different, if not adversary or threatening "other", in this case migrants, refugees and/or Muslims. Othering works linguistically though the attribution of incompatible binary categories that are perceived as essential and static, like modern/traditional,

---

17 Enemy images are very well researched. For an extensive analysis of the psychological mechanisms they are based on see Flohr 1991.

18 For details on the linguistic mechanisms of "othering", see Said 1978.

civilised/uncivilised, good/bad; often heard in the discourse on migration. Emphasising the difference between 'us' and 'them' strengthens the coherence and thus the identity of the in-group while constituting an insurmountable distance to the out-group.

All these securitizing narratives exemplarily described above culminate in a fear climate which spreads easily in times of manifold uncertainties due to the financial crisis, violent conflicts in Europe's near neighborhood and the ever growing complexity of the globalizing world. From literature, we know that it is not necessarily poor people, but people fearing economic decline who are especially receptive to narratives producing a climate of fear (Poutvaara and Steinhardt 2015). In this climate, the refugee has become a placeholder, or scapegoat, for the projection of all kinds of fears. The phenomenon is not limited to a xenophobic discourse, but spills over to respective social practice, as the worrying increase in attacks against refugees illustrates (ZDF heute 2016). Radicals can find acceptance when they frame their xenophobic violence as a preemptive countermeasure against the allegedly vital threat deriving from the refugees. Another source of legitimation for xenophobic attitudes is the respective practice of European and national migration regimes. By drawing increasingly on border defense, the migration regime makes those who seek shelter appear as something like an enemy. To cite a concrete example, recent approaches to channel the influx of refugees through transit camps are also a securitizing practice insofar as these camps look like prisons, hence evoking the narrative of the illegal, criminal and threatening migrant. Although statesmen are not the only fear entrepreneurs, their institutionalized power assigns them much more responsibility, and they should therefore be recognized as decisive actors in the process of securitization.[19]

5 Discourse and counter-discourse on the "refugee crisis": Talking among deaf

"The process of fear construction is not deterministic but rather dynamic and involves also 'de-securitizing actors', such as asylum and migrants law experts, human rights organizations or associations of migrants that may counteract the securitizing moves of fear entrepreneurs by offering a different interpretation of the social reality." (Blanc 2011, 16) Their counter-discourse does not draw on the ideal of a culturally and ethnically homogenous nation or state, but on Germany's national identity as a constitutional democracy, based on the rule of law – includ-

19 For a thorough analysis of securitization in the European Council's discourse on migration, see Saulich 2015.

ing minority rights – and thus irrespective of ethnicity or religion. Here, refugees or migrants in general are not automatically excluded, but have at least a chance to become members of the national in-group. Another, even wider concept of identity within the counter-discourse is embedded in cosmopolitism, drawing on universal human rights that trump the limited concept of civil rights.[20] In the counter-discourse, notions like "flood", "tsunami", or "landslide" are refuted; threatening pictures of masses of young and angry men are deliberately contrasted with humanizing pictures showing individuals, especially women and children in vulnerable situations. Utilitarian logics shape the counter-discourse on economic fears, such as the narrative on a migrant's added value as a potential to regenerate Germany's aging society or to overcome a shortage of skilled labour (Bruckner 2012; European Commission 2015). Stories of refugees succeeding in the job market add to the counter-discourse on economic fears, while stories of successful integration into society fuel the counter-discourse on societal fears. All these personal stories of refugees who have a name, a face and an individual fate are intended to facilitate identification and thereby to open the door to empathy. Last but not least, the agency of the refugees themselves matters in the discursive struggle. Increasingly, they are making their own voices heard, be it through interviews or projects in the cultural or social sector.[21]

This counter-discourse is so strong that there is no consensus even on whether it is a *counter*-discourse at all. After all, it was Chancellor Merkel who started it when she opened the borders and proclaimed "wir schaffen das". From the perspective of those who resented this decision it is therefore the other way round. PEGIDA successfully claims to give a voice to those whose fears are being overlooked by what it sees as the "established elites", ignoring the fact that the pro-refugee movement is not elitist at all, but extremely heterogeneous, uniting people from all walks of life. The claimed struggle against a hegemonic pro-refugee discourse meets with the approval of many people who might not be as radical and hateful as PEGIDA, but who are emotionally responsive to the securitizing discourse. There is no reliable empirical data to prove who dominates the discourse and who is dominated, but it is obvious that the struggle between the two camps is as productive as a dialogue among deaf. The phenomenon of societies so deeply divided that there is hardly any communication left is confined neither to Germany nor to the policy field of migration. In fact, it can be observed in Hungary, Poland, France, the UK and,

20 For critical reflections on a renewed cosmopolitanism, see Friese 2010, 325.

21 Elfriede Jelinek's theatre play "Die Schutzbefohlenen", performed in many theatres in Austria and Germany, is a prominent case in point. But there are also hundreds of small and local projects such as Kaleidoskop, a playback theatre working together with refugees in Hamburg. Their play "Stop Checkpoint" was performed at Helmut Schmidt University in November 2015 as a contribution of the Dahrendorf workshop on Fortress Europe.

since the latest elections, also in the US. Xenophobia is only one of many items that are splitting Western societies today, challenging what used to be, or at least claimed to be, a community of values. Thus, the question of how to overcome the deep rift in Western societies goes far beyond this case study on xenophobia, even though it is a good case in point to exemplarily discuss the problem. The maintenance of dialogue is of utmost importance because democracy builds on consensus, and consensus can only be attained through communication.

It is known from literature on cognitive psychology that it is difficult to approach people who have already incorporated xenophobic attitudes into their belief system.[22] The fact that xenophobic enemy images are based on the binary construction of a totally different "other" that has absolutely nothing in common with oneself makes it almost impossible for these people to empathize with a refugee. To develop empathy, they would first of all have to admit that there are commonalities between the "we" and the "other". Admitting commonalities, however, would produce cognitive dissonance and thereby severely challenge their own identity (Flohr 1991, 47ff.). To avoid such emotional unsettlement, any information which could deconstruct the enemy image is either deliberately ignored or allowed to fall through the unconscious grid of selective perception (ibid.). Manifold mechanisms of selective perception make xenophobic attitudes almost immune to any challenge from outside.

We do not know to what extent these mechanisms stabilize the attitudes of xenophobic fear entrepreneurs in contrast to people who would not see themselves as xenophobic, but still feel insecure and unsettled when confronted with strangers. Such differentiations between degrees of conscious or unconscious xenophobia might be somewhat artificial, because we know neither whether fear entrepreneurs believe their securitizing narratives themselves nor to what extent those who claim to simply feel insecure might want to disguise racist attitudes.[23] Since it is impossible to look into people's heads, denouncing people as xenophobic without proof is quite a sensitive matter. If the aim is to counteract xenophobic attitudes, such condemnations are even counterproductive because they impede open dialogue. I hold that to counteract xenophobia, it is of the utmost importance to reach out and to open arenas for communication and exchanges with people who perceive strangers as a threat for whatever reason. This, however, is easier said than done: Where and how could a productive dialogue take place? Not least due to the rising usage of social media, the tendency to communicate preferably with like-minded people has increased, too. Thus, securitising narratives are always

22 For the role of emotional beliefs see Mercer 2010.

23 On more or less open manifestations of xenophobia see the contribution of Jana Sinram in this edited volume.

produced and re-produced in the same fora, creating ideal conditions for fear entrepreneurs to spread their messages uncontested. Communication is all too often limited to these "filter bubbles" in which the same positions are shared, liked and thus reinforced again and again, fostering the climate of fear as described above. This makes it extremely difficult to counteract xenophobic attitudes. Neither de-securitizing narratives addressing the emotional level nor facts and figures addressing the cognitive level reach the recipients; they remain in the "filter bubble" of like-minded people consenting the admission of refugees.

6 Conclusion: Creating arenas for overcoming the fatal logic of inclusion and exclusion

The image of two camps communicating in two exclusive bubbles is an analytical model that needs differentiation. In social reality, the dividing line on the issue of migration is not as clear-cut because it does not divide well-defined milieus. As stated in the introduction, the people who spontaneously decided to voluntarily support refugees in the summer of 2015 came from all walks of life. What they had in common was the ability to empathize with the deprived refugees, which prompted them to develop strong feelings of compassion. Since empathy is at least in part a human disposition, it does not go hand in hand with the affiliation to specific segments of society, nor does it correlate significantly with class, age or gender.[24] If anything, the receptiveness to prejudice correlates with lower levels of education; nevertheless, the movement in support of refugees is not restricted to urban and academic elites. On the contrary, the activist network is extremely heterogeneous, uniting people from urban elites, known for having a liberal and cosmopolitan outlook, with people from rather conservative rural milieus, represented for example by the "Landfrauen". This is an association of women farmers and farmer's wives, the majority of whom, like farmers in most parts of the world, belong to the conservative down-home spectrum of society.[25] Local football-clubs also play a positive role for the integration of refugees. Due to this heterogeneity, the discursive dividing line on the "refugee crisis" sometimes even splits families or circles of friends, resulting in unusual and sometimes painful situations as exemplified in the quote of an activist: "Tonight I will meet my xenophobic friends."[26]

24 For a deeper analysis on the motivations and dispositions for voluntary engagement see Anheier and Scherer 2015. In the specific context of voluntary work in support of refugees see Han-Broich 2012.

25 See Ruske 2016; see also Aumüller and Gersemann 2016.

26 Quote from a refugee support activist in March 2015.

This unusual mélange, however, might be a starting point for opening up the communication bubbles described above. When volunteers share their experiences of working together with refugees by word of mouth with their families, friends or colleagues, the information might appear more credible than when it is obtained from media or other anonymous sources. What might add to the credibility of such personal information is the fact that it does not reproduce the well-known discourse, because neither the securitizing nor the de-securitizing narratives play a decisive role in the everyday work with refugees. In contrast to that, the everyday lives of refugees are shaped by the manifold problems they face in trying to settle down in Germany. These are often as banal as the struggle with bureaucracy, which is easy to identify with, but they also comprise problems refugees have due to their very specific fate.

Working for and together with refugees, activists often move from an initial, sometimes even paternalistic feeling of charity to a much more complex form of "social empathy" defined as the ability to understand people more deeply by perceiving or experiencing their life situations and as a result to gain insight into structural inequalities and disparities. (Segal 2011, 266) This most of all concerns the political context of the European and German asylum regimes, with all their merits, deficits and contradictions, that together shape the living conditions of the refugees. But it is not only that. In addition to the differences in cultural, social, and political backgrounds, it is also, and perhaps foremost, the extreme violence that most of them experienced in their homelands and often also on their long journey to Europe that complicates empathic understanding of refugees. Only very few people in Germany personally share such traumatic experiences and therefore can only conclude from their knowledge of the situation what impact war, terror and other forms of violence might have on the emotions of the people who escaped from all that. To grasp this dimension of social empathy, volunteers have to go through a long and sometimes stony learning process that ideally takes them onto an equal footing with the refugees they want to support[27]. From this position, they can function as mediators and reach out to the xenophobic sceptics within their own peer groups[28]. Word of mouth communication on refugees is one way, the other is direct contact with refugees when they come to private homes or work-places and thereby get access to the respective peer groups. Direct contact

27 For deeper insights in the problematics of voluntary work, often shaped by paternalistic attitudes and unconscious expectations, see Friese 2010; Dunn 2004.

28 It is known from statistical inquiry that xenophobia is slightly more dominant in the eastern parts of Germany, where fewer foreigners live compared to the western parts of the country, especially urban areas such as Berlin and Hamburg, where comparatively more foreigners live. For details on the development of right-wing and xenophobic attitudes in Germany, see Decker et al. 2016.

can help a lot to de-prove securitizing narratives, especially when it takes place in a familiar environment. Their mere presence, literally or in the frequent conversations and encounters of their supporters, blurs the dividing line between the in- and the out-group and facilitates identification and – empathy.

To sum up, it can be said that against the backdrop of rising xenophobia in Germany, the findings of this article are rather pessimistic and the strategies offered to counteract in the discourse on the "refugee crisis" are fairly modest. The starting point of this article was Neta Crawford's argument that empathy and fear co-relate with each other in a way that empathy can function as an antidote against xenophobia. My findings fully confer the dense nexus between empathy and the emotion of fear. However, Crawford's conclusions seem to me to be overoptimistic because the argument also works the other way round: Fear is one of the most decisive factors impeding empathic identification. For empathy to unfold the productive power Crawford ascribes to it, it is necessary to actively reach out to those who hold xenophobic attitudes. Against the background of an overtly split society, this is easier said than done. Approaches to tackle the problem through rational arguments alone have proved to be ineffective for two reasons: firstly, because xenophobic resilience is preserved through unconscious mechanisms of selective perception and, secondly, due to new forms of filtered communication in exclusive bubbles. But strategies shifting to the emotional level also achieve little success, at least when restricted to overtly positive counter-narratives on refugees, because these are also filtered off. To get out of this impasse, the suggestion was made for the very few remaining arenas allowing unfiltered communication and dialogue to be sought out. Having people with deviant opinions – including xenophobia – in peer-groups like families, circles of friends and colleagues, was identified as a starting point. Almost private settings enhance the possibilities to shatter deeply engrained xenophobic attitudes, all the more when refugees themselves gain access to such in-groups and so get a chance to personally de-prove the enemy image of the threatening migrant.[29] Given the fact that the number of people who are actively involved in the support of refugees is rather large, they have quite some potential to open doors for the development of empathy with refugees in Germany.

29 See in this context Foroutan et al. 2015. Here she describes the positive long-term impact of mixed milieus on attitudes on the "other", dissolving the traditional categories of in- and out-group.

References

Anheier, Helmut and Nikolas Scherer. 2015. Voluntary Actions and Social Movements. In The Oxford Handbook of Social Movements, D. Della Porta and M. Diani (eds.), 494–510. Oxford: University Press.

Aumüller, Jutta and Frank Gersemann. 2016. Flüchtlinge aufs Land? *APuZ* 46-47, 29–34.

Bargetz, Brigitte and Birgit Sauer. 2010. Politik, Emotionen und die Transformation des Politischen. Eine feministisch-machtkritische Perspektive. Österreichische Zeitschrift für Politikwissenschaft 39 (2), 141–155.

Bauer, Joachim. 2014. Motivation, Empathy, Aggression: How Neurobiology Adds to Our Understanding of the Psyche. *Dynamische Psychatrie,* 1.01.2014.

Baumann, Mechthild. 2009. Migration und Sicherheit. *WISO direkt, Analysen und Konzepte zur Wirtschafts- und Sozialpolitik.*

Blanc, Emmanuelle. 2011. From the Barcelona Process to the Arab Spring: The Role of Emotions in the EU Migration Policy towards the Mediterranean Countries. *KAS Working Paper* 112/2011.

Bordermonitoring-eu. 2015. Of Hope. Hungary and the Long Summer of Migration. http://bordermonitoring.eu/ungarn/2015/09/of-hope-en/. Accessed: 28th October 2016.

Bruckner, Elke. 2012. *Migration und demographischer Wandel.* Gütersloh: Bertelsmann Stiftung.

Buzan, Barry, Ole Wæver, and Jaap de Wilde. 1998. *Security: A New Framework for Analysis.* Boulder, Boulder: Lynne Rienner.

Chumacov, Alexander M., Ivan I. Mazour, and William C. Gay (eds.). 2014. *Global Studies Encyclopedic Dictionary.* Amsterdam, New York: Rodopi.

Crawford, Neta C. 2014. Institutionalizing passion in world politics: fear and empathy. *Forum: Emotions and World Politics, International Theory* 6 (3), 535–557.

Decker, Oliver, Johannes Kiess, and Elmar Brähler (eds.). 2016. *Die enthemmte Mitte. Die Leipziger "Mitte"-Studie 2016.* Gießen: Psychosozial Verlag.

Dunn, Jennifer. 2004. The politics of empathy: Social movements and victim repertoires. *Sociological Focus* 37 (3), 225–250.

European Commission. 2015. *Determining labor shortages and the need for labor migration from third countries in the EU.* Synthesis Report for the EMN Focussed Study.

Flohr, Anne K. 1991. *Feindbilder in der internationalen Politik: Ihre Entstehung und ihre Funktion.* Bonner Beiträge zur Politikwissenschaft.

Foroutan, Naika et al. 2015. *Deutschland postmigrantisch II. Einstellungen von Jugendlichen und jungen Erwachsenen zu Gesellschaft, Religion und Identität.* Humboldt-Universität zu Berlin.

Fratzke, Susanne. 2015. *Not adding up. The Fading Promise of Europe's Dublin System.* Migration Policy Institute Europe. Brussels.

Friese, Heidrun. 2010. The limits of Hospitality: Political Philosophy, Undocumented Migration and the Local Arena. *European Journal of Social Theory* 13 (3), 323–341.

Godwin, Jeff, James M. Jasper, and Francesca Poletta. 2000. The Return of the Repressed. The Fall and Rise of Emotions in Social Movement Theory. *Mobilization, An International Journal* 5 (1), 65–83.

Götsch, Katharina. 2016. Alleged Terrorists, Refugees and Radicalized Muslims in Europe: A Wicked Diskursive Conjunction. *S+F Security and Peace* 34 (1), 38–45.

Hahn, Dirk. 2006. Zur Wahrnehmung des Islams und zur sozio-kulturellen Teilhabe der Muslime in Deutschland. Projektbericht Universität Duisburg-Essen. http://www.fes.de/BerlinerAkademiegespraeche/publikationen/islamundpolitik/documents/WahrnehmungHalmEndbericht_2_.pdf. Accessed: 16th November 2016.

Han-Broich, Misun. 2012. *Ehrenamt und Integration. Zur Bedeutung sozialen Engagements in der (Flüchtlings-)Sozialarbeit*. Wiesbaden: Springer VS.

Hutchison, Emma and Roland Bleiker. 2014. Theorizing emotions in world politics. *International Theory* 6 (3), 491–514.

Jervis, Robert. 1976. *Perception and Misperception in International Politics*. Princeton: University Press.

Koschut, Simon. 2015. Keine Angst vor Gefühlen! Konstruktivistische Emotionsforschung in den IB. zip-online, https://zib-online.org/2015/12/07/keine-angst-vor-gefuehlen-konstruktivistische-emotionsforschung-in-den-ib/. Accessed: 25th November 2015.

Mercer, Jonathan. 2010. Emotional Beliefs. *International Organization* 64 (1), 1–31.

Mercer, Jonathan. 2014. Feeling like a state: social emotion and identity. *Forum: Emotions and World Politics, International Theory* 6 (3), 515–535.

Pedwell, Carolyn. 2014. *Affective Relations. The Transnational Politics of Empathy*. London: Palgrave Macmillan.

Poutvaara, Panu and Max F. Steinhardt. 2015. Bitterness in life and attitudes towards immigration. *SOEP papers on Multidisciplinary Panel Data Research at DIW Berlin* 800.

Ruske, Jennifer. 2016. Flüchtlinge – ein Thema, das auf den Nägeln brennt. *Bauernblatt*.

Said, Edward W. 1978. *Orientalism*. New York: Pantheon Books.

Saulich, Christina. 2015. Irreguläre Migration. In *Handbuch Sicherheitsgefahren, Globale Gesellschaft und Internationale Beziehungen*, ed. T. Jäger, 483–492. Wiesbaden: VS-Springer.

Schieder, Siegfried and Manuela Spindler. 2014. *Theories of International Relations*. Abingdon, New York: Routledge.

Segal, Elizabeth A. 2011. Social Empathy: A Model Built on Empathy, Contextual Understanding, and Social Responsibility that Promotes Social Justice. *Journal of Social Service Research* 37 (3), 266–277.

Wolf, Reinhardt. 2012. Der "emotional turn" in den IB. Plädoyer für eine theoretische Überwindung methodischer Engführung. *Zeitschrift für Außen und Sicherheitspolitik* 5 (4), 605–624.

ZDF heute. 2016. Staat verkennt Rassismus. http://www.heute.de/rechte-gewalt-ai-staat-tut-zu-wenig-gegen-rassismus-43884486.html, Accessed: 30th November 2016.

Contributors

Ummuhan Bardak, *European Training Foundation*
Ummuhan Bardak is a senior labour market specialist at the European Training Foundation (ETF) in Turin, Italy. At the ETF, she has worked on the "Patterns of Migration and Human Resources Development" project and the implementation of the Euro-Mediterranean Partnership's (MEDA) "Education and Training for Employment" (ETE) program. She has also been involved in the joint ETF/MPC project on migrant support measures from the employment and skills perspective (MISMES Project). Before joining the ETF, she worked for the Turkish Ministry for Labour. Ummuhan Bardak studied political science and International Relations in Turkey and holds a Master's degree from the London School of Economics.

Nicolas Fromm, *Helmut Schmidt University*
Nicolas Fromm is a PhD candidate at Helmut Schmidt University. He holds a Master's degree in political science from Freie Universität Berlin and a Master's degree in international security from Sciences Po Paris, Paris School of International Affairs (PSIA). He has worked as a parliamentary assistant at the European Parliament, as a researcher in the Gulf region and as a public affairs consultant in Berlin. Between 2014 and 2016, he was a research associate at Helmut Schmidt University. Since 2016, Nicolas Fromm has been working as a consultant in the field of international politics. His research and teaching focus on the Arab world from the International Relations perspective.

Prof. Dr. Naika Foroutan, *Humboldt University*
Naika Foroutan is the vice director of the Berlin Institute for Integration and Migration Research. She is a professor for integration studies and social policy at Humboldt University and head of the "Hybrid European-Muslim Identity Models (HEYMAT)" research project, which is funded by the Volkswagen Foundation.

Since 2011, she has been the head of the "Young Islam-Related Topics in Germany" research group in the framework of the "Young Islam Conference", which is funded by the Stiftung Mercator. Her research focuses on migration and integration, images of Islam and Muslims in Germany, identity and hybridity, political Islam and the transformation of countries of immigration.

Parastou Hassouri, *independent researcher, currently consulting UNHCR*
Parastou Hassouri is an independent researcher and consultant in international refugee law and migration policy. She has been serving as a consultant with the Refugee Status Determination (RSD) Unit at the UNHCR office in Ankara, Turkey. Her previous consultancies with the UNHCR were at the Zaatari Refugee Camp in Jordan and the UNHCR office in Moscow. Parastou Hassouri has taught international refugee law at the American University of Cairo. She has also worked as an attorney advisor at the Immigration Courts of New York City and Los Angeles and as an immigration attorney in private practice in New York City.

Prof. Dr. Annette Jünemann, *Helmut Schmidt University*
Annette Jünemann teaches International Relations at Helmut Schmidt University/ University of the Federal Armed Forces Hamburg, Germany. She is a member of the Dahrendorf "Europe and the MENA Region" working group. Her main areas of research are International Relations, Euro-Mediteterranean relations, Migration, and Gender Studies. Among her recent publications are "Euro-Mediterranean Relations after the Arab Spring: Persistence in Times of Change" (ed. with Jakob Horst and Delf Rothe, Routledge 2014); Geschlechterpolitik für die arabische Welt: Die EU-Förderpolitik zwischen Staatsfeminismus und Islamismus [Gender democracy for the Arab World: EU policies between state feminism and Islamism], VS-Verlag 2015.

Prof. Dr. Michael Köhler, *European Commission*
Michael Köhler serves as Director Neighbourhood-South at the Directorate-General for Neighbourhood and Enlargement Negotiations, where he is responsible for cooperation with Mediterranean Arab countries and Israel. Before his appointment, he was Head of Cabinet to the Commissioner for Energy, Günther Oettinger, and Head of Cabinet to the Commissioner for Maritime Affairs and Fisheries, Joe Borg. Michael Köhler holds a Dr. phil. in history and Middle Eastern studies from Hamburg University. He has authored about thirty books, articles in international Islamic studies and foreign policy reviews. Since 1997, he has taught at the College of Europe in Bruges, Belgium, and since 2000 he has been a senior Fellow of the Center for European Integration Studies at Bonn University, Germany.

Prof. Dr. Mehdi Lahlou, *INSEA Rabat*
Mehdi Lahlou is a professor at the National Institute of Statistics and Applied Economics (INSEA – Ministry of Planning) in Rabat. He is a research supervisor on Moroccan and international migration, on sustainable development (in North African and Sub-Saharan countries) and on water issues in North African countries. In 2006, he founded the Open University on "migration, human rights and development". Since 1992, he has published a number of studies and articles on international migration between Africa and the EU. Mehdi Lahlou is vice president of the Mediterranean Society of Comparative Education (MESCE) and a former member of the executive bureau of the National Union of Higher Education in Morocco.

Prof. Dr. Hannes Schamman, *Hildesheim University*
Hannes Schammann is a junior professor of migration policy at Hildesheim University. Before that, he worked as a project manager in the field of migration and integration at the Robert Bosch Foundation, as an advisor for integration at the Federal Office for Migration and Refugees and as a coordinator of integration projects at the Federal Association of Evangelical Youth Social Work. He has designed and realized numerous projects on migration and integration, for instance, on "refuge and asylum", "Islam in Germany", "migration and the labour market" and the "culture of welcome and interculturality". His research focuses on migration, integration and refugee policy in Germany from the institution perspective.

Nikolas Scherer, *Hertie School of Governance*
Nikolas Scherer is a PhD candidate at the Hertie School of Governance and was a research associate to the Dahrendorf Forum's "Europe and the MENA Region" working group. His main research interests include security politics, finance capitalism and catastrophe insurances. In his PhD thesis, he explored the career of "climate risk insurances" across the Global South. In 2015, he was a visiting PhD fellow at LSE IDEAS, London School of Economics. Since 2016, Nikolas Scherer has been working as project manager in the areas of climate and security and climate finance. He studied International Relations (MA) at the University of Warwick and Governance & Public Policy (BA) at the University of Passau and Rome (La Sapienza).

Dr. Jana Sinram, *journalist at Deutschlandfunk*
Jana Sinram works as a news editor at Deutschlandfunk, a German public radio station in Cologne. Her journalistic work concentrates on various aspects of immigration and integration in Germany and Europe. She is a graduate of the German School of Journalism in Munich. Jana Sinram studied at the universities in Kiel, Stockholm and Münster and holds a doctoral title in political science and

Scandinavian studies. Her dissertation focuses on immigration into Denmark and the Muhammad cartoons controversy.

Catherine Teule, *European Association for the Defense of Human Rights*
Catherine Teule is the vice president of the European Association for the Defense of Human Rights (AEDH). She has also worked at the French Human Rights League (LDH), first as a general secretary, then as vice president. Before that, she conducted research missions for the International Federation for Human Rights (FIDH). In her research, she is particularly interested in issues concerning the right of asylum and migration and its application. She publishes articles and briefings on related questions and provides training sessions and debates at community and trade union level.

Dr. Gerasimos Tsourapas, *University of Birmingham*
Gerasimos Tsourapas is a lecturer in Middle East Politics at the Department of Political Science and International Studies at the University of Birmingham. He holds a BA from Yale University and MSc degrees from the London School of Economics and SOAS. In 2016, he received his PhD from SOAS University of London. Between 2009 and 2011, he worked as a researcher for the Hellenic Ministry of Foreign Affairs. In 2013, he was a visiting fellow at the Centre for Migration and Refugee Studies, American University of Cairo. His research interests include diaspora politics, the interplay between migration and authoritarianism and the politics of the Middle East, with a focus on Egypt, Jordan and Tunisia.

Dr. Jan Claudius Völkel, *Vrije Universiteit Brussel*
Jan Claudius Völkel is Marie Sklodowska Curie Fellow at the Institute for European Studies, Vrije Universiteit Brussel, researching the role of Arab parliaments in the current transformation processes. Before, he was four years DAAD longterm lecturer at Cairo University's Faculty of Economics and Political Science. He is fellow of the Arab German Young Academy of Sciences and Humanities (AGYA) and Regional Coordinator for the Middle East and North Africa at the Bertelsmann Transformation Index (BTI). He has had teaching assignments with the universities of Freiburg, Salzburg, Innsbruck and Duhok (Iraqi Kurdistan) and spent one year as a research assistant at the European University Institute in Florence. In his publications, he primarily focuses on Democratization in the Middle East, EU–MENA relations and EU migration policy.

FSC
www.fsc.org
MIX
Papier aus verantwortungsvollen Quellen
Paper from responsible sources
FSC® C105338

If you have any concerns about our products,
you can contact us on
ProductSafety@springernature.com

In case Publisher is established outside the EU,
the EU authorized representative is:
Springer Nature Customer Service Center GmbH
Europaplatz 3, 69115 Heidelberg, Germany

Printed by Libri Plureos GmbH
in Hamburg, Germany